AF499266

# PSYCHODIAGNOSTICS
## MPCE-12

*For*

Master of Arts (Psychology) (MAPC)

IGNOU, KSOU (Karnataka), Bihar University (Muzaffarpur), Nalanda University, Jamia Millia Islamia, Vardhman Mahaveer Open University (Kota), Uttarakhand Open University, Kurukshetra University, Seva Sadan's College of Education (Maharashtra), Lalit Narayan Mithila University, Andhra University, Pt. Sunderlal Sharma (Open) University (Bilaspur), Annamalai University, Bangalore University, Bharathiar University, Bharathidasan University, HP University, Centre for distance and open learning, Kakatiya University (Andhra Pradesh), KOU (Rajasthan), MPBOU (MP), MDU (Haryana), Punjab University, Tamilnadu Open University, Sri Padmavati Mahila Visvavidyalayam (Andhra Pradesh), Sri Venkateswara University (Andhra Pradesh), UCSDE (Kerala), University of Jammu, YCMOU, Rajasthan University, UPRTOU, Kalyani University, Banaras Hindu University (BHU) and all other Indian Universities.

**GullyBaba Publishing House Pvt. Ltd.**

ISO 9001 & ISO 14001 CERTIFIED CO.

**Regd. Office:**
2525/193, 1st Floor, Onkar Nagar-A,
Tri Nagar, Delhi-110035
(From Kanhaiya Nagar Metro Station Towards Old Bus Stand)
Call: 9991112299, 9312235086
WhatsApp: 9350849407

**Branch Office:**
1A/2A, 20, Hari Sadan,
Ansari Road, Daryaganj,
New Delhi-110002
Ph.011-45794768
Call & WhatsApp:
8130521616,8130511234

**E-mail:** hello@gullybaba.com, **Website**: GullyBaba.com

**Author:** Gullybaba.com Panel

**ISBN:** 978-93-90557-34-9



## Disclaimer

Although the author and publisher have made every effort to ensure that the information in this book is correct, the author and publisher do not assume and hereby disclaim any liability to any party for any loss, damage, or disruption caused by errors or omissions, whether such errors or omissions result from negligence, accident, or any other cause.

If you find any kind of error, please let us know and get reward and or the new book free of cost.

The book is based on IGNOU syllabus. This is only a sample. The book/author/publisher does not impose any guarantee or claim for full marks or to be passed in exam. You are advised only to understand the contents with the help of this book and answer in your words.

All disputes with respect to this publication shall be subject to the jurisdiction of the Courts, Tribunals and Forums of New Delhi, India only.

# About Publisher

Gullybaba Publishing House is the brainchild of Mr Dinesh Verma, his name alone evokes profound respect and admiration. He is the pioneer of providing quality materials to the students of IGNOU because, having been a student of IGNOU, he understood the difficulty and pain of the non-availability of quality materials himself. He is serving the students with the following services:

### EXAM-SUCCESS GUIDES

Important questions, solved question papers, guess papers - all in one! to score good marks in lesser time and effort.

### FREE BOOK

As our love and care for our students, here is a Free Gift – A Famous Book "Secrets to Pass IGNOU Exams with Less Study" for you. You can download it now! https://www.gullybaba.com/ignou-free/

### YOUR CONTRIBUTION TO MOTHER-EARTH

When you read our books, you save our mother earth as we use recycled paper to make these books. On every purchase, we contribute something to plant a plant.

### SOLVED ASSIGNMENTS PDFs / HAND-WRITTEN

Best and genuine solved assignments PDFs you can instantly download from Gullybaba.com or our App.

### PROJECT REPORTS/SYNOPSIS

Best Quality No-Rejection projects/synopsis by professionals researchers in ready to refer format.

### MOBILE APP

You can download 'Gullybaba' app from Google Play Store to enjoy all above services at one place.

# Why Gullybaba's IGNOU Help Books

Is Fear of Exams making you stressful? Are you not getting good marks in your IGNOU exams? Are you looking for sure-shot solution get ahead in your IGNOU studies? Look no further than the answer: Gullybaba.com! With our expertly crafted course help-books, you'll be ready to face any exam with ease-guaranteed. What's more, we offer a huge discount on IGNOU Help Books Combo Deals – Save BIG.

Now, complete IGNOU courses more quickly and with Good Marks in Lesser Time & Effort.

# Home Delivery of GPH Books

You can order Gullybaba Books online from Gullybaba.com or Gullybaba App. We dispatch books on the same day of receiving the order through our fastest courier partners.
You can also order books through WhatsApp on 9350849407 or by email at order@gullybaba.com.
We also provide "Cash On Delivery" through our courier partners and sometimes Govt. Postal Department.

# Important Note to Sellers

Selling this book on any online platform like Amazon, Flipkart, Shopclues, Rediff, etc. without prior written permission of the publisher is prohibited and hence any sales by the SELLER will be termed as ILLEGAL SALE of GPH Books which will attract strict legal action against the offender.

# How to Use This Book

To make the most of this book, please study all the sections thoroughly. First section is Important Exam Study Material which contains : Highly Asked Questions with Answers, Medium Asked Questions, and Some Less Asked questions. All is in a flow of the subject to understand the concept and write best answers for more marks. The second section is previous questions papers with solutions. If the subject is new and no exam is conducted, you will find sample papers with answers. These are based on our years of experience in helping IGNOU students.

| **Chapters are Based on** |
|---|
| Very High Asked Questions |
| Highly Asked Questions |
| Medium Asked Questions |
| Less Asked Questions |
| Exam Important Questions |
| Exam Notes |

For your exams, you need to be thorough with every page of this book if you are only reading it to study.

# Pattern of the Question Paper

Here, we are providing an outline of your question paper and some tips on how to write the exams so that you can plan your studies more effectively.

**Paper Pattern***

| TOTAL MARKS: 100 | |
|---|---|
| **Description** | **Marks** |
| **Section A** | |
| Answer any five from the following questions in 400 words | 5 x 10 = 50 |
| **Section B** | |
| Answer any four questions in 250 words | 4 x 5 = 20 |
| Answer any two questions in 600 words | 2 x 15 = 30 |

**Note:** Paper pattern may vary from paper to paper.

# How to Write Exam Answers like a Pro!!!

Make your answer as neat and presentable as possible in order to get the best marks. You can use the following points as a guide when writing your answers:

- Keep paragraphs short and leave a line between each paragraph for easier reading.
- Make sure your answer is broken down into logical subsections. Whenever possible, divide each subheading into smaller points. Using a pencil, underline each subheading.
- Begin each answer after giving 2-3 lines of gap.

**For More Exam Writing Tips**
Refer our Famous Book "Secrets to Pass IGNOU Exams with Less Study".

**You can download it now!**
https://www.gullybaba.com/ignou-free/

# Preface

This GPH book ***"Psychodiagnostics (MPCE-12)"*** is the ultimate guide for students who want to achieve top grades. If you're preparing for your next exam, don't worry! We have created the help book to pass IGNOU exams in lesser time and effort, even if you are busy or working. Using 18+ years of rich experience and compiled based on historical data from the past ten years, we've accurately predicted at least 50-90% of questions that will come up in upcoming exams. Our IGNOU help books have helped millions to achieve higher scores than ever before possible (and get onto those good jobs, further studies, and achieve the desired goal).

An attempt has been carefully made to present this book more useful and meet the requirement and challenges of the course prescribed by IGNOU University. We hope that this effort will fulfil the readers' expectations and help them excel in exams. Referring to University study material alongside this book is like "icing on the cake".

We wish you a successful and rewarding career. If you have any feedback to improve our books/products, please email at feedback@gullybaba.com. Because we believe, "Feedback is breakfast of champions" and our readers are our strength.

**– Gullybaba.com Panel**

# Table of Contents



# Question Papers

# 1 INTRODUCTION TO PSYCHODIAGNOSTICS

## INTRODUCTION

These days psychologists not only provide assessments but treat a wide variety of disorders in an equally wide variety of settings, consult, teach, conduct research, help to establish ethical policies, deal with human engineering factors, have a strong media presence, work with law enforcement in profiling criminals, and have had increasing influence in the business world and the realm of advertising, to identify just a few of the major activities in which they are engaged. This shows that the scope of activity of clinical psychologists has increased exponentially. The chapter starts with the definition and concept of psycho diagnostics. It covers methods of behavioural assessment. It also deals with the definition and purpose of clinical assessment and the application of assessment in the field of clinical psychology. At last, it covers the main ethical considerations involved in psychological assessment.

**Q1. Describe the concept of psychodiagnostics in detail.**

**Ans.** Psychodiagnostics is the discipline that deals with psychological assessment and diagnosis, personology and psychopathology, through the use of an integrated repertoire of questionnaires, personality inventories, batteries and test techniques (psychometric and projective), clinical interviews, neuropsychological examinations and observational evaluations; the type of techniques and tools used vary from time to time, based on the context and purpose of the assessment, age and type of possible difficulties of the assessed subjects.

Even if all the psychologists (in particular, but not only, the clinical ones) have a basic technical training and the relative authorisation of Law for carrying out the psychodiagnostic activity, the complexity and technical articulation of some of its applicative sub-sectors and/or of various psychodiagnostic techniques, at times, suggests the attainment of further post-graduate specialist training in the specific areas of interest (e.g., in neuropsychological, psychotherapeutic, legal, for the use specific projective tests, etc.).

Psychological diagnosis is not limited to the recognition and classification of symptoms or the classification of a disease (as in the medical field) but, taking into account the complexity and uniqueness of each individual, it is proposed to arrive at a psychological understanding that it necessarily passes through the emotional and cognitive sharing of profound aspects of oneself.

The use of the psychological tests completes and integrates the information collected during the interviews, allows the evaluation of specific functions or characteristics of personality and allows to have, in a relatively short time, a confirmation or disconfirmation of the clinical observations.

The diagnostic process is also structured according to its purpose.

Within a clinical context the diagnosis acts as a guide and pragmatic criterion on the feasibility of treatment and is configured as a proposal for a therapeutic project: deepening the knowledge related to personal, relational and contextual characteristics, the patient is placed in the condition of autonomously make decisions and make choices that facilitate the realisation of their needs and aspirations.

The diagnosis is not a "label" that is affixed to the patient, but a dynamic description of a mode of operation, always subject to change over time.

The psychodiagnostic evaluation allows a global assessment of the functioning of a person and can also be requested in the forensic field to ascertain the psychic conditions within legal, civil and criminal procedures.

Korchin and Schuldberg (1981) define psychodiagnostic as a process that:

- uses several procedures,
- intended to tap various areas of psychological functions,
- both at a conscious and unconscious level,
- using projective techniques as well as more objective and standardised tests,
- in both cases, interpretation may rest on symbolic signs as well as scoreable responses,
- to describe individuals in personological rather than normative terms.

The term psychodiagnostic might be applied more aptly to the neutral term clinical assessment. The central difference between clinical assessment and other testing applications is that the clinician, rather than the test, is at the centre of the assessment process. The clinician has two distinct functions, both of which are essential to the assessment process.

First, the clinician must gather data. Although standardised tests are used in clinical assessment, projective tests, interviews, and behavioural observations represent the clinician's most important measurement tools.

Second, the clinician must integrate data from various tests, interviews, and observations to form an overall assessment of the individual. The data gathering function has clear implications for the quality of psychological measurement. A clinician who makes inaccurate observations conducts poorly structured interviews or misinterprets or misreports responses-to open-ended questions or ambiguous stimuli (e.g., responses to Rorschach cards) is not likely to produce valid assessments. The clinician often functions as a measurement instrument, and it is important to assess the reliability and validity of the clinical data he or she gathers. Although it may not be immediately obvious, the clinician's second function the integration of clinical data-also affects the quality of psychological measurement in clinical settings. An assessment represents an attempt to arrive at a valid classification of each patient or client. In some cases, clinicians may be called on to diagnose or assist in the diagnosis of mental or behavioural disorders.

**Testing, Assessment and Clinical Practice:** Since the early 1980s, the practice of clinical psychologists has shifted steadily from an emphasis on assessment and diagnosis to an emphasis on psychotherapy and adjustment. Several reviews of research and practice, however, suggest that testing will remain an important activity and that many of the tests now widely used (e.g., standardised measures of intelligence, the MMPI-2) will remain popular even if they are partially supplemented by new testing technologies.

Although clinicians do not appear to devote as much of their time to testing as in the past, psychological testing still represents an important activity for practising clinicians. Wade and Baker's (1977) survey suggested that over 85 per cent of practising clinical psychologists used tests and that over one-third of their therapy time was devoted to testing administration and evaluation. Patterns of test users have been quite stable since the 1970s and probably will remain so for the foreseeable future. Psychological testing appears to be a common activity, regardless of the psychologist's therapeutic orientation (e.g., behavioural, cognitive).

The most widely used clinical tests can be divided into three types:

- Individual tests of general mental ability,
- Personality tests, and
- Neurological tests.

The Wechsler Intelligence Scales (WISC-ill and WAIS-ill) and the StanfordBillet represent the most popular tests of general mental ability. These tests serve a dual function· in forming assessments of individuals. First, an evaluation of general mental ability often is crucial for understanding an individual's behaviour, since many behavioural problems are linked to intellectual deficits. Second, individual intelligence tests present. An opportunity to observe the examinee's behaviour in response to several intellectually demanding tasks, and thus they provide data regarding the subject's persistence, maturity, problem-solving styles, and other characteristics.

The Rorschach, the Thematic Apperception Test (TAT), and the Minnesota Multiphasic Personality Inventory (MMPI) represent three of the most popular personality tests. Of the three, the MMPI is most closely associated with the diagnosis of psychopathology, whereas the TAT is most closely associated with the assessment of motives and drives. The Rorschach may be used for a variety of purposes, ranging from the assessment of specific personality traits to the diagnosis of perceptual disorders, depending on the scoring system used.

The Bender-Gestalt and the Luria-Nebraska Neuropsychological Test Battery are widely used in the diagnosis of neurological disorders. The Bender-Gestalt is used in the assessment of perceptual disorders and organic dysfunctions, although it may be used for a wide range of diagnostic purposes, whereas the Luria Nebraska Battery provides a wide ranging assessment of perceptual, motor, and intellectual functions that might be affected by damage to specific portions of the brain.

**Q2. Explain the variable domains of psychological assessment.**

**Ans.** Assessment pervades nearly every aspect of psychological or psychotherapeutic work with older adults. Thorough evaluation of the psychological status of an older person is an important but oftentimes complex and daunting process, even for experienced clinicians. In general, psychological assessment techniques are designed to evaluate a person's cognitive, emotional, social, and personality functioning. In clinical settings, the purposes of assessment are to find out what kinds of problems an older person is experiencing, to clarify personality features, to identify psychiatric disorders, to develop case conceptualisation and intervention plans, and to evaluate effects of treatment. Traditional assessment strategies require some modification for older persons, given their often complex problems, unique socialisation and life circumstances, and frequent comorbid health problems.

Within the limits of this distinction, the following summary list help to illustrate the scope of behavioural variables for which assessment procedures have been developed.

- **Performance Variables:** These include measures of sensory processes (for example tactile sensitivity, visual acuity, colour vision proficiency, auditory intensity threshold); perceptual aptitudes (tactile texture differentiation, visual closure, visual or auditory pattern recognition, memory for faces, visuo spatial tasks, etc.). Measures of attention and concentration (tonic and phasic alertness; the span of attention, distractibility, double performance tasks, vigilance performance over time), psychomotor aptitudes (including a wide variety of speed of reaction task designs), measures of learning and memory (short-term vs long-term memory, memory span, intentional vs. incidental memory, visual/auditory/kinesthetic memory), assessment of cognitive performance and intelligence (next to general intelligence a wide range of primary mental abilities like verbal comprehension, word fluency, numerical ability, reasoning abilities, measures of different aspects of creativity, of social or emotional intelligence; assessment of language proficiency (developmental linguistic performance, aphasia test systems, etc.); measures of social competence.

- **Personality Variables:** These include the assessment of primary factors of personality (especially of the so-called Big Five and numerous more specific personality measurement scales); special clinical schedules and symptom checklists (to assess anxiety, symptoms of depression, schizotypic tendency, personality disorders, etc.); motivation structures and interests; styles of daily living; pastime and life goals; assessment of incisive life events; assessment of stress tolerance and stress coping (including coping with serious illnesses and ailments); plus a wide range of still more specific assessment variables, like measures for the assessment of specific motives or specific styles of coping with illness or stressful life events. By now even the number of Psychodiagnostic assessment methods meeting high psychometric standards must have already reached many tens of thousands, rendering it impossible to give more than an informative overview within the limitations of this unit.

**Q3. Discuss the various data sources for psychological assessment.**

**Ans.** By present understanding and professional standards, psychological assessments and tests cannot be applied responsibly without proper psychometric and ethical/legal grounding. Psychological assessment procedures in general and psychological tests in particular, must not be mistaken for stand-alone procedures, they cannot be applied responsibly in the absence of profound psychometric qualification and sufficient familiarity with the conceptual basis of an assessment procedure, within which it has been developed and beyond which its results should not be interpreted. For example, tests of intelligence originate in specific operationalisations of what is to be understood by intelligence. Individual scores on a test of intelligence must not be interpreted beyond the limits set by the theoretical-conceptual basis of that test. Of course, from this follow also stringent rules of professional procedure as regards minimum qualifications to be requested from persons who may apply methods of assessments outside contexts of supervision (Bartram, 1998).

**(1) Actuarial and Biographical Data:** This category refers to descriptive data about a person's life history, educational, professional and medical record, possibly also a criminal record. Age, type and years of schooling, nature of completed professional education/vocational training, marital status, current employment and positions held in the past, leisure activities, and past illnesses and hospitalisations are examples of actuarial and biographical data. As a rule, such data is available with optimum reliability and often represents indispensable information, for example, in clinical and industrial/organisational assessments. Special biographical check list-item assessment instruments may be available in a given language and culture for special applications.

**(2) Behaviour Trace:** This refers to physical traces of human behaviour like handwriting specimen, products of art and expression (drawings, compositions, poems or other kinds of literary products), left-over's after the play in a children's playground, style (tidy or untidy, organised or 'chaotic') of the self-devised living environment at home, but also attributes of a person's appearance (e.g., bitten finger nails!) and attire. While at times perhaps intriguing, also within a wider humanistic perspective, the validity of personality assessments based on behaviour traces can be rather limited. For example, graphology (handwriting analysis) has been known for a long time to fall short of acceptable validity criteria in carefully conducted validation studies (Guilford, 1959; Rohracher, 1969). On the other hand, behaviour trace variables may provide valuable information in clinical contexts and at the process stage of developing assessment hypotheses.

**(3) Behaviour Observation:** In some sense, behaviour observation will form part of every assessment. In the present context the word observation is used in a more restricted sense, though, referring to direct recording/monitoring, describing, and operational classification of human behaviour, over and above what may be already incorporated in the scoring rationale of a questionnaire, an interview schedule, or an objective test. Examples of behaviour observation could be: studying the behaviour of an autistic child in a playground setting; monitoring the behaviour of a catatonic patient on a 24-hour basis; observing a trainee's performance in a newly designed workplace; starting in the 1920s and 1930s, has pushed careful, systematic behaviour observation to the side of the assessment process. Only in recent years, especially within clinical assessment and treatment contexts following behaviour therapeutic approaches, is the potential value of behaviour ratings for the assessment process being rediscovered.

**(4) Behaviour Ratings:** In behaviour rating assessments a person is asked to evaluate her/his own behaviour or the behaviour of another person with respect to given characteristics, judgemental scales, or checklist items. The method can be applied to concurrent behaviour under direct observation (as in modem assessment centre applications) or, and more typically, to the rater's explicit or anecdotal memory of the rate's behaviour at previous occasions, in (pastor imagined) concrete situations, or in a general sense. Behaviour rating methods may tell more about the mental representations that raters hold (developed, believe in) regarding the assessed person's behaviour than about that behaviour itself. Behaviour ratings constitute an essential methodology in clinical and industrial organisational psychology, in psychotherapy research and, last but not the least, in basic personality research. Modem textbooks of personality research usually give detailed accounts of how to devise behaviour rating scales and how to compensate for common sources of error variance in ratings.

**(5) Expressive Behaviour:** As a technical term, expressive behaviour refers to variations in the way in which a person may look, move, talk, express her/his current state of emotion, feelings or motives. Making a grim-looking face, trembling, getting a red face, sweating on the forehead, walking in a hesitant way, speaking loudly or with an anxiously soft voice, would be examples of variations in expression behaviour. Thereby expression refers to stylistic attributes in a person's behaviour which will induce an observer to draw explicitly or implicitly inferences about that person's state of mind, emotional tension, feeling state, or the like. Assessing another person from her/his expressive behaviour has a long tradition which goes back to pre-scientific days. More recently this approach has been extended to the study of gross bodily movement expression (Feldman & Rim'e, 1991). This research is relevant also for developing teaching aids in psychological assessment and observer training.

**(6) Projective Technique:** In the 1930s and 1940s many clinical psychologists, often influenced by psychoanalysis and other forms of depth psychology, placed high expectations in projective techniques, believing that they would induce a person to express her/his perception of the ambiguous stimulus material, thus willingly or even unwillingly 'uncovering' her/his personal individuality, including motives and emotions that the person may not even be aware of. Later, in the1950s and 1960s, research has clearly shown that such assessment methods not only tend to lack in scoring objectivity and psychometric reliability but, and still more important, also turned out to be of very limited validity, if any.

Nevertheless, projective tests still keep some of their appeals today, and research in the 1960s and thereafter succeeded in improving techniques like the Rorschach test at least as far as scoring objectivity and reliability are concerned. Further, more thematic association techniques like the TAT maintain their status as assessment methods potentially useful for deducing assessment hypotheses. In addition, special TAT forms have been devised for assessing specific motivation variables such as achievement motivation (McClelland, 1971). In the clinical context, once their prime field of application, projective techniques are no longer considered a tenable basis for hypothesis testing and theory development, let alone therapy planning and evaluation. Most psych diagnostics assessments will include an interview at least as an ancillary component and be it only for establishing personal contact and an atmosphere of trust. Extensive research on interview structure, interviewer influences, and interviewee response biases has given rise to a spectrum of interview techniques for different purposes and assessment contexts. As a rule, clinical assessments will · start out with an exploratory interview in which the psychologist will seek to focus the problem at hand and collect information for deriving assessment hypotheses. An interview is called unstructured if questions asked by the psychologist do not follow a predetermined course and, largely if not exclusively, depends on the person's responses and own interjections. Today most assessment interviews are semi-structured or fully structured. In the first case, the interviewer is guided by a schedule of questions or topics, with varying degrees of freedom as to how the psychologist may choose to follow up on the person's responses. Fully structured interviews follow an interview schedule containing all questions to be asked, often with detailed rules about which question(s) to ask next depending on a person's response to previous questions. An example of such a structured clinical interview schedule is the Structured Clinical Interview (SCID; Spitzer, Williams, & Gibbon, 1987) for clinical assessments according to the Diagnostic and Statistical Manual (DSM).

**(7) Questionnaires:** Originally, personality inventories, interest surveys, and attitude or opinion schedules were devised as structured interviews in written, following a multiple-choice response format (rather than presenting questions open-ended as in an interview proper). In a typical questionnaire, each item (question or statement) will be followed by two or three response alternatives such as 'Yes, do not know, No' or 'True, Cannot Say, Untrue'. Early clinical personality questionnaires like the Minnesota Multiphasic Personality Inventory (MMPI) drew much of their item content from confirmed clinical symptoms and syndromes. By contrast, personality questionnaires designed to measure extraversion, introversion, neuroticism, and other personality factors in healthy normal persons rely on item contents from empirical (mostly factor analytic) studies of these primary factors of personality. As in behaviour ratings, the research identified a number of typical response sets also in questionnaire data, including acquiescence (readiness to choose the affirmative response alternative, regardless of content) and social desirability (preference for the socially more acceptable response alternative). One way to cope with these sources of deficient response objectivity was to introduce special validity scales (as early as the MMPI) to control for response sets in a person's protocol. Yet individual differences in response sets may and in fact, do relate also to valid personality variance themselves.

There is common agreement today that a person's responses to a questionnaire must not be interpreted as behaviourally veridical, but only within empirically established scale validities. For example, a person's response to the questionnaire item frequently feels fatigued without being able to give a reason' must not be interpreted, for example, as being behaviourally indicative of the so-called fatigue syndrome. Rather subjects may differ in what they mean by 'frequently', by 'fatigued', by 'without reason' and on how broad a time and situation sample they base their response. After all, questionnaire data is assessment data about mental representations (perception, memory, evaluation) of behaviour variations in a person's self-perception and self-cognition. They tell us a lot about the awareness persons develop of tl1eir own behaviour which may, but need not, turn out veridical in objective behavioural terms. So the aforementioned item will carry its diagnostic value only as contributing to the validity of a psychmetrically reliable questionnaire scale, in this case, the scale 'neuroticism', with proven high clinical validity.

**(8) Objective Test:** Tests constitute the core of psychological assessment instruments; it is through them that psychological assessment has reached its level of scientific credibility and wide range of applications. A test is a sample of items, questions, problems, etc. chosen so as to sample, in a representative manner, the universe of items, questions or problems indicative of the trait or state to be assessed, for example, an aptitude or personality trait or a mood state like alertness. The adjective 'objective' refers to administration, scoring, and response objectivity in test development. Objective tests have been developed for the full spectrum of behaviour variables mentioned above. Their number goes into tens of thousands. A test is called an individual test, if it needs an exan1iner to administer it individually to the person assessed. Psychomotor and other performance tests are typical examples of tests still given individually. Still, the most widely used intelligence test system, the Wechsler Adult Intelligent Scale (WAS; Wechsler, 1958; and later editions) and its derivatives are administered individually throughout. The other test design, group tests, are devised so that one examiner can administer them to a number of persons (typically 20 to 30) at the same time in the same setting. Traditionally group tests were developed in so-called paper-and-pencil form, with the test items printed in a booklet and the person answering on a special answer sheet. While the development of objective behaviour tests of performance has been brought to a high level of proficiency and psychometric quality, objective behaviour tests of personality still linger in a far from the final phase of development that is despite massive, continuing efforts by Eysenck,

Cattell and many others (Cattell & Warbmton, 1965; Hundleby, Pawlik, & Cattell, 1963). There is confirmed empirical evidence to the fact that personality variables, i.e., measures of mode and style of typical behaviour (rather than of optimum performance), are more difficult to assess through objective tests than through conventional questionnaire scales, behaviour observations, or behaviour ratings.

**(9) Psycho Physiological Data:** All variations in behaviour and conscious experience are nervous system based, while ancillary input from the hormone and the immune system, respectively, and from peripheral organic processes. This should lead us to expect that individual differences as revealed in psychological assessment should be accessible also, and perhaps even more directly so, through monitoring psychophysiological system parameters that relate to the kind of behaviour variations that an assessment is targeted at. These psychophysiological variables include measures of brain activity and brain function plasticity (electroencephalogram, EEG; functional magnetic resonance imaging, fMRI; magnetoencephalogram, MEG) of hormone and immune system parameters and response pattern, and of peripheral psycho physiological responses mediated through the autonomic nervous system (cardiovascular system response patterns: electrocardiogram, ECG; breathing parameters: pneumogram; variations in sweat gland activity: electro dermal activity, EDA; in muscle tonus: electro myogram, EMG; or in eye movements and in pupil diameter: pupillometry).

**Q4. Discuss some frequently used methods of psychological assessment.**

*Or*

**What do you understand by psychological assessment in clinical context? Discuss the practical application of psychological assessment.**

**[Dec-2019, Q.No.-6]**

*Or*

**Discuss the application of psychological assessment.**

**[Dec-2020, Q.No.-6]**

**Ans.** Some frequently used methods of psychological assessment for three frequently encountered assessment problems: testing of intellective and other aptitude functions; psychological assessment in clinical contexts; and vocational guidance testing are described below:

**Assessment of Intelligence and Other Aptitude Functions:** The scaling proposal of mental age (age equivalence, in months, of the number of test item & solved correctly) as suggested by Binet and Henri (1896) in their prototype scale of intellectual development in early childhood, the German psychologist William Stem suggested an intelligence quotient (IQ), defined as tile ratio of mental age over biological age, as a measurement concept for assessing a gross function like intelligence in a score that would be independent of the age of the person tested. When subsequent research revealed psychometric inadequacies with this formula, the US psychologist David Wechsler proposed in his test (Wechsler, 1958) an IQ computed as age-standardised normalised standard score (with mean of 100 and standard deviation of 15). Now available in redesigned and standardised form as Wechsler Adult Intelligence Scale (WAIS), Wechsler Intelligence Scale for Children (WISC) and Wechsler Pre-School Test of Intelligence, this test package has become the trend-setting intelligence test system of widest application, also internationally through numerous foreign language adaptations. So a closer look at its assessment structure seems in order. The WAIS, for example, contains ten individually administered tests of two kinds:

(1) verbal tests (general information, general comprehension, digit memory span, arithmetic reasoning, finding similarities of concepts) and

(2) five performance tests (digit symbol substitution, arranging pictures according to tile sequence of a story, completing pictures, mosaic test block design, object assembly of two-dimensional puzzle pictures).

A person's test performance is assessed in three IQ scores, viz.,

(i) Verbal IQ,

(ii) Performance IQ, and

(iii) Total IQ

Surprisingly enough, this kind of overall test of cognitive functioning is still maintained in practical assessment work, despite indisputable and overwhelming empirical evidence that general intelligence as a trait will only account for part, at most perhaps about 30 per cent of individual difference variation in cognitive tests (Carroll, 1993). More recent examples of general intelligence type tests are the Kaufman Assessment Battery (Kaufman & Kaufman, 1983, 1993). An alternative, theoretically more developed approach is called differential aptitude assessment. Tests in this tradition are usually based on the results of factor analytic multi-trait studies of intelligence, originating in the work of Thurstone, Guilford and their students. Thurstone's Primary Mental Abilities Test (PMA, Thurstone & Thurstone, 1943), the Differential Aptitude Tests Battery (DAT; Bennettet al.,1981), the Kit of Reference Tests for Cognitive Factors (French, Ekstrom, & Price, 1963) are typical examples of this assessment approach that provides separate standardised scales for each selected primary intelligence factor. In addition to these tests of intellective functions, numerous more specialised aptitude tests have been developed such as the Wechsler Memory Scale (Wechsler & Stone, 1974), special performance tests for neuropsychological assessment, e.g., of brain-damaged patients (Lezak, 1995), for assessing mentally handicapped persons and the diagnosis of dementia, as well as for special sensory and psychomotor functions.

**Psychological Assessment in the Clinical Context:** In addition to some assessment questions mentioned in the preceding paragraph, in clinical psycho diagnostics, one faces questions of testing for personality variables, for behaviour disorders and or specific symptomatologies (as in the hyperactivity attention deficit disorder or posttraumatic stress disorder syndrome, for example). The MMPI was a classical prototype clinical personality test, which like the Wechsler tests of intelligence, has frequently been adapted and translated into other languages. Also, the large item stock of the MMPI (more than 550 items) has been utilised as a base from which a great number of special questionnaire scales were developed, perhaps best known among them the Taylor Manifest Anxiety Scale (MAS by Taylor, 1953). More recent personality questionnaires used in clinical psycho diagnostics would include, for example, the 16 Personality Factors Questionnaire (16 PF; Cattell, Cattell, & Cattell, 1994; also adapted and translated into many other languages). Besides these broad-band multi-scale questionnaires numerous assessment instruments of narrower focus have been developed. Examples are the Beck Depression Inventory, assessment instruments for studying phobic or obsessive symptoms or, more recently, interview and diagnostic inference schedules implementing the DSM and ICD approaches of descriptive disease classification. Often introduced as the master methodology of clinical psycho diagnostics, DSM IV- and ICD 10-based assessment strategies, have recently received increasing · criticism because of their purely descriptive, at theoretical nature, without recourse to aetiology of behaviour disorders and their development. It yet remains to be seen if tl1is criticism will give rise to novel, more etiologically oriented clinical assessment philosophies.

**Assessment in Vocational Guidance Testing and Job Selection/Placement:** Ever since the 1920s a multitude of tests of varying conceptual bandwidth have been developed to assess specific aptitudes and interest variables related to different vocational training curricula and on the job work demands. In vocational guidance testing, integrated multidimensional systems like one inaugurated by Paul Host in the 1950s for the US State of Washington have since become a model of approach in many countries. For example, the German *Bundesanstalt f'urArbeit* (Federal Office of Labor) developed its multidimensional testing and prognosis system for vocational guidance counselling at the senior high school level. A similar, CAT formatted multidimensional test system has been developed by the German Armed Forces Psychological Service Unit. Comparable assessment systems for guidance and placement have been devised, for example, in the UK and the US. Compared to these broadband assessment systems, job selection/placement testing in industrial and organisational psychology typically is narrower in scope, though more demanding in specific functions and job-related qualifications. Before implementing such an assessment system, a careful analysis of the job structure, the nature of professional demands and contextual situational factors is absolute! compulsory. The literature offers developed instrumentalism for carrying out such analyses (Kleinbeck & Rutenfranz, 1987). Since the 1970s/1980s a new methodology called 'assessment centre' has been introduced to provide for behaviour observation, behaviour rating, and interview assessment data in selected social situations devised to mirror salient demand situations in future on the job performance (Lattrnann, 1989). In continental Europe, the assessment centre approach has even become something like the method of choice, in selecting, for example, persons for higher-level managerial positions. Moreover, single-stage assessment and testing is now being replaced by on the job personnel development programs and special training offered to devise a more intervention oriented, multi-stage approach to assessment in organisational development.

**Q5. What do you mean by behavioural assessment?**

**Ans.** Behavioural assessment is a tool from the field of psychology that is used for observing, describing, explaining and predicting behaviour. Behavioural assessments are now being used outside the clinical settings too, especially in educational and corporate sectors, considering their insightful and predictive nature.

Behaviourists assert that both 'disordered' and 'non-disordered' behaviour can be explained using a common set of principles describing classical and operant conditioning. Behaviourists believe that behaviours are best understood in terms of their function. Two 'symptoms' may differ in form while being similar in function. For example, Jacobson (1992) describes topographically diverse behaviours such as walking away or keeping busy that all function to create distance between a client and his partner. Conversely, topographically similar behaviours may serve different functions. For example, tantrums may serve to elicit attention from adults or maybe an indication that the present task is too demanding. Behaviour therapists try to understand not only the form but also the function of problem behaviours within the client's environment.

**Goals of Assessment:** The initial goals of assessment are to identify and construct a case formulation of the client's difficulties that will guide the clinician and patient towards potentially effective interventions. For the behaviour therapist, this involves identifying problem behaviours, stimuli that are present when the target behaviours occur, along with associated consequences, and organism variables including learning history and physiological variables. The results of this functional analysis are used to design a behavioural intervention that is tailored to the individual client and conceptually linked to basic learning principles.

**Behavioural Assessment and Traditional Assessment:** Behavioural assessment is one of a variety of assessment traditions such as projective testing, neuropsychological assessment, and objective testing. Behavioural assessment distinguishes itself by being a set of specific techniques as well as a way of thinking about behaviour disorders and how these disorders can be changed. One of its core assumptions is that behaviour can be most effectively understood by focussing on preceding events and resulting consequences. Out of this core the assumption has come a surprisingly diverse number of assessment methods, including behavioural interviewing, several strategies of behavioural observation, measurement of relevant cognitions, psycho physiological assessment, and a variety of self-report inventories. Behavioural assessment can be most clearly defined by contrasting it with the traditional assessment. One of the most important comparisons is the emphasis that behavioural assessment places on situational determinants of behaviour. This emphasis means that behavioural assessment is concerned with a full understanding of the relevant antecedents and consequences of behaviour.

In contrast, traditional assessment is often perceived as more likely to view behaviour as a result of enduring, underlying traits. It is this underlying difference in conceptions of causation that explains most of the other contrasts between the two traditions. An extension of this conceptual difference is that behavioural assessment goes beyond the attempt to understand the contextual or situational features of behaviour and, more importantly, concerns itself with ways to change these behaviours. There is a close connection between the assessment itself and its implications for treatment. Thus, behavioural assessment is more direct, utilitarian, and functional. The perceived limitations of traditional assessment were a major factor in stimulating the development of behavioural assessment. Specifically, the traditional assessment was considered to focus too extensively on abstract, unobservable phenomena that were distant from the actual world of the client. Also, behaviourists felt that traditional clinical psychology had stagnated because its interventions were not sufficiently powerful and too much emphasis was placed on verbal therapy. A further contrast between behavioural and traditional assessment is that behavioural assessment is concerned with clearly observable aspects in the way a person interacts with his or her environment. A typical behavioural assessment might include specific measures of behaviour (overt and covert), antecedents (internal and external), conditions surrounding behaviours, and consequences. This knowledge can then be used to specify methods for changing relevant behaviours. Although some behavioural assessors might take selected personality traits into account, these traits would be considered relevant only if they had direct implications for therapy, For example, certain personality styles interact with the extent and type of depressive cognitions, and the existence of a personality disorder typically predicts therapeutic outcome. This focus on the person and his or her unique situation are quite different from psychodynamic, biochemical, genetic or normative trait models.

**Focus of Behavioural Assessment:** The behavioural approach stresses that different behaviour disorders are typically expressed in a variety of modes. These might include overt behaviours, cognitions, changes in physiological states, and patterns of verbal expressions. This implies that different assessment strategies should be used for each of these modes. An inference based on one mode does not necessarily generalise to another. For example, anxiety for one person may be caused and maintained primarily by the person's cognitions and only minimally by poor social skills. Another person might have a few cognitions relating to anxiety but be anxious largely because of inadequate social skills. The person with inadequate social skills might be most effectively treated through social skills training and only minimally helped through approaches that alter irrational thoughts.

It should also be noted that altering a person's behaviour in one mode is likely to affect other modes, and these effects might have to be considered. Whereas the preceding information presents a relatively rigid and stereotyped distinction between traditional and behavioural assessment, most practising clinicians, including those who identify themselves as behaviour therapists, typically combine and adapt techniques from both traditions.

**Assumptions and Perspectives of Behavioural Assessment:** The assumptions and perspectives of behavioural assessment have resulted in an extremely diverse number of approaches and an even wider variety of specific techniques. These approaches and their corresponding techniques can be organised into the areas of behavioural interviewing, behavioural observation, cognitive behavioural assessment, psycho physiological assessment, and self-report inventories. The book you can believe most– GPH book.

**Q6. Explain the self-report methods of behaviour assessment.**

*Or*

**Describe self-report inventory highlighting its strengths and weaknesses. Discuss the various formats of self-report inventory.**

**[June-2020, Q.No.-4]**

**Ans.** A self-report is any method which involves asking a participant about their feelings, attitudes, beliefs and so on. Examples of self-reports are questionnaires and interviews; self-reports are often used as a way of gaining participants' responses in observational studies and experiments.

Self-report measures have been used by many researchers to assess the behavioural, cognitive, and affective aspects of task engagement.

Items relating to the cognitive aspects of engagement often ask the subjects to report on factors such as their attention versus distraction during a task, the mental effort they expend on these tasks (e.g., to integrate new concepts with previous knowledge), and task persistence (e.g., reactions to perceived failures to comprehend the concerned material). Subjects can also be asked to report on their response levels during class time (e.g., making verbal responses within group discussions, looking for distractions and engaging in non-academic social interaction) as an index of behavioural task engagement. Affective engagement questions typically ask the subjects to rate their interest in and emotional reactions to learning tasks on indices such as choice of activities (e.g., selection of more versus less challenging tasks), the desire to know more about particular topics, and feelings of stimulation or excitement in beginning new projects. A variety of self-report questionnaires have been used in research on subjects' engagement, reflecting the multi-faceted nature of the construct. Wigfield (1997) suggested that high levels of task engagement were often reflected in factors such as the subjects' learning beliefs and expectations (e.g., Miller, et al, 1996), self-efficacy (Pintrich & Schrauben, 1992), task interest levels (Schiefele, 1995), and use of effective and/or deep, rather than "shallow" or "surface" learning strategies. Researchers have used different combinations of these indicators in empirical evaluations. Thus, typical assessment protocols comprise several separate indices for assessing the cognitive, affective or behavioural manifestations of task-related engagement. This reflects the fact that no one instrument is likely to be able to comprehensively assess the subject's engagement on all of the construct dimensions listed. Using separate indices also allows educators to adapt the focus of their protocols more towards their own instructional goals: Attitudes towards, and interests in, learning tasks are highly interrelated constructs and thus often assessed within the same scale.

**Examples of Self-Report Inventories:**

- **The MMPI-2:** Perhaps the most famous self-report inventory is the Minnesota Multiphasic Personality Inventory (MMPI). This personality test was first published in the 1940s, later revised in the 1980s and is today known as the MMPI-2. The test contains more than 500 statements that assess a wide variety of topics including interpersonal relationships, abnormal behaviours and psychological health as well as political, social, religious and sexual attitudes.

- **The 16 Personality Factor Questionnaire:** Another well-known example of a self-report inventory is the questionnaire developed by Raymond Cattell to assess individuals based on his trait theory of personality. This test is used to generate a personality profile of the individual and is often used to evaluate employees and to help people select a career.
- **California Personality Inventory:** California personality inventory is based on the MMPI, from which nearly half questions are drawn. The test is designed to measure such characteristic as self-control, empathy and independence.

**Strengths and Weaknesses of Self-Report Inventories:** Self-report inventories are often a good solution when researchers need to administer a large number of tests in relatively short space of time. Many self-report inventories can be completed very quickly, often in as little as 15 minutes. This type of questionnaire is an affordable option for researchers faced with tight budgets. Another strength is that the results of self-report inventories are generally much more reliable and valid than projective tests. Scoring of the tests a standardised and based on norms that have been previously established. However, self-report inventories do have their weaknesses. For example, while many tests implement strategies to prevent "faking good" or "faking bad," research has shown that people can exercise deception while taking self-report tests (Anastasi & Urbina, 1997). Another weakness is that some tests are very long and tedious. For example, the MMPI takes approximately 3 hours to complete. In some cases, test respondents may simply lose interest and not answer questions accurately. Additionally, people are sometimes not the best judges of their behaviour. Some individuals may try to hide their feelings, thoughts and attitudes. There are several formats for collecting self-report data. These include interviews, questionnaires and inventories, rating scales, think aloud, and thought sampling procedures. It is most often the case that an assessment would include several of these methods.

**Formats of Self-Report Inventories**

- **Interviews:** The clinical interview is the most widely used method of clinical assessment and is particularly advantageous in the early stages of assessment. The most salient of its advantages is flexibility. The typical interview begins with a broad-based inquiry regarding the client's functioning. As the interview progresses, it becomes more focussed on specific problems and potential controlling variables. Interviewing also provides an opportunity to directly observe the client's behaviour, and to begin developing a therapeutic relationship. The clinical interview also has important disadvantages. Interviews elicit information from memory that can be subject to errors, omissions, or distortions. Additionally, the interview often relies heavily on the clinician to make subjective judgements in selecting those issues that warrant further assessment or inquiry. One could reasonably expect that different clinicians could emerge from a clinical interview with very different conceptualisations of the client. Structured and semi-structured interviews were developed to facilitate consistency across interviewers. Structured interviews are designed for administration by non-clinicians such as research assistants in large scale studies. A structured interview follows a strict format that specifies the order and exact wording of questions. Semi-structured interviews are more frequently used by trained clinicians. They provide a more flexible framework for the course of the interview while providing enough structure to promote consistency across administrations. While specific questions may be provided, the interviewer is free to pursue additional information when this seems appropriate. In general, the goal of enhanced reliability has been attained with the use of structured and semi-structured interviews. However, the majority of these interviews are designed for purposes of diagnosis rather than more particular target behaviours or functional assessment. Just as the clinical interview proceeds from a general inquiry to a more focussed assessment of behavioural targets, other self-report measures vary in the degree to which they assess general areas of functioning versus particular problem behaviours. In general, those measures that assess general constructs such as depression or general domains of functioning are developed using group data and are meant to apply to a wide range of clients. Examples of these nomothetic measures include personality inventories and standardised questionnaires. Other self-report methods can be tailored more towards individual clients and particular problem responses. These include rating scales and think-aloud procedures.

- **Questionnaires:** Questionnaires are probably the next most common assessment tool after interviews. Questionnaires can be easily and economically administered. They are easily quantified and the scores can be compared across time to evaluate treatment effects. Finally, normative data is available for many questionnaires so that a given client's score can be referenced to a general population. There has been a rapid proliferation of questionnaires over the last few decades. Some questionnaires focus on stimulus situations provoking the problem behaviour, such as anxiety-provoking situations. Other questionnaires focus on particular responses or positive or negative consequences. The process of choosing questionnaires from those that are available can be daunting. Fischer and Corcoran (1994) have compiled a collection of published questionnaires accompanied by summaries of their psychometric properties. Many behaviourists have expressed concern with the apparent reliance on questionnaires both in clinical and in research settings. These criticisms stem in part from repeated observations that individuals evidence very limited ability to identify those variables that influence their behaviour. Additionally, behaviourists point out that we tend to reify the constructs that we measure. This may lead to a focus on underlying dispositions or traits in explaining behaviour rather than a thorough investigation of environmental factors and the individual's learning history. Behaviourists do make use of questionnaires but tend to regard them as measures of behavioural responses that tend to correlate rather than as under-lying traits or dispositions.
- **Rating Scales and Self-Ratings:** Rating scales can be constructed to measure a wide range of responses. They are often incorporated into questionnaires or interviews. For example, a client may be asked to rate feelings of hopelessness over the past week on a scale of 0-8. Clinicians might also make

ratings of the client's noticeable behaviour during the interview or the client's apparent level of functioning. The main advantage of rating scales is its flexibility. They can be used to assess problem behaviours for which questionnaires are not available. Additionally, rating scales can be administered repeatedly with greater ease than questionnaires. For example, rather than pausing to complete an anxiety questionnaire, a client might provide periodic self-ratings of discomfort during an anxiety-provoking situation. The main disadvantage of rating scales is the lack of normative data.

- **Thought Listing and Think Aloud Procedures:** Clinicians are sometimes interested in the particular thoughts that are experienced by a client in a situation such as phobic exposure or role play. The use of questionnaires may interfere with the situation and may not capture the more idiosyncratic thoughts of a particular client. Think aloud and thought sampling procedures may be used under these circumstances. These procedures require the client to verbalise thoughts as they occur in the assessment situation. Thoughts can be reported continually in a think-aloud format or the client may periodically be prompted to report the most recently occurring thoughts in a thought sampling procedure. When the requirements of think-aloud procedures may interfere with the client's ability to remain engaged in the assessment situation, the client may be asked to list those thoughts that are recalled at the end of the task. These procedures carry the advantage of being highly flexible. Like other highly individualised methods, they also carry the disadvantage of lacking norms.

**Q7. Explain direct observation and self-monitoring methods of behavioural assessment.**

*Or*

**Write a short note on disguised field observations.**

**[June-2019, Q.No.-11][June-2021, Q.No.-10]**

*Or*

**Write a short note on analogue observation. [Dec-2020, Q.No.-11]**

**Ans.** Behaviour-modification procedures often require subjects to self-observe their own behaviour. The present study was undertaken with the belief that the effects of self-monitoring may be predictable and that self-observation may have important applications for behaviour-change programs. Undergraduate students were asked to observe and record their studying behaviour for a college course. It was predicted that self-observation would increase study output for these students and thereby effect an increase in their course grades. Two control groups were included: *(1)* a group of students who self-observed dating activities, and *(2)* another group of students who volunteered but were randomly not accepted into the study. The results indicate that students who self-observed study behaviour achieved significantly higher grades, during the latter part of the academic term, than the control group of unaccepted volunteers. Subjects in the dating group achieved higher grades than the control group and lower grades than the study group but these differences were not significant. These findings suggest that self-observation procedures may often be reactive and that this reactivity may be successfully used as an agent for behaviour change.

There are several ways to decrease the demands on the observer and thereby facilitate more faithful data collection. One option is the use of brief observation periods. For example, a parent might be asked to record the frequency of the target behaviour at intervals during those specific situations when the behaviour is probable. When the target behaviour is an ongoing response, the observer might employ momentary sampling procedures and periodically check to see if the behaviour is occurring. The features of direct observation are listed in the box given below:

- Behaviour is observed in a natural setting.
- Behaviour is recorded or coded as it occurs.
- Impartial, objective observers record behaviour.
- Behaviour is described in clear, crisp terms, requiring little or no inference by the observer.

**Disadvantages of Direct Observation:** Direct observation carries some disadvantages. It can be costly and time-consuming. In the strictest sense, it would be favourable to utilise multiple observers so that the concordance of their recording could be checked. It has been shown that the reliability of observations is enhanced when observers know that the data will be checked. However, this may not be practical, particularly in clinical settings. The use of participant-observers may be a less costly alternative in many cases. Direct observation can also result in reactive effects. Reactivity refers to changes in behaviour that result from the assessment procedure. Making clients aware that they are being observed can alter the frequency or form of the target response. This can occur even with the use of participant-observers. The variables that influence observe reactivity are not well understood. For ethical reasons, it may be unwise to conduct observations without the client's awareness.

Also indirect observations, people know that you are watching them. The only danger is that they are reacting to you. As stated earlier, there is a concern that individuals will change their actions rather than showing you what they're like. This is not necessarily bad, however. For example, the contrived behaviour may reveal aspects of social desirability, how they feel about sharing their feelings in front of others, or privacy in a relationship. Even the most contrived behaviour is difficult to maintain over time. A long-term observational study will often catch ·a glimpse of the natural behaviour. Other problems concern the gerieralisability of findings. The sample of individuals may not be representative of the population or the behaviours observed are not representative of the individual (you caught the person on a bad day). Again, long-term observational studies will often overcome the problem of external validity.

**Types of Direct Observation:** There are two commonly used types of direct observations:

- **Continuous Monitoring:** This involves observing a subject or subjects and recording (either manually, electronically, or both) as much of their behaviour as possible. Continuous monitoring is often used in organisational settings, such as evaluating performance. Yet this may be problematic due to the Hawthorne Effect. The Hawthorne Effect states that workers react to the attention they are getting from the researchers and in turn, productivity increases. Observers should be aware of this reaction. Other CM research is used in education, such as watching teacher-student interactions. Also in nutrition where researchers record how much an individual eats. CM is relatively easy but a time consuming endeavor. You will be sure to acquire a lot of data.
- **Time Allocation:** This involves a researcher randomly selecting a place and time and then recording what people are doing when they are first seen and before they see you. This may

sound rather bizarre but it is a useful tool when you want to find out the per cent of time people are doing things (i.e. playing with their kids, working, eating, etc.). There are several sampling problems with this approach. First, to make generalisations about how people are spending their time the researcher needs a large representative sample. Sneaking up on people all over town is tough way to spend your days. Also, questions such as when, how often, and where should you observe are often a concern. Many researchers have overcome these problems by using nonrandom locations but randomly visiting them at different times.

**Unobtrusive Observation:** Unobtrusive measures involve any method for studying behaviour where individuals do not know they are being observed (don't you hate to think that this could have happened to you!). Here, there is not the concern that the observer may change the subject's behaviour. When conducting unobtrusive observations, issues of validity need to be considered. Numerous observations of a representative sample need to take place to generalise the findings. This is especially difficult when looking at a particular group. Many groups possess unique characteristics, which make them interesting studies. Hence, often such findings are not strong in external validity. Also, replication is difficult when using non-conventional measures (non-conventional meaning unobtrusive observation). Observations of a very specific behaviours are difficult to replicate in studies especially if the researcher is a group participant (we'll talk more about this later). The main problem with unobtrusive measures, however, is ethical. Issues involving informed consent and invasion of privacy are paramount here. An institutional review board may frown upon your study if you need to inform your subjects. There are two types of unobtrusive research measures you may decide to undertake in the field and these are given below:

- **Behaviour Trace Studies:** Behaviour trace studies involve findings things people leave behind and interpreting what they mean. This can be anything to vandalism to garbage. The University of Arizona Garbage Project one of the most well-known trace studies. Anthropologists and students dug through household garbage to find out about such things as food preferences, waste behaviour, and alcohol consumption. Again, remember, that in unobtrusive research individuals do not know they are being studied. Surprisingly Tucson residents supported the research as long as their identities were kept confidential. As you might imagine, trace studies may yield enormous data.

- **Disguised Field Observations:** In Disguised field analysis the researcher pretends to join or is a member of a group and records data about that group. The group does not know they are being observed for research purposes. Here, the observer may take on several roles. First, the observer may decide to become a complete participant in which they are studying something they are already a member of. For instance, if you are a member of a sorority and study female conflict within sororities you would be considered a complete participant observer.

  On the other hand, we may decide to only participate casually in the group while collecting observations. In this case, any contact with group members is by acquaintance only. Here you would be considered an observer participant. Finally, if you develop an identity with the group members but do not engage in important group activities consider yourself a participant observer. An example would be joining a cult but not participating in any of their important rituals (such as sacrificing animals). However, considered a member of the cult and trusted by all of the members. Ethically, participant observers have the most problems. Certainly, there are degrees of deception at work. The sensitivity of the topic and the degree of confidentiality are important issues to consider.

**Analogue Observation:** Analogue Observation is a method of direct observation, but it occurs in a contrived, carefully structured setting, designed specifically for the assessment. By contrast, direct observation occurs in a naturalistic setting. In analogue assessment or observation, after the setting has been structured, direct observation of behaviour follows, using many of the principles of observation previously described.

**Self-Monitoring:** In self-monitoring procedures, the client is asked to act as his or her observer and to record information regarding target behaviours as they occur. Self-monitoring can be regarded as a self-report procedure with some benefits similar to direct observation. Because target behaviours are recorded as they occur, self-monitored data may be less susceptible to memory-related errors. Like other self-report methods, self-monitoring can be used to assess private responses that are not amenable to observation. Self-monitored data also have the potential to be more complete than that obtained from observers, because the self-monitor can potentially observe all occurrences of target behaviours. There are several formats for self-monitoring. Early in assessment, a diary format is common. This allows the client to record any potentially important behaviours and their environmental context in the form of a narrative. As particular target behaviours are identified, the client may utilise data collection sheets for recording more specific behavioural targets and situational variables. Whim behaviours are highly frequent or occur with prolonged duration, the client may be asked to estimate the number of occurrences at particular intervals or the amount of time engaged in the target response. It is often desirable to check the integrity of self-monitored data. Making the client aware that their self-monitored data will be checked is known to enhance the accuracy of data collection, Self-monitored data can be checked against data obtained from external observers or can be compared to measured by products of the target response. For example, self-monitored alcohol consumption can be compared to randomly tested blood alcohol levels. Among the disadvantages of self-monitoring are its demands on the client for data collection and the lack of available norms. Like direct observation, self-monitoring also produces reactive effects. However, this disadvantage in terms of measurement can be advantageous in terms of treatment. This is because reactive effects tend to occur in the therapeutic direction, with desirable behaviours becoming more frequent and undesired behaviours tending to decrease.

**Q8. What do you mean by Psychophysiological Assessment?**

*Or*

**Write as short note on Psychophysiological Assessment.**

**[Dec-2019, Q.No.-11]**

**Ans.** Psychophysiological assessment involves recording and quantifying various physiological responses in controlled conditions using electromechanical equipment (e.g., electromyography, electroencephalography, electrodermal activity, respiratory activity, electrocardiography). Which response or response system is measured depends on the purpose of the assessment. Psychophysiological measurement has been used to assess autonomic balance (e.g., heart rate, diastolic blood pressure, salivation), habituation to environmental stimuli, reactivity to traumatic imagery, orientation response, and other physiological systems.

Frequently, the behavioural assessor is not so much interested in the behaviour measured by the equipment as what may be inferred from the behaviour. For example, a large literature exists with regard to the psychophysiological measurement of responses to anxiety-eliciting stimuli. Keane and co-workers in 1998 showed that male military veterans with posttraumatic stress disorder (PTSD) exhibited greater changes in psychophysiological responding (i.e., increased heart rate, skin conductance, systolic and diastolic blood pressure) when presented a series of trauma-related cues than did veterans without PTSD. Other studies have found increased physiological responsively in females with PTSD and increased heart rate responses to startling tones in individuals with PTSD.

Physiological measures can be sensitive to subtle changes and to physiological processes that occur without the client's awareness. They can also provide both discrete and continuous data about physiological processes while requiring only passive participation from the client. Additionally, most clients lack familiarity with psychophysiological measurement, making deliberate distortion of responses improbable. The main disadvantage of psychophysiological measurement is the cost of equipment and training. This problem is compounded by the observation that it is often desirable to include measures of multiple physiological channels. For example, there can be substantial variance across individuals in the degree of response exhibited on a given physiological index. Those measures that are most sensitive for a given individual may not be included in a limited psychophysiological assessment. With technological advances in this area, less costly instrumentation will likely become more available.

**Q9. Define and describe the psychological assessment in clinical setting.**

**Ans.** In order for a mental health professional to be able to effectively treat a client and know that the selected treatment actually worked (or is working), s/he first must engage in the clinical assessment of the client. Clinical assessment refers to collecting information and drawing conclusions through the use of observation, psychological tests, neurological tests, and interviews to determine what the person's problem is and what symptoms s/he is presenting with. This collection of information involves learning about the client's skills, abilities, personality characteristics, cognitive and emotional functioning, social context (e.g., environmental stressors), and cultural factors particular to them such as their language or ethnicity.

**Definition of Psychological Assessment:** Psychological assessment can be formally defined in many ways. Clinical assessment involves an evaluation of an individual's strengths and weaknesses, a conceptualisation of the problem at hand (as well as possible etiological factors), and some prescription for alleviating the problem; all of these lead us to a better understanding of the client. Assessment is not something that is done once and then is forever finished. In many cases, it is an ongoing process-even an everyday process, as in psychotherapy. Whether the clinician is making decisions or solving problems, clinical assessment is the means to the end. Intuitively, we all understand the purpose of diagnosis or assessment. Before physicians can prescribe a treatment, they must first understand the nature of the illness. Before plumbers can begin soldering pipes, they must first determine the character and location of the difficulty. What is true in medicine and plumbing is equally true in clinical psychology. Aside from a few cases involving pure luck, our capacity to solve clinical problems is directly related to our skill in defining them. Most of us can remember our parents' stem admonition: "Think before you act!" In a sense, this is the essence of the assessment or diagnostic process.

**Psychological Assessment:** Physicians run "tests" to identify illnesses of diseases. Sometimes one test identifies the source of problems such as an x-ray revealing a tumour or a blood test showing low iron levels or anaemia. However, some illnesses aren't so clear-cut, requiring a battery of tests and medical procedures to accurately diagnose complex conditions. Clinical psychologist's tools also are used to diagnose learning disabilities, determine competency to stand trial for a crime, and guide individuals into a deeper understanding of their vocational and vocational likes and dislikes. Clinical psychologists similarly use various tools, called psychological tests to help diagnose mental illness and disease. But like complex medical conditions, tests often don't provide all the answers, so psychologists rely on a broader educational tool called an "assessment" to more accurately diagnose psychological conditions. Based on assessments, psychologists develop and apply effective treatment plans and interventions.

**Psychologists as Detectives:** Psychologists conducting assessments are likes detectives trying to solve a case. The assessment requires a gathering of information from multiple sources, from written tests, personal interviews, job history records, and reports and records from other physicians, therapists, and counsellors. The clinical psychologist compiles an entire "case history" or in-depth story of a person's inner and outer life, a sort of journey into the intricacies of psyche and behaviours. Past and present life situations are also considered. According to Wikipedia, 91 per cent of clinical psychologists perform some type of assessment. But the complexity of the assessment depends on several factors, such as the clinical setting, the severity of the condition, and the age and ability of the particular client. For example, an assessment done on a child struggling in school will be quite different from an assessment conducted with a suspected criminal. And an assessment given to a soldier in Afghanistan experiencing symptoms of trauma will differ dramatically from individual seeking treatment for depression from a psychotherapist who uses a form of "talk therapy" to diagnose and treat clients. A "full" assessment of the soldier probably isn't likely given the conditions of war and fighting, yet military psychologists are trained to assess soldiers using other methods, such as observational or interview-type approaches, to determine an effective immediate intervention, or to determine if the soldier needs to be removed from the situation and admitted to a military facility for a more thorough assessment and longer term therapy. Likewise, psychotherapists in private settings have more flexibility in the type of assessment given to clients than psychotherapists working in a mental health facility or hospital, which often recommends standard, commonly used tools for tests and assessments.

**Comprehensive Assessments:** The strength of the psychological assessment process stems from its comprehensive, scientific methodology. Testing implies something like a blood test where you just give a test and get a number," explained Smith, also in private practice and a faculty member at the University of California, Berkeley. "Assessment is a much more complex enterprise where you integrate data points from various places to get a more comprehensive understanding. Psychologists must be able to select the best assessment tools available for certain client populations and to become, in a sense, wise consumers of psychological research. Also, a post-assessment must occur after a psychological intervention has been applied, assessing the impact on the client's behaviour and progress towards healing.

**Psychological Assessment as Important Tools:** Scientific research in clinical psychotherapy has evolved since its beginnings after World War II, as psychologists attempted to understand and treat soldiers with shell shock- what today is called post-traumatic stress disorder. Over the years, many in the scientific community have questioned the reliability and validity of psychological testing as compared to medical testing. Studies conducted over the past few decades have proven the efficacy of psychological tests, according to professionals working in the field. In the American Psychological Association's journal "Monitor," an article by Jennifer Draw explored the results from a study conducted by the American Psychological Association's Psychological Assessment Work Group. The PAWG researchers found that many psychological tests produce results of comparable validity to medical tests such as Pap smears, mammography, magnetic resonance imaging (MRI) and electrocardiograms. As an example, the researchers cited test scores from the Minnesota Multiphasic Personality Inventory (MMPI) that had an average ability to detect depressive or psychotic disorders with the same reliability that Pap tests detect cervical abnormalities. The researchers also went a step further to conclude that some psychological tests work as well as medical tests in detecting the same illnesses. They point to neuropsychological testing for dementia producing results with the same level of effectiveness as an MRI.

**Reliability and Validity:** Reliability means that an experiment or test reports the same results after a repeated number of trials. Independent researchers must be able to replicate experiments using the same controls as the original researchers, making the research generalisable. Validity determines if the experiment measures exactly what the researchers attempted to measure- or the specific concept under study.

**Q10. State the types of psychological assessment.**

***Or***

**Write a short note on addiction assessment. [June-2020, Q.No.-11]**

**Ans.** Psychological tests provide a way to formally and accurately measure different factors that can contribute to people's problems. Before a psychological test is administered, the individual being tested is usually interviewed. In addition, it is common for more than one psychological test to be administered in certain settings.

Thousands of psychological tests exist all falling in one of the following categories:

- Intelligence or IQ tests, such as WAIS IV, WICS IV, Stanford Binet,
- Cattell Culture Fair III,
- Woodcock Johnson Tests of Cognitive Abilities III.
- Attitude scales such as Thurstone scale or Liket scale and
- Personality tests such as the MMPI, MCMI III,
- Beck Depression Inventory and vii) Child Behaviour Check List.
- The Rorschach Test used less frequently is also a personality test.
- Direct Observation tests, such as the Parent-Child Interaction Assessment II, the MacArthur Story Stem Battery and the Dyadic Parent-child Interaction Coding System.

**Addiction Assessments:** The assessment of client functioning is a critical component of both treatment outcome evaluation and assessment of the individual level of need for individual treatment planning and service delivery selection. This is especially true for the dually diagnosed client with multiple concomitant needs, on a variety of levels. The Functional Assessment of Mental Health and Addiction scale (FAMHA) was specifically designed to meet both criteria. While it is beneficial to note the positive client changes that occur due to the effects of treatment, it is perhaps more important to have a functional baseline or clinical yardstick with which to plan effective strategies of biopsychosocial interventions. This is of utmost importance for dually diagnosed clients, with multiple service needs in mental health, addiction treatment, and medical interventions.

A basic, core goal of all treatment is to produce substantial and enduring changes in client behaviours, cognitions and moods and more useful strategies for managing their day-to-day lives. The only other goal of treatment is then to reduce a client's distress to the greatest degree possible. By determining a client's specific level· of functioning across all major biopsychosocial domains and an overall level of functioning, specific symptom and functional deficit profiles emerge that can then be used for more effective treatment planning. Such assessments are client centered by their very nature and specifically relate to the distress and difficulties that each patient must endure in their daily lives. Thus, functional assessments like the FAMHA are the key to not only measuring the outcomes of treatments on a broad scale but crucial to the clinician's full understanding of the patient's individual needs.

**Description of the FAMHA:** The Functional Assessment of Mental Health and assessment(FAMHA) is a clinician rating scale, specifically designed to accurately assess dually diagnosed, across a broad range of symptom and functional domains. It was developed in response to clinical and outcome research goals identified by the Department of Health (1996) which emphasised the need for extending research on the outcome of treatment for substance misuse problems. It is meant for three different types of addicts.

- mentally ill substance users (MISU),
- substance-using mentally ill (SUMI), and
- medically compromised substance-using patients (MCSU)

The assessment scale is specifically tailored to assess the multifaceted needs of severely distressed patients and to identify specific areas for effective therapeutic interventions. The 46 items of the scale document functional deficits across all biopsychosocial functional domains in such a way as to capture the current state of overall functioning, whilst demonstrating specific areas of need. Thus, it can be used as both an indicator of current functioning for diagnostic assessment and as a repeated measure to demonstrate the changes that occur to patients throughout the clinical cycle. Sciacca (1991) noted significant differences between various subpopulations of dually diagnosed patients (in both mental health and addiction treatment settings) that have an impact on treatment planning and service delivery for each patient population.

The term dual diagnosis is somewhat broad and misleading (for example; mental illness and learning disabilities are dual diagnoses). The distinction between MISU, SUMI, and MCMU patients has a significant impact on the selection and use of a variety of intervention techniques and strategies. MISU patients generally present with symptoms of severe and enduring mental illness that has been complicated by the use of psychotropic substances. SUMI patients are characterised by their excessive use of psychotropic agents with the subsequent development of a concomitant severe and persistent mental illness. MCSU patients characteristically use large amounts of psychotropic agents in the presence of a long-term or severe physical injury, illness or ongoing medical condition. Traditionally, MISU patients have gravitated towards mental health treatment systems, SUM! patients have generally sought treatment in addiction treatment settings; while MCSU patients have relied on medical treatment facilities to seek therapeutic relief. Mental illness, substance use/misuse and medical conditions must be approached differently for each group to achieve effective therapeutic outcomes (Sciacca, 1991). The severe and persistent mental illness of MISU patients make it difficult for them to engage in motivational interviewing or more restrictive treatments often used in addiction treatment settings (Bachrach, 1984). On the other hand, SUMI and MCSU patients often require relief from the effects of addiction and withdrawal before they can fully focus on their treatment for the medical, psychological and social issues that have emerged or intensified as a result of tl1eir substance use. For this reason, the FAMHA was designed to assess individual differences in symptomatology, whilst differentiating these two populations on a functional level. Effective treatment of MISU, SUMI and MCSU patients require diagnostic clarification as to the initial step in successful care planning. To address the problem of multiple diagnoses of mental illness, medical conditions and substance abuse. clinicians from addiction, medical, and psychiatric backgrounds must learn to make the clinical formulations for each of the concomitant disorders, using clear diagnostic standards and evidence-based assessments.

A major advantage of using the FAMHA is that it can be quickly and effectively administered to provide diagnostic indicators and monitor the effects of treatment over time. The following list identifies many of the characteristics that distinguish MISU, SUMI and MCSU patients which can be quantitatively assessed on the FAMHA:

**MISU Characteristics**

- Severe mental illness exists independently of substance abuse; persons would meet the diagnostic criteria of a major mental illness even if there were not' a substance abuse problem present.

- MISU persons have a DSM-N-R, Axis I (American Psychiatric Association, 1987) diagnosis of a major psychiatric disorder, such as schizophrenia or major affective disorder.
- MISU persons usually require medication to control their psychiatric illness; if medication is stopped, specific symptoms are likely to emerge or worsen.
- Substance abuse may exacerbate acute psychiatric symptoms, but these symptoms generally persist beyond the withdrawal of the precipitating substance.
- MISU persons, even when in remission, frequently display the residual effects of major psychiatric disorders (for example, schizophrenia), such as marked social isolation or withdrawal, blunted or inappropriate affect, and marked lack of initiative, interest, or energy. Evidence of these residual effects often differentiates MISU from populations of substance abusers who are not severely mentally ill.

**SUMI Characteristics**

- SUMI patients have severe substance dependence (alcoholism; heroin, cocaine, amphetamine, or other addictions), and frequently have multiple substance abuse and/or polysubstance abuse or addiction.
- SUMI persons usually require treatment in alcohol or drug treatment programs. SUMI persons often have the coexistent personality or character disorders.
- SUMI patients may appear in the mental health system due to "toxic" or "substance-induced" acute psychotic symptoms that resemble the acute symptoms of a major psychiatric disorder. In this instance, the acute symptoms are always precipitated by substance abuse, and the patient does not have a primary Axis I major psychiatric disorder.
- SUMI patients' acute symptoms remit completely after a period of abstinence or detoxification. This period is usually a few days or weeks but occasionally may require months.

- SUMI patients do not exhibit the residual effects of a major mental illness when acute symptoms are in remission.

**MCSU Characteristics**

- MCSU patients continued to use large amounts of substances even after their medical conditions have gone into remission or have been successfully treated.
- These patients begin using psychotropic agents to seek relief from physical pain due to a medical condition.
- MCSU patients often have long-term medical conditions (i.e. HIV, Heart Conditions, Autoimmune deficiencies, etc.) that reduce their level of physical functioning and make them vulnerable to a substance use disorder.
- The hopeless and helpless feelings associated with long-term or severe medical conditions produce depressive states that are reduced by the use of intoxicating or pain-relieving substances.
- The loss of physical function and range of motion often produces a reduction in psychological functioning and increases the reliance on pharmacological agents.

**Development of the Scale:** The FAMHA was developed with a variety of criteria in mind. To adequately assess MISU, SUMI, and MCSU patients in naturalistic settings, specific criteria developed by Green and Greely (1987) were applied to the scale as it was modified in development phases and pilot trials. It was felt that the FAMHA should not only assess the obvious symptom categories of major mental illness and addiction but should also:

- include functional domains that are deemed important for community-based treatment clinics;
- demonstrate reliability and validity;
- possess sensitivity to treatment-related change;
- be appropriate and relevant to the dually diagnosed population that it functionally assesses;
- be a useful tool for treatment planning and clinical governance;
- have low administration costs;
- be relatively easy to use by all levels of clinical staff.

The current version of the FAMHA meets all of these criteria and can be administered in as little as 8 minutes by a trained, experienced rater. The FAMHA builds on the strengths of the Specific Level of Functioning scale (SLOF) (Schnieder & Struening - 1983), Symptom Checklist 90 (SCL90R) (Derogatis, 1975), the Bellevue Psychiatric Audit (BPA) (Hardesty & Burdock, 1962) and the Addiction Severity Index, 5th Edition (ASI) (McLellan et al, 1997). It combines a variety of clinical and functional dimensions into a 46 item clinician rating scale that is subdivided into 6 biopsychosocial dimensions:

- Socio-legal
- Social-Community Living
- Social - Interpersonal Skills
- Mood
- Psychological Functioning
- Physical Functioning.

In addition to the dimensional scales, data as to the patient's primary and secondary chug of choice, alcohol consumption, prior mental health and addiction treatment episodes, demographics, and current medical, mental health and addiction diagnoses are also collected to add to the clarity of the diagnostic profile. It is expected that continued statistical analysis, including factor analyses of further trials, will yield more refined, discrete scale dimensions and add to the overall utility of the instrument. Similar to the SLOF in appearance, the FAMHA uses a seven-point, three-way anchored Likert like scale, ranging from extremely dysfunctional symptoms or behaviours (Score 1) to normative levels of these behaviours and symptoms (Score 7). The low end, mid-point and high points of functioning are anchored by descriptors for each item. This allows for enhanced inter-rater reliability and validity of patient/clinic-wide functional assessments. Like the SLOF and SCL-90R, each of the 46 items of the FAMHA is evaluated on the Likert-like scale. Due to the specific nature of each of these 46 functional items, the FAMHA assumes a high degree of assessor familiarity with the patient. The scale was designed to quantify patient functional levels more systematically than the Global Assessment of Functioning (GAF)(APA, 1994) and provides for the systematic rating of functional deficits in critical areas of that could not otherwise be assessed in this population. Also, FAMHA overall scores are designed with a coefficient that readily converts the total score to overall GAF scores. Thus, it refines the diagnostic profile for individual patients that is necessary for appropriate diagnosis within both ICD-10 (WH0-1996) and DSM-N (APA 1994) diagnostic systems.

**Validity and Reliability:** The concordance rates between the FAMHA total scores, sub-scores and GAF scores are currently in clinical trials and cannot yet be reported on. However, due to the high degree of similarity between the SLOF and the FAMHA, it is assumed that patient scores on each FAMHA dimension will significantly correlate with overall GAF scores and subscores. The SLOF concordance rates for the various components were reported to be r =.67 for the social component, .60 for the psychological, and .50 for the physical component. Moderate associations ·were found between the SLOF substance abuse scale and the Drake et al. (1990) substance abuse scale (r =.73) (Uehara et al. 1994).

This concordance rate should be mirrored in the FAMHA since most of these specific SLOF items are embedded in the FAMHA as well. Further clinical trials should conclusively demonstrate the usefulness of combining the level of functioning information across mental health and addiction dimensions and ultimately, validate the FAMHA as an ideal instrument for assessing dually diagnosed patients in mental health and addiction treatment settings. To sum up this section, the FAMHA documents the outcomes of treatment by quantifying the substantial and enduring changes in client behaviours, cognitions, moods and day-to-day client functioning It also notes reductions in distress due to the effects of treatment. By determining a client's specific level of functioning across a number of domains and an overall level of functioning. specific profile emerge that can then be used for more effective treatment planning. FAMHA assessments are client centred by their very nature and specifically relate to the distress and difficulties that each patient must endure in their daily lives. Thus, such assessments are crucial to a clients mental health, substance use, and medical recovery.

**Q11. Explain assessment in clinical psychology.**

*Or*

**Explain the role of psychological assessment in deciding, planning, conducting and evaluating therapy. [June-2020, Q.No.-2]**

*Or*

**Discuss the phase of planning, conducting and evaluating therapy in Clinical Psychology. [June-2021, Q.No.-5]**

**Ans.** Clinical assessment is a way of diagnosing and planning treatment for a patient that involves evaluating someone in order to figure out what is wrong. There are many types of psychological assessments, all of which have their own strengths and weaknesses.

Differential diagnosis involves drawing on assessment information to describe an individual's psychological characteristics and adaptive strengths and weaknesses. These descriptions provide a basis for determining What type of disorder an individual may have, The severity and chronicity of this disorder and the circumstances in which it is likely to be manifest, and The kinds of treatment that are likely to provide the individual relief from this disorder. With respect to further treatment planning, adequate assessment information helps to guide treatment strategies and anticipate possible obstacles to progress in therapy. As for outcome evaluation, pre-treatment assessments establish an objective baseline against which treatment progress can be monitored in subsequent evaluations, and by which the eventual benefits of the treatment can be judged at its conclusion. These clinical contributions of psychological assessment can be implemented during each of four sequential phases in delivering psychological treatment: deciding on therapy, planning therapy, conducting therapy, and evaluating therapy.

**Deciding on Therapy:** The first step in the clinical utilisation of assessment information consists of deciding whether a patient needs treatment and is likely to benefit from it. An accurate differential diagnosis identifies pathological conditions (e.g. depression, paranoia) and maladaptive characteristics (e.g. passivity, low self-esteem) for which treatment is usually indicated, and adequate psychological evaluation helps to distinguish such conditions and characteristics from normal range functioning that does not call for professional mental health intervention. Assessment methods also provide valuable information concerning two factors known to predict whether people are likely to become involved in and profit from psychotherapy: their motivation for treatment and their accessibility to being treated.

The motivation for treatment usually corresponds to the amount of subjectively felt distress that people are expeliencing. Accessibility to psychological treatment typically depends on how willing people are to examine themselves, to express their thoughts and feelings openly, and to make changes in their customary beliefs and preferred ways of conducting their lives. Information derived from appropriate assessment procedures can provide clinicians with objective indices of each of these variables, and these assessment data can, in turn, be used as a basis for determining whether to recommend and proceed with some form of treatment.

**Planning Therapy**

- Planning therapy for patients who need and want to receive psychological treatment involves.
- Deciding on the appropriate setting in which to deliver the treatment,
- Estimating the duration of the treatment, and
- Selecting the particular type of treatment to be given.

With respect to deciding on the treatment setting, assessment data provide reliable information concerning the severity of a patient's disturbance, the patient's ability to distinguish reality from fantasy, and his or her likelihood of becoming suicidal or dangerous to others, all of which bear on whether the person requires residential care or can be treated safely and adequately as an outpatient. The more severely disturbed people are, the farther out of touch with reality they are, and the greater their risk potential for violence, the more advisable it becomes to care for them in a protected environment. Regarding treatment duration, clinical experience and research findings consistently indicate that mild and acute problems of recent onset can usually be treated successfully in a shorter period of time than severe and chronic problems of longstanding duration. A variety of psychodiagnostic measures provide clues to the chronicity as well as the severity of symptomatic and characterological mental and emotional problems, and pretreatment data obtained with these measures can accordingly help clinicians formulate some expectation of how long treatment is likely to last. Having available such assessment-based inforn1ation on expected duration, in turn, assists clinicians in presenting treatment recommendations to prospective patients (Hurt, Reznikoff & Clarkin, 1991). As for treatment selection, people who are relatively psychologically minded, self-aware, and interested in gaining fuller self-understanding are relatively likely to respond positively to an uncovering, insight-oriented, and conflict focussed treatment approach. Patients whose preference is to feel better without having to examine themselves closely, on the other hand, are more likely to become actively engaged in supportive and symptom-focussed approaches to treatment than in exploratory psychotherapy.

Psychologically minded people are inclined to feel dissatisfied with supportive treatment because it does not get at the root of their problems, whereas relief-minded people tend to feel uncomfortable in uncovering treatment because it makes unwelcome demands on them. Additionally, there is reason to believe that some kinds of conditions and difficulties, especially in people who are problem-oriented, respond relatively well to cognitive behavioural forms of treatment, whereas other kinds of disorders and maladaptive tendencies, especially in people who are interpersonally oriented, respond better to psychodynamic-interpersonal than cognitive behavioural therapy (Beutler & Harwood, 1995; Hayes, Nelson & Jarrett, 1987). Psychological mindedness and preferences for problem-oriented or interpersonally oriented approaches to life situations are among a vast array of personality characteristics that can be measured with assessment methods. Accordingly, adequately conceived pre-therapy psychological assessment can facilitate treatment planning by differentiating among psychological states and orientations of the individual that have known implications for a successful response to particular treatment approaches.

**Conducting Therapy:** Psychological assessment can play a key role in conducting therapy by helping to identify in advance:

- Treatment targets on which the therapy should be focussed and
- Possible obstacles to progress towards these treatment goals.

Appropriately collected assessment data, and particularly the results of a multi method test battery, typically contain many normal range findings and often some indications as well as notably good personality strengths and especially admirable personal qualities. At the same time, especially in people who are being evaluated for symptoms or difficulties that have led them to seek professional help, test data are likely to reveal specific adaptive shortcomings and coping limitations. One person may show a penchant for circumstantial reasoning and poor judgement; another person may give evidence of poor social skills and interpersonal withdrawal; a third may exhibit considerable emotional inhibition with the restricted capacity to express feelings and feel comfortable in emotionally charged situations. In short, any assessment findings that fall outside of an established normal range and are known to indicate specific types of cognitive dysfunction, affective distress, coping deficit, personal dissatisfaction, or interpersonal inadequacy, in turn, assist therapists and their patients in deciding on the objectives of their work together and directing their efforts accordingly. Some psychological characteristics of patients that fit constitute targets in their treatment may so pose obstacles to their becoming effectively engaged in therapy and making progress towards their goals. For example, people who are set in their ways and characteristically rigid and inflexible in their views often have difficulty reframing their perspectives or modifying their behaviour in response even to well-conceived and appropriately implemented treatment interventions. People who are interpersonally aversive or withdrawn may be slow or reluctant to form the kind of working alliance with their therapist that facilitates progress in most forms of therapy. People who are relatively satisfied with themselves and not experiencing much subjectively felt distressed may have little tolerance for the demands of becoming seriously engaged in a course of psychological treatment. Characteristics of these kinds do not preclude effective psychotherapy, but they can result in slow progress, and they may cause patients and therapists to become discouraged and terminate prematurely a treatment that does not appear to be going well.

Pretreatment assessment data serve to alert therapists in advance to possible treatment obstacles, which can help them understand and be patient with initially slow progress and also guide them in dealing directly with these obstacles, as by concentrating in the early phases of therapy on encouraging flexibility and open-mindedness, building a comfortable and trusting treatment relationship, or generating some motivation for the patient's involvement in the therapy.

**Evaluating Therapy:** Psychological assessment provides valuable data for monitoring the progress of therapy and measuring its eventual benefit. For this potential benefit of assessment to be realised, it is vital for assessment data to be collected from patients before their beginning treatment. In addition to helping to identify treatment targets and the long-term objectives of therapy, pre-treatment data provide an objective baseline for comparison with the results of subsequent assessments. Periodic reevaluations can then shed light on whether the treatment is making a difference, how close it has come to meeting its aims, in what way the focus of continued treatment should be adjusted, and whether a termination point has been reached. For example, if a reliable test index shows abnormally high anxiety, low self-esteem, poor self-control, or excessive anger, and a retest during treatment shows the same or a worse result for any of these treatment targets, there is objective evidence that no progress has been made on this front. Such results can then lead to an informed decision to alter the type or focus of the treatment, change the therapist, or await the next re-assessment before making any change. On the other hand, should retesting show an index closer to an adaptive range than initially, there is reason to conclude that progress is being made on the treatment target related to that index but that further improvement remains to be made in that area. When an initially abnormal test result is found on retesting to be in an adaptive range, then therapists and their patients can conclude with confidence that they have achieved the objective to which this result relates and do not need to address it further. At the point when retesting indicates that most or all of the treatment targets have reached or are approaching as much resolution as could real, statically be expected, then the assessment process helps to indicate that an appropriate termination point has been reached.

**Q12. What are the ethics in assessment?**

***Or***

**Write a short note on perfect conditions fallacy.**

**[June-2020, Q.No.-12]**

**Ans.** Every profession has distinct ethical obligations to the public. These obligations include professional competency, integrity, honesty, confidentiality, objectivity, public safety, and fairness, all of which are intended to preserve and safeguard public confidence. Unfortunately, all too often we hear reports in the media of moral dilemmas and unethical behaviour by professionals. These reports naturally receive considerable attention by the public, whose confidence in the profession is undermined with each report. Those who are involved with assessment are unfortunately not immune to unethical practices. Abuses in preparing students to take tests as well as in the use and interpretation of test results have been widely publicised. Misuses of test data in high-stakes decisions, such as scholarship awards, retention/promotion decisions, and accountability decisions, have been reported all too frequently. Even claims made in advertisements about the success rates of test coaching courses have raised questions about truth in advertising. Given these and other occurrences of unethical behaviour associated with assessment, the purpose of this digest is to examine the available standards of ethical practice in assessment and the issues associated with implementation of these standards.

It must be remembered that there are certain important fallacies in psychological assessment. These have to be kept in mind while doing the assessment. Also, we have many ethical considerations that have to be considered which are given in the sections below.

There are 10 common fallacies and pitfalls that plague psychological testing and assessment. They are:

- mismatched validity;
- confirmation bias;
- confusing retrospective and prospective accuracy (switching conditional probabilities)
- un standardising standardised tests;
- ignoring the effects of low base rates;
- misinterpreting dual high base rates;
- perfect conditions fallacy;
- financial bias;
- ignoring the effects of audio-recording, video-recording, or the presence of third-party observers; and
- uncertain gatekeeping.

These assessment fallacies and pitfalls are discussed in more detail below:

- **Mismatched Validity:** Some tests are useful in diverse situations, but no test works well for all tasks with all people in all situations. Hence selecting assessment instruments involves complex questions, such as, "Has research established sufficient reliability and validity (as well as sensitivity, specificity, and other relevant features) for this test, with an individual from this population, for this task (i.e., the purpose of the assessment), in this set of circumstances?" It is important to note that as the population, task, or circumstances change, the measures of validity, reliability, sensitivity, etc., will also tend to change. To determine whether tests are well-matched to the task, individual, and situation at hand, the psychologist must ask a basic question at the outset: Why exactly am I conducting this assessment?

- **Confirmation Bias:** Often we tend to seek, recognise, and value information that is consistent with our attitudes, beliefs, and expectations. If we form an initial impression, we may favour findings that support that impression, and discount, ignore or misconstrue data that do not fit. This premature cognitive commitment to an initial impression which can form a strong cognitive set through which we sift all subsequent findings is similar to the logical fallacy of hasty generalisation.

  To help protect ourselves against confirmation bias (in which we give preference to information that confirms our expectations), it is useful to search actively for data that disconfirm our expectations and to try out alternative interpretations of the available data.
- **Confusing Retrospective and Predictive Accuracy:** It begins with the individual's test results and asks: What is the likelihood, expressed as a conditional probability, that a person with these results has a condition (or ability, aptitude, quality, etc.) X? Retrospective accuracy begins with the condition (or ability, aptitude, quality) X and asks: What is the likelihood, expressed as a conditional probability, that a person who has X will show these test results? Confusing the "directionality" of the inference (e.g., the likelihood that those who score positive on a hypothetical predictor variable will fall into a specific group versus the likelihood that those in a specific group will score positive on the predictor variable) causes many errors. This mistake of confusing retrospective with predictive accuracy often resembles the affirming the consequent local fallacy.
- **Unstandardising Standardised Tests:** These tests gain their power from their standardisation. Norms, validity, reliability, specificity, sensitivity, and similar measures emerge from an actuarial base, that is a well-selected sample of people providing data (through answering questions, performing tasks, etc.) in response to a uniform procedure in (reasonably) uniform conditions. When we change the instructions, or the test items themselves, or the way items are administered or scored, we depart from that standardisation and our attempts

to draw on the actuarial base become questionable. There are other ways in which standardisation can be defeated. People may show up for an assessment session without adequate reading glasses, or having taken cold medication that affects their alertness, or having experienced a family emergency or loss that leaves them unable to concentrate, or having stayed up all night with a loved one and now can barely keep their eyes open. The professional conducting the assessment must be alert to these situational factors, how they can threaten the assessment's validity, and how to address them effectively. It is our responsibility to recognise the limits of competence and to make sure that any assessment is based on adequate competence in the relevant areas of practice, the relevant issues, and the relevant instruments.

- **Ignoring the Effects of Low Base Rates:** Ignoring base rates can play a role in many testing problems but very low base rates seem particularly troublesome. Imagine a psychologist has been commissioned to develop an assessment procedure that will identify crooked judges so that candidates for the judicial appointment can be screened. It's a difficult challenge, in part because only 1 out of 500 judges is (hypothetically speaking) dishonest. Let us say that the psychologist pulls together all the actuarial data that he can locate and finds that he can develop a screening test for crookedness based on a variety of characteristics, personal history, and test results. Let us say that his method is 90 per cent accurate.

  When this method is used to screen the next 5,000 judicial candidates, there might be 10 candidates who are crooked (because about 1 out of 500 is crooked). A 90 per cent accurate screening method will identify 9 of these 10 crooked candidates as crooked and one as honest. The problem is the 4,990 honest candidates. Because the screening is wrong 10 per cent of the time, and the only way for the screening to be wrong about honest candidates is to identify them as crooked, it will falsely classify 10 per cent of the honest candidates as crooked. Therefore, this screening method will into) Tectly classify 499 of these 4,990 honest candidates as crooked. So out of the 5,000 candidates who were screened, the 90 per cent accurate test has classified 508 of them as crooked (i.e., 9 who were crooked and 499 who were honest). Every 508 times the screening method indicates crookedness, it tends to be right only 9 times. And it has falsely branded 499 honest people as crooked.

- **Misinterpreting Dual High Base Rates:** As part of a disaster response team, let us say a psychologist is flown in to work at a community mental health centre in a city devastated by a severe earthquake. Taking a quick look at the records the centre has compiled, he notes that of the 200 people who have come for services since the earthquake, there are 162 who are of a particular religious faith and are diagnosed with PTSD related to the earthquake, and 18 of that faith who came for services unrelated to the earthquake. Of those who are not of that faith, 18 have been diagnosed with PTSD related to the earthquake, and 2 have come for services unrelated to the earthquake. It seems almost self-evident that there is a strong association between that particular religious faith and developing PTSD related to tire earthquake. That is, 81 per cent of the people who came for services were of that religious faith and had developed PTSD. Perhaps this faith makes people vulnerable to PTSD. Or perhaps it is a more subtle association, in that this faith might make it easier for people with PTSD to seek mental health services. But the inference of an association is a fallacy because ninety per cent of all people who seek services at this centre happen to be of that specific religious faith (i.e., 90 per cent of those who had developed PTSD and 90 per cent who had come for other reasons) and 90 per cent of all people who seek services after the earthquake (i.e., 90 per cent of those with that particular religious faith and 90 per cent of those who are not of that faith) have developed PTSD. The 2 factors appear to be associated because both have high base rates, but they are statistically unrelated.
- **Perfect Conditions Fallacy:** When we are in haste, we like to assume that "all is well," that in fact "conditions are perfect." If we do not check, we may not discover that the person we are assessing for a job, a custody hearing, a disability claim, a

criminal case, asylum status, or a competency hearing took standardised psychological tests and completed other phases of formal assessment under conditions that significantly distorted the results. For example, the person may have forgotten the glasses they need for reading, be suffering from a severe headache or illness, be using a hearing aid that is not functioning well be taking medication that impairs cognition or perception, have forgotten to take needed psychotropic medication, have experienced a crisis that makes it difficult to concentrate, be in physical pain, or have trouble understanding the language in which the assessment is conducted.

- **Financial Bias:** It is a very human error to assume that we are immune to the effects of financial bias. But a financial conflict of interest can subtly affect how we gather, interpret, and present even the most routine data. Thus, the principle is reflected in well established forensic texts and formal guidelines prohibiting liens and any other form of fee that is contingent on the outcome of a case. The Specialty Guidelines for Forensic Psychologists, for example, state: "Forensic psychologists do not provide professional services to parties to a legal proceeding based on 'contingent fees,' when those services involve the offering of expert testimony to a court or administrative body, or when they call upon the psychologist to make affirmations or representations intended to be relied upon by third parties."
- **Ignoring Effects of Audio Recording, Video Recording or the Presence of Third Party Observers:** Empirical research has identified ways in which audio recording, video recording, or the presence of third parties can affect the responses (e.g., various aspects of cognitive performance) of people during the psychological and neuropsychological assessment. Ignoring these potential effects can create an extremely misleading assessment. Part of adequate preparation for an assessment that will involve recording or the presence of third parties is reviewing the relevant research and professional guidelines.
- **Uncertain Gate Keeping:** Psychologists who conduct assessments are gatekeepers of sensitive information that may

have profound and lasting effects on the life of the person who was assessed. The gatekeeping responsibilities exist within a complex framework of federal (e.g., HIPAA) and state legislation and case law as well as other relevant regulations, codes, and contexts. The following scenario illustrates some gatekeeping decisions psychologists may be called upon to make. Clarifying issues to the client regarding whom the information will be conveyed when asked for while planning an assessment is important because if the psychologist does not clearly understand them, it is impossible to communicate the information effectively as part of the process of informed consent and informed refusal. Information about who will or will not have access to an assessment report may be the key to an individual's decision to give or withhold informed consent for an assessment.

**Q13. Explain the APA ethics code.**

**Ans.** The American Psychological Association's (APA's) Ethical Principles of Psychologists and Code of Conduct (hereinafter referred to as the Ethics Code) consists of an Introduction, a Preamble, five General Principles (A-E), and specific Ethical Standards. The Introduction discusses the intent, organisation, procedural considerations, and scope of application of the Ethics Code. The Preamble and General Principles are inspirational goals to guide psychologists towards the highest ideals of psychology. Although the Preamble and General Principles are not themselves enforceable rules, they should be considered by psychologists in arriving at an ethical course of action. The Ethical Standards set forth enforceable rules for conduct as psychologists. Most of the Ethical Standards are written broadly, in order to apply to psychologists in varied roles, although the application of an Ethical Standard may vary depending on the context. The Ethical Standards are not exhaustive. The fact that a given conduct is not specifically addressed by an Ethical Standard does not mean that it is necessarily either ethical or unethical.

**(1) Ethical Principles:** The Ethics Code contains six general principles:

(i) **Competence:** Psychologists maintain high standards of competence, including knowing their limits of expertise. Applied to testing, this might suggest that it is unethical for the psychologist to use a test with which he or she is not familiar to make decisions about clients.

(ii) **Integrity:** Psychologists seek to act with integrity in all aspects of their professional roles. As a test author, for example, a psychologist should not make unwarranted claims about a particular test.

(iii) **Professional and Scientific Responsibility:** Psychologists uphold professional standards of conduct. In psychological testing, this might require knowing when test data can be useful and when it cannot. This means, in effect, that a practitioner using a test needs to be familiar with the research literature on that test.

(iv) **Respect for People's Rights and Dignity:** Psychologists respect the privacy and confidentiality of clients and have an awareness of cultural, religious, and other sources of individual differences. In psychological testing, this might include an awareness of when a test is appropriate for use with individuals who are from different cultures.

(v) **Concern for Others' Welfare:** Psychologists are aware of situations where specific tests (for example, ordered by the courts) may be detrimental to a particular client. How can these situations be resolved so that both the needs of society and the welfare of the individual are protected?

(vi) **Social Responsibility:** Psychologists have professional and scientific responsibilities to community and society. About psychological testing, this might cover counselling against the misuse of tests by the local school.

**(2) Ethical Standards:** In addition to these six principles, there are specific ethical standards that cover eight categories, ranging from "General standards" to "Resolving ethical issues." The second category is titled, "Evaluation, assessment, or intervention" and is thus the area most explicitly related to testing; this category covers 10 specific standards:

(i) Psychological procedures such as testing, evaluation, diagnosis, etc., should occur only within the context of a defined professional relationship.

(ii) Psychologists only use tests in appropriate ways.

(iii) Tests are to be developed using acceptable scientific procedures.

(iv) When tests are used, there should be familiarity with and awareness of the limitations imposed by psychometric issues, such as those discussed in this course.

(v) Assessment results are to be interpreted in light of the limitations inherent in such procedures.

(vi) Unqualified persons should not use psychological assessment techniques.

(vii) Tests that are obsolete and outdated should not be used.

(viii) The purpose, norms, and other aspects of a test should be described accurately.

(ix) Appropriate explanations of test results should be given.

(x) The integrity and security of tests should be maintained.

**(3) Standards for Educational and Psychological Tests:** In addition to the more general ethical standards discussed above, there are also specific standards for educational and psychological tests (American Educational Research Association, 1999), first published in 1954, and subsequently revised several times.

**Q14. What are the ethical issues in assessment?**

**[June-2019, Q.No.-3]**

***Or***

**Write a short note on invasion of privacy. [June-2019, Q.No.-12]**

***Or***

**Discuss ethical issues in assessment. [June-2021, Q.No.-4]**

**Ans.** Ethical standards and guidelines for testing are necessary, as they promote and regulate professional behaviour. While there are many professional association codes of conduct promoting ethical issues in testing and assessment, The Universal Declaration of Ethical Principles for Psychologists is discussed, as it is a document reflecting the principles and values expected of a code of conduct. In addition and more specifically, standards, guidelines and the responsibilities for ethical test usage are reflected on, such as that found in the International Test Commission, which promotes effective testing and assessment policies. There are a variety of issues pertinent to tests and assessment and these are discussed, namely cross-cultural applicability and transportability of tests, translation guidelines, telepsychology, computer and Internet-based assessment, privacy and confidentiality, feedback and assessment, test publishers and authors, culturally competent career assessment practice, and special populations such as children and adolescents.

**Informed Consent:** The term informed consent is commonly used throughout the field of psychology; for example, consent to treatment, consent to participate in research, and consent to release information are but a few of the contexts in which consent is given and sought Consent, however, is a legal term, and care should be given to its application within the realm of psychological assessment While the intent here is to provide a general understanding of informed consent, the information presented should not be used in substitution for state law or ethical guidelines. Informed consent in assessment implies that the test taker (or his or her legal guardian) has agreed to be evaluated before testing and after being informed of reasons for testing, intended uses of data, possible consequences (including risks and benefits), what information will be released (if any), and to whom the information will be released (APA, 1996). The APA Committee on Psychological Tests and Assessment (1996) indicated that informed consent may be desirable to obtain even when not required (e.g., court-ordered assessment). Further, even when informed consent is not required, it is advisable to inform test takers of the testing process, including who may have access to the report, unless such information will threaten the psychometric properties of the instrument or test (APA, 1996). Typically, consent consists of three separate aspects: voluntariness, competence, and information.

First, voluntariness implies that the examiner must obtain the test taker's consent "without exercising coercion or causing duress, pressure, or undue excitement or influence" (Koocher & Keith-Spiegel, 1998, p. 417).

Second, the test taker must be considered legally competent to grant consent. Unless legally deemed incompetent, all adults are assumed competent to give consent. Children, however, generally are not presumed to be competent, although the legal age to give consent varies by state. In assessing children or adults deemed legally incompetent, substitute consent should be obtained from parents, legal guardians, or the court as applicable. Everstine and colleagues (1980) recommended obtaining consent from both the required substitute and from the incompetent person whenever possible. At the very least, information about testing in developmentally-appropriate language should be given to the legally incompetent person, and assent, or agreement, should be obtained.

Finally, the test taker must have the requisite information to consent. Sufficient information must be provided to the test taker to allow the individual the opportunity to make an informed decision regarding his or her participation in assessment. While it is unnecessary (and perhaps impossible) to review all possible outcome scenarios with the client, it is necessary to provide facts a reasonable person would need in arriving at an informed decision. Whether test results will be used in decision-making, if copies of test reports will be kept in the client's file and the right to refuse testing or to withdraw at any time are examples of information that should be given to each potential test taker.

Information on feedback policies is particularly important, as it appears that psychologists do not routinely provide feedback to test takers. As recently as 1983, Berndt's survey of psychologists found that a majority favoured only limited feedback to test takers, suggesting that most examiners viewed full disclosure regularly as an unrealistic goal. However, APA (1996) clearly has stated that test takers have the right to feedback about testing results unless this right is waived by the test taker before testing or prevented by law (e.g., when courts mandate testing for competency to stand trial). A feedback session is recommended to serve two main purposes (Welfel, 1998). First, a feedback session allows the test taker an opportunity to respond to incorrect or misleading conclusions. Second, feedback may be therapeutic for the client, promoting symptom reduction and improved client-therapist rapport. However, special care should be given in how information is presented to the individual client. Many psychological assessment instruments are complex, even for the professional trained in its usage, psychometric properties, and interpretation.

Reports should be written in a manner that is clear and simple and free from the technical language to avoid misinterpretation and misunderstanding. Examiners should be available to answer specific questions about assessment results and to clarify questions raised by the client.

In summary, a good rule of thumb is "to provide as full a description as time, interest, and test security allow, omitting or postponing a review of results that the counsellor judges would be harmful to the client's current wellbeing" (Welfel, 1998, p. 230). Regardless of the method of feedback utilised, a description of the examiner's feedback policy should be reviewed during informed consent procedures. Information on obsolete data policies should also be reviewed with each test taker. APA (2002) requires that examiners refrain from basing recommendations or decisions on obsolete or outdated testing data. How long a psychologist. may rely on certain test results depends primarily on the construct being measured (Welfel, 1998). Tests that measure rapidly changing constructs, such as depressed or anxious moods (e.g., Beck Depression Inventory, Beck Anxiety Inventory) may be valid only for several days or weeks. Other tests that measure more stable personality constructs (e.g., Minnesota· Multiphasic Personality Inventory) may be valid for several months. Regardless of the tests employed, examiners should inform potential test takers of their policies on the removal of such data. Much information should be provided to test takers before the examination.

Following the presentation of this information, common practice entails asking the client to state the concept in his own words. This practice gives the examiner some degree of certainty regarding the client's understanding of consent. Use of written documents to record the terms of consent is standard. Both client and clinician can benefit from a written contract specifying client rights and responsibilities, limitations of confidentiality, and fees for services. Documentation of informed consent should be reviewed verbally with the client in language appropriate to the client's level of understanding and free from technical jargon or colloquial terminology. As a rule of thumb, consent forms should be written at no higher than a 7th-grade reading level. Additionally, the client should be allowed to look over such documentation and ask questions before signing, to ensure understanding. Research conducted on the effects of written informed consent forms generally has found positive effects. For example, Handelsman (1990) found that the use of written consent forms increased clients' positive judgements of therapists' experience, likeability, and trustworthiness.

**Confidentiality:** There are many issues of concern when it comes to ethics, one such issue being the right to privacy. The concepts of individual rights and privacy are an essential part of our society and must be taken seriously when students are involved. The Ethical Principles assert individual rights to privacy and confidentiality as well as self-determination. The term confidentiality indicates that individuals are guaranteed privacy in terms of all personal information that is disclosed and that no information will then be disclosed without the individual's direct permission. There are times, however, that confidentiality is breached because managers, for example, will seek out psychological information about their employees. Another example is that teachers may seek test scores for students, however, with the good intention of understanding issues of performance (Mcintire & Miller, 2007). Another ethical concern is the right to informed consent.

Self-determination is a right to every individual which means that individuals are entitled to receive complete explanations in regards to why exactly they are being tested as well as how the results of the test will be used and what their results mean. These complete explanations are commonly known as informed consent and should be conveyed in such a way that is straight-forward and easy for students to understand. In situations involving minors or those with limited cognitive abilities, informed consent needs to come from both the student themselves as well as their parent or guardian. However, parental permission should not be confused with informed consent. Educators have a responsibility to ensure that the student, as well as their parent or guardian, understand and implications and requirements that will be involved in any test before it is even administered (Mcintire & Miller, 2007). Koocher and Keith-Spiegel defined confidentiality as "a general standard of professional conduct that obliges a professional not to discuss information about a client with anyone". Confidentiality between clinician and client cannot be overstated as a critical ingredient for candid and cooperative participation. It can be argued that confidentiality is what allows psychological services to be effective since without candid client participation assessment results can be invalid, diagnoses inaccurate, and therapy ineffective.

The basis for most clients agreeing to receive psychological services is an understood agreement of confidentiality and is among the primary reasons why informed consent is requested and documented. It is important to ensure that clients have an understanding of the limits of confidentiality. For example, in the USA, all 50 states have legal statutes which mandate disclosure of various information, including child abuse, elder abuse, suicide, and/or imminent harm to others. Also, assessment and testing are frequently conducted for third parties that have a vested interest in the outcome of test data. For example, insurance companies and health maintenance organisations (HMOs) can and do request assessment information to determine eligibility for coverage or reimbursement for services rendered. Furthermore, employers, legal representatives, and schools often request testing results to aid in decision-making.

The amount of information requested can vary widely from full disclosure of all test data in legal proceedings to summary reports prepared for prospective employers. Releasing information to individuals or entities other than the client presents a myriad of ethical and legal obstacles. Psychologists should refer to the APA Ethics Code (2002) for guidance. To comply with the Ethics Code, psychologists should inform test-takers, before the assessment, of any mandatory, as well as any likely, releases of information. Also, when requests from third parties are received, psychologists should have test takers sign their consent to release specific testing information. Finally, psychologists, once granted consent, should exercise extreme caution in releasing only the necessary information to satisfy the inquiry of the third party rather than releasing the entire contents of the client's chart. As stated previously, examiners should not release secure test materials (e.g., protocols, test items) unless permission is granted from the testing publisher. Child test-takers pose special dilemmas for examiners. Unless granted by law, children are not considered capable of consenting to assessment. Therefore, testing results may be shared with the legal guardian who consented to the child's participation in assessment. However, a good rule of the thumb is to follow the same procedures utilised for release of information to third parties. In other words, examiners must clarify limits of confidentiality with the child and legal guardian at the outset of testing and should only release relevant information to the legal guardian.

**Invasion of Privacy:** One of the main difficulties examinees can encounter psychological tests is that the examiner might discover aspects of the client that he or she would rather keep secret. Also of concern is that this information may be used in ways that are not in the best interest of the client. The Office of Science and Technology (1967), in a report entitled Privacy and Behavioural Research, has defined privacy as "the right of the individual to decide for him/herself how much he will share with others his thoughts, feelings, and facts of his personal life". This right is considered to be "essential to ensure dignity and freedom of self-determination".

The invasion of privacy issue usually becomes most controversial with personality tests because items relating to motivational, emotional, and attitudinal traits are sometimes disguised. Thus, persons may unknowingly reveal characteristics about themselves that they would rather keep private. Similarly, many persons consider their IQ scores to be highly personal. The ethical code of the American Psychological Association (1992) specifically states that information derived by a psychologist from any source can be released only with the permission of the client. Although there may be exceptions regarding the rights of minors, or when clients are a danger to themselves or others, the ability to control the information is usually clearly defined as being held by the client. Thus, the public is often uneducated regarding its rights and typically underestimates the power it has in determining how the test data will be used. Despite ethical guidelines relating to the invasion of privacy, dilemmas sometimes arise. For example, during personnel selection, applicants may feel pressured into revealing personal information on tests because they aspire to a certain position. Also, applicants may unknowingly reveal information because of subtle, non-obvious test questions, and, perhaps more important, they have no control over the inferences that examiners make about the test data.

However, if a position requires careful screening and if serious negative consequences may result from poor selection, it is necessary to evaluate an individual as closely as possible. Thus, the use of testing for personnel in the police, delicate military positions, or important public duty overseas may warrant careful testing. In a clinical setting, obtaining personal information regarding clients usually does not present problems. The agreement that the information be used to help clients develop new insights and change their behaviour is generally clear and straight forward. However, should legal difficulties arise relating to areas such as child abuse, involuntary confinement, or situations in which clients may be a danger to themselves or others, ethical questions often arise.

Usually, there are general guidelines regarding the manner and extent to which information should be disclosed. These are included in the American Psychological Association's Ethical Principles of Psychologists and Code of Conduct (1992), and test users are encouraged to familiarise themselves with these guidelines. Adequate handling of the issue of an individual's right to privacy involves both a clear explanation of the relevance of the testing and obtaining informed consent. Examiners should always have a clear conception of the specific reasons for giving a test. Thus, if personnel are being selected based on their mechanical abilities, tests measuring areas such as general maladjustment should not ordinarily be administered. Examiners must continually evaluate whether a test or series of tests, is valid for a particular purpose and whether each set of scores has been properly interpreted about a particular context. Furthermore, the general rationale for test selection should be provided in clear, straightforward language that can be understood by the client. Informed consent involves communicating not only the rationale for testing but also the kinds of data obtained and the possible uses of the data. This does not mean the client should be shown the specific test subscales beforehand, but rather that the nature and intent of the test should be described in a general way.

❑❑❑

# 2 PSYCHODIAGNOSTICS IN PSYCHOLOGY

## INTRODUCTION

Different types of assessment have different goals, and these purposes are articulated. It presents the different stages in psycho diagnostics. The practice of psychological assessment involves *considerably* and *qualitatively* more than merely administering tests, questionnaires, or behaviour ratings in a uniform way and shows a condensed summary process of psychological assessment according to present-day conceptualisation. Without interview data, most psychological tests are meaningless. As interviews are the primary means for developing rapport and can serve as a check against the meaning and validity of test results. It continues defining and describing test batteries, followed by the use of test batteries. At last, it deals with the psychological report which is the end product of assessment. It represents the clinician's efforts to integrate the assessment data into a functional whole so that the information can help the client solve problems and make decisions.

**Q1. Write short notes on the followings:**

**(i) Differences between Psychodiagnostic Assessment and Psychiatric Consultation**

**Ans.** A psychiatric consultation consists of a thorough clinical interview, review of records, and observation of the patient's behaviour by a psychiatrist or psychologist. For many psychiatric concerns, this is the most appropriate referral and connects the patient with a mental health provider.

Psychodiagnostic testing is a specialised diagnostic procedure that identifies and quantifies degrees of psychopathology. In contrast to psychiatric consultation, it uses written, oral and projective instruments to evaluate a patient's mental processes and to assess how their thinking and emotions are likely to impact their behaviour. Therefore, psychodiagnostic testing provides objective data on a patient's psychological functioning and is a useful tool for clarifying confusing clinical presentations.

Psychodiagnostic testing enhances diagnostic accuracy by controlling for subjective opinion because it uses highly reliable, standardised tests that have been validated in clinical trials. Because it can provide both accurate diagnostics and grade the severity of impairment, psychodiagnostic testing helps the physician or psychiatrist to make pharmacological or psychotherapeutic treatment recommendations that have the highest likelihood of success.

Psychodiagnostic testing, because of its standardised and objective qualities, aids the practitioner in developing differential treatment recommendations.

**(ii) Referral for Psychodiagnostic Testing**

**Ans.** Patients sometimes presents confusing clinical pictures. They require sophisticated and extensive workups to distinguish the psychological contributions that confound accurate diagnoses. Referral for psychodiagnostic testing is a valuable tool in arriving at a diagnostic decision.

Examples of appropriate referrals for psychological testing include the following:

- Patients having substance abuse problems
- Patients with possible learning disabilities

- Patients with suspected mental retardation or poor intellectual functioning
- Patients with mood disorders
- Patients with anxiety and panic disorders
- Patients who have experienced trauma
- Children and adolescents who are "acting-out"
- Patients with suspected personality disorders.

**(iii) The Psychodiagnostic Report**

**Ans.** The psychodiagnostic report is designed to answer specific referral questions, These may include questions regarding diagnostic clarification, differentiation between transient "state" disorders and long-standing "trait" disorders (DSM Axis I versus Axis II disorders), intellectual functioning, learning style, current psychosocial stressors, and adaptive ability.

Reports also include treatment recommendations that are based on the synthesised results of the clinical interview, mental status examination, patient's personal, family and cultural history, and findings from the standardised tests. Clinicians can use these objective recommendations to develop interventions with the highest likelihood of success.

**(iv) Application of Psychodiagnostic Testing**

**Ans.** Psychodiagnostic testing is a widely recognised diagnostic procedure that is used in a variety of non-medical settings. Examples include:

- **Forensics:** In this context, 80 per cent of psychological testing is ordered when the defendant's psychiatric condition is seen as important in a criminal case. Other legal uses of psychodiagnostic testing include child custody evaluations, contested estates, wrongful termination and harassment cases, etc.
- **Insurance Settlements:** Insurance companies rely on psychodiagnostic testing for a variety of disability and Workman's Compensation cases. Similarly, the Department of Social Services routinely uses psycho-diagnostic tests to make Social Security determinations. Psychodiagnostic testing is particularly useful in ruling out malingering.

- **Employment Environments:** Psychodiagnostic testing was originally developed during World War II a screening device to increase the efficacy in deploying military personnel in stressful situations. It is still used extensively by police departments, the military, and other employers to ensure that recruits are psychologically suited to the required tasks.
- **School Settings:** Psychodiagnostic testing is used by counsellors in schools and universities to help students make career choices based on their aptitudes and abilities. It is also the mainstay of assessments for special education placement, admission to gifted programs, and learning disability assessment.

The function of assessment in clinical practice varies greatly and can include any and all of the following objectives:

- Diagnosis and/or evaluation of clients' reason for seeking treatment
- Case conceptualisation
- Treatment planning
- Monitoring of client response to treatment
- Change clients' behaviour or cognitions through increased self-awareness (e.g., self-monitoring, behavioural experiments)
- Programme evaluation or individual clinician evaluation of effectiveness.

**(v) Reasons for Psychodiagnostic Testing**

**Ans.** There are many reasons for conducting a psychological assessment, and each reason requires the assessor to initiate different tasks. Likewise, selecting methods and techniques for acquiring clinical information depends on the nature and function of the assessment. Therefore, before learning how to conduct an assessment, practitioners of clinical psychology must understand why or for what purpose assessments are conducted.

In general, the major aims of assessments are to gather information about persons, systems, environments, or phenomenon (or some combination of these), and to enable classification, description, and comprehension or evaluation of current circumstances. Assessments also may be directed to predict future behaviours (dangerousness, suicide) or circumstances (maintaining employment). Commonly, assessments seek to respond to more than one of these goals at a time and can be tailored to address several clinical or research questions. Therefore, there will be overlap among the strategies and techniques used for collecting information for each purpose.

**(vi) The Purpose of Diagnostic Assessment**

**Ans.** The purpose of diagnostic assessment is to differentiate between "normal" and "abnormal" behaviour, to differentiate among various "abnormal" constellations of symptoms, and to classify individuals based on identified abnormalities or "presentation of disease" (Chaplin, 1985).

The purpose of the diagnostic interview is to arrive at an understanding of a client's presenting problem through an assessment of current life situations, developmental processes, family and developmental background, enduring personality trends, assets, and vulnerabilities, as well as manifest behaviour and responsiveness in the interview situation.

In order to conduct such psycho diagnostics, the clinician must have the following steps: (1) Signed consent form(s). (2) Audio/Video tape of the interview session. (3) Verbatim transcript of audio/videotape. (4) Case report.

***Conducting the Interview:*** The clinical psychologist is expected to explore the presenting problem and its precipitating factors in some depth. How he chooses to do so should be based on his clinical judgement, and procedures used.

**(vii) Areas to be Covered in Diagnostic Interview**

*Or*

**Discuss the areas to be covered in a diagnostic interview.**

**[Dec-2019, Q.No.-9]**

**Ans.** Areas to be covered in diagnostic interview are as follows:

- **Identifying Information:** Description of interview setting and role of the interviewer in establishing an intake process.

  Include client's sex, age, social class, race, religion, marital status, occupation, education, and current living situation of the client (with a description of the family constellation at the time of interview). Also, include a current level and effectiveness of functioning when you describe the current living situation.

- **Presenting Complaints**: Current symptoms, anxieties, moods, difficulties in personal and/or occupational relationships and activities. Overt reason(s) for seeking help and referral route to the interviewer.
- **Presenting Appearance:** Description of salient aspects of physical appearance and mannerisms, as well as observations of significant interactions with the interviewer. Specify significant behavioural, affective, interactional observations that helped in assessing the client's problems and strengths.
- **Precipitating Factors and History of the Problem:** Events and/or life changes that accompanied the appearance of psychological distress, or appear associated with such distress. Development and course of problems since the client first noticed their appearance. Previous efforts at resolution and apparent consequences.
- **History of the Person/Social Context:** Areas of information developed will depend on the type of problem and interviewer's orientation and rationale for the interview.

  Integrate, as applicable issues of diversity, including, but not limited to gender, sexual orientation, race, age, cultural background, socio-economic status, religious or spiritual identifications, and ability or disability when addressing the following subsections.
- **Developmental History**: Developmental milestones and attendant stresses (e.g. early separations from family, adolescent stresses, young adult crises, etc.). The "Developmental History" and "Family History" sections can be integrated.
- **Family History**: Family of origin, constellation, ages, ethnic racial and religious backgrounds, description of parents, siblings, and quality of relationships with such figures at critical times in childhood and adolescence, major losses, changes, and traumas within family history as evidence. Whether there has been any severe or mild psychological disturbance in family members. Such problems should be mentioned here if not included fully in earlier sections. Include

the inter-factional consequences of behaviour within the family.

- **School History:** Achievements, problems, aspirations significant relationship with authority figures.

**Q2. Briefly discuss about DSM IV (TR) diagnosis.**

**Ans.** DSM-IV-TR classifies PTSD as an anxiety disorder with the major criteria of an extreme precipitating stressor, intrusive recollections, emotional numbing, and hyperarousal.

The DSM-IV-TR diagnostic criteria for ADHD, which are currently applied to all ages and both genders, require the individual to demonstrate a minimum of six symptoms of hyperactivity or inattention that have persisted for a minimum of 6 months and are maladaptive plus inconsistent with developmental level.

**Recommendations:** The nature of recommendations should flow from the needs of the client and the orientation of the interviewer. If interviewer's orientation emphasises treatment goals and specific modalities of therapy, recommendations along these lines should be included. If the orientation of interviewer is along with a more expressive/exploratory modality, recommendations will be far less structured or definite. Rather, the the interviewer might note possible areas deserving some focus in the therapy.

The interview is to last no more than 50 minutes and no less than 45 minutes. A 60 minute interview will be allowed.

Questions that diagnostic assessments can answer include the following examples.

- A 6-year-old child is having trouble in school, and not staying in his seat during lessons: Does the child have an attention deficit disorder, an anxiety disorder, or conduct disorder?
- A 68-year-old female has been increasingly forgetful, less energetic, and confused: Is she depressed or suffering from the onset of dementia?
- Why is the 35-year-old male having chest pains and rapid heart rates without any biological explanation for these symptoms?

Answering such questions through diagnostic assessments may lead to recommendations for treatment, the establishment of the clients' eligibility (or ineligibility) for disability services (e.g., disability accommodations, reimbursement from insurance companies), or simply increased understanding of patients' symptoms, which will enable other healthcare practitioners to work more effectively with them.

Diagnostic assessments in a psychological setting are similar in concept to physicians' medical examinations. Medical patients arrive in physicians' offices for many reasons. Depending on the motivation for the visit, physicians either focus on a specific complaint presented by the patient, or' may evaluate the entire person in the search for "what's wrong?"

There is a clear mission to search for abnormality or pathology, identify the malady, and report the findings. Typically, such an examination would lead to treatment if a disease or abnormality were found. Seldom does a physician examine a patient only to identify optimal functioning; information is typically a by-product of the diagnostic or physical examination. Similarly, diagnostic psychological assessments tend to be disease focussed and are criticised for following a deficit model, rather than a balanced model of strengths and deficits.

Furthermore, behavioural and cognitive behavioural psychologists criticise diagnostic assessments for excluding contextual information about antecedents, consequences, and social, physical, and cultural environmental factors from the evaluation of persons' reported problems and symptoms. Partially, this phenomenon is a function of the classification systems that guide diagnostic evaluations.

**Classification Systems:** The Diagnostic and Statistical Manual of Mental Disorders (4th Edition; DSM IV-TR; American Psychiatric Association, 2000) is the guide most commonly used by mental health professionals in the United States for diagnosing psychological, psychosocial, interpersonal and environmental problems in children, adolescents, and adults. The International Classification of Disorders-10 (ICD 10; WHO, 1992) is also used worldwide and is the preferred classification system by physicians. Classification systems, as the basis for diagnostic assessments, are derived from enormous amounts of research on very large samples of the population. Their purpose is to provide nomothetic information. Nomothetic information is information that establishes general principles, norms, or laws.

With regard to the DSM-IV-TR (American Psychiatric Association, 2000) or ICD-10 (WHO,1992), nomothetic information informs us how many people with certain characteristics, features, or symptoms may behave, interact with others, or reportedly feel about themselves, others, and the world around them. The information differentiates persons with such characteristics, features, or symptoms from data collected on large volumes of "normal" people, or individuals who do not have difficulty in personal, social, occupational, or academic functioning.

For example, we know that many adults with major depressive disorders often have persistent feelings of extreme hopelessness about their future, and they have felt this way for an extended period (2 weeks or more; American Psychiatric Association, 2000). Non-depressed, normal persons, while in a temporary negative mood state, may endorse intermittent feelings of hopelessness about specific situations or momentary feelings of hopelessness about their futures, but they do not typically report enduring feelings of hopelessness under ordinary circumstances. It is important to remember, however, that information in the DSM-IV-TR and ICD-10 is based on average scores and commonalities in self-reports or evaluations, and that there are variations within the group and exceptions to the rules and criteria established. Therefore, not all persons who meet criteria for a Major Depressive Disorder will endorse having persistent feelings of hopelessness, but they will likely overlap with the majority group in other symptomatology.

The classification systems continue to evolve in accordance with the development in the fields of clinical and social psychology, anthropology, and epidemiology. The DSM-IV-TR is revised periodically to include information about populations and variables that had been under represented in the past. In the most recent revision, the task forces in charge of improving on the DSM-IV-TR have increased attention to diversity and cultural factors and strive to increase understanding and classification of patterns of symptoms that may warrant a diagnosis or specific nomenclature in future additions.

Diagnostic manuals have significant merits and have allowed for a certain degree of standardisation in the field of clinical psychology. They provide a means for professionals to communicate about clients or patients and disseminate synthesised conclusions from volumes of research. Psychologists gear diagnostic assessments, in part, to seek confirmation or disconfirmation of persons' fit with nomothetic information.

The DSM-IV-TR provides a starting point for understanding clients' clinical presentations and for determining general directions for treatment planning. However, to solely rely on nomothetic information would be equivalent to taking a cookbook approach to identify persons' problems and solutions to their problems. As you know from your own experience with others, people are much more complex. Relying on group norms and typical or common presentations would be misleading in diagnosis and treatment. Psychologists also have an ethical obligation to consider personal characteristics of individuals assessed to ensure tests are valid for the person tested, interpretation of data is appropriate, and recommendations based on test data are culturally and individually relevant (APA, 2003, 9.0). As such, nomothetic information is balanced and integrated with ideographic (individual) information.

**Logistics and Details of Diagnostic Assessments:** Mental health professionals who have training and experience using the DSMIV TR or ICD-10, and specialised measures, inventories, or structured interviews use these tools to conduct diagnostic assessments for a variety of purposes. The APA Ethical Principles and Code of Conduct (APA, 2003) specifies that only trained qualified individuals should use psychological tests, and outlines the cautions to be taken. Clients or family members of clients might request a diagnostic assessment. Clinicians routinely incorporate diagnostic assessments into their standard practices for evaluating new clients for treatment planning. Non-mental health professional colleagues (medical professionals, school administrators, teachers), or mental health professionals who desire a more precise understanding of their patients' presentations of symptoms may request a consultation with professionals trained to conduct diagnostic assessments. Diagnostic assessments may also be conducted to screen, classify, or assign individuals for clinical research studies according to the information obtained. Likewise, forensic psychologists may conduct diagnostic assessments to determine clients' mental competencies to stand trial or mental states related to committed crimes.

Depending on the complexity of the client's presentation of symptoms, a diagnostic assessment may be accomplished through interviewing alone or may require interviewing in combination with other tests and measurements. A diagnostic assessment may be one component of a comprehensive evaluation of an individual, or it may be the sole purpose of an assessment. Although diagnostic assessments may be repeated over time to determine whether temporal symptoms have been alleviated, certain diagnoses are considered unremitting, lifelong conditions (antisocial personality disorder, borderline personality disorder, narcissistic personality disorders; A. T. Beck, Freeman, Davis, & Associates, 2004), and therefore, reevaluation may not occur. Unlike some forms of behavioural assessment, practitioners may conduct diagnostic assessments in almost any setting in which they work. These evaluations are not dependent on viewing clients in their naturalistic environments.

**Clinical Examples**

***Example 1:*** For a client who is self-referred to a psychologist specialising in sleep disorders, a diagnostic assessment is necessary to determine if the client indeed has a sleep disorder, and if so, what kind; or to determine if the sleep difficulties are secondary to other medical or psychological problems. Once the psychologist determines the nature of the client's difficulty, treatment interventions may be offered, or an appropriate referral made if the sleep difficulties are determined to be secondary to another psychological or medical problem.

***Example 2:*** In psychiatric emergency rooms, psychologists may conduct diagnostic assessments to determine patients' needed level of care, and to communicate this information to triage facilities (inpatient unit, partial program, or outpatient clinic) before discharging or admitting patients to other units for follow up care.

***Example 3:*** If someone you know told you that her child has a reading disability, would you know how to help your friend assess the services that her child needs? Most professionals would need more specific information to develop recommendations or a treatment plan. For starters, what are the child's current learning strengths and difficulties, environmental supports, learning strategies used individual and family expectations, and self-efficacy beliefs? Note that you can ethically help a friend consider services that might be appropriate for a particular disorder, but you cannot ethically give recommendations or treatment plans on a casual basis to personal friends and acquaintances. Assessments, just like therapy, must always be conducted within the boundaries of a formal professional relationship (APA, 2002).

**Descriptive Assessments:** Descriptive assessments, broadly described, are conducted to learn more about clients' cognitive functioning, psychosocial functioning, academic achievement, personality, behaviour, or specific needs within an identified area of interest (e.g., caregivers' needs). Assessment questions may focus on individuals, families, groups of people (e.g., group home setting; hospital unit), or person-environment interactions (e.g., the goodness of fit between a developmentally disabled adult and her social rehabilitation programme setting).

Mental health professionals conduct these assessments to obtain background and general information necessary for better understanding of clients' problems and factors contributing to those problems. Such assessments aid professionals in planning treatment, providing academic or occupational counselling, and designing group or individual behaviour modification interventions. Researchers or programme evaluators may use descriptive assessments to provide end-users of their work with information about populations or programs under study.

Descriptive assessments are often combined with diagnostic assessments, and some methods of evaluation will accomplish data collection for both purposes. Data collection techniques for descriptive assessments include a combination of interviews, observation, self-report inventories and questionnaires, reports by others, computerised assessment, and physiological assessment. Clinical psychologists with proper training can conduct most types of descriptive assessments. Psychologists also commonly specialise in assessments for specific aged populations (e.g., children/adolescents, adults, senior adults), disorders (e.g., learning disabilities, traumatic brain injury, Huntington's chorea)or psychosocial problems (e.g., the court adjudicated offenders).

**Prediction Assessments:** While evaluation of current functioning is critical to most types of assessment, under certain circumstances, psychologists are also asked or required to predict clients' future behaviours or the effect or impact that situations or life events will have on individuals' thoughts, feelings, behaviours, or overall functioning.

Predictive assessments are often necessary for or for medical, forensic, and occupational settings, and traditional mental health in and outpatient settings. Given the uniqueness of individuals and the inconsistency of behaviours characteristic of persons with certain personality disorders or other problems, most predictive assessments remain tentative and qualified as best estimations.

The accuracy of any assessment, but especially of predictive assessments, relies on the availability, accuracy, and reliability of data about the predictor and predicted variables. Predictor variables are those factors that are presumed to proceed or co-occur with the behaviour to be predicted and to be causally related in some way.

Some behaviours are more easily predictable than others. Assuming we have comprehensive information leading to the diagnosis, it is likely that a young adult with social anxiety, without treatment, will have difficulty delivering his 30-minute presentation to the 75 students in his college course; an older adult who had little social support other than her recently deceased spouse, who also has a history of poor coping skills, may be likely to have difficulty adjusting to widowhood and may suffer from complicated bereavement. Such predictions are fairly easy to make, given a thorough assessment of past behaviour, current functioning, and other psychosocial variables, and the predictable nature of the behaviours in question.

When more difficult predictions of future behaviour are requested or necessary, significant consequences may be associated with the outcome of the evaluation. For example, predictions of suicide risk, dangerousness, psychological suitability for specific medical treatments, or prediction of psychological preparedness for parenthood (adoption) require psychologists to gain as much certainty as possible, since the consequences related to poor or inadequate assessment can obviously be grave.

The APA Code of Ethics cautions that predictions or recommendations made based on assessments should specify the sources of data collected and that for mandated individuals specifically and all others, generally), appropriate informed consent must be obtained. Some examples of prediction assessments will illustrate the complexities of this work.

Psychologists working in almost any clinical setting will be faced with the need to conduct suicide and dangerousness risk assessments. Current suicide symptoms and homicidal ideation are standard components of most psychologists' intake assessment and mental status examination. When clients endorse suicidal or homicidal ideation (thoughts), further evaluation is necessary to determine the severity of these thoughts, the clients' likelihood of acting on these thoughts and plans to do so, and their ability or access to the means by which they could execute their plans.

Based on thorough assessments, clinical psychologists are expected to make predictions about a client's safety and the safety of others, before they can release the client from their presence. However, Rudd and Joiner (1998) emphasise that although the court system seems to imply that clinicians should be able to predict suicide, empirical data show that prediction" models of suicide consistently fail; therefore, the complexity of this task cannot be overstated.

Based on the research reviewed by Rudd and Joiner, clinicians' "risk" assessments (focussing on patients' current state) are more accurate and reliable than actual predictions (implying future behaviour) of suicide attempts or completion. Risk assessment for suicide consists of evaluation of predisposing factors (e.g., age, sex, previous psychiatric diagnosis, history of sociality), acute and chronic risk factors and precipitating factors (current stressors or losses, such as job, loved ones, physical or cognitive ability, chronic pain, affective disorders, poor problem-solving skills, social isolation, poor impulse control), and protective factors (active involvement in treatment, good physical health, good problem-solving ability, social support, hopefulness).

In medical settings, physicians constantly make decisions and predictions about patients' likely physical response to medications, medical interventions (e.g., surgery, radiation, organ transplantation), and treatments (e.g., light therapy). However, many physicians recognise that biological responses are not the only concern. Patients' compliance with medical regimens and the ability to cope with the necessary lifestyle and behavioural changes can be equally important. Clinical (or clinical health) psychologists aid physicians decision-making and treatment planning for patients by conducting predictive assessments relating to these issues

For example, organ transplant recipients must comply with medication and behavioural (bone marrow transplant recipients must stay away from crowds for 6 months to 1 year, due to low immune functioning) regimens following transplants. Many recipients take as many as 5 to 10 medications following the transplant, including anti-rejection medications to prevent their bodies from rejecting the new organ. If patients do not comply with this requirement, fatal consequences could result.

Physicians, therefore, want to be as certain as possible that treatment is truly in an individual's best interest. Likewise, individuals with histories of drug or alcohol abuse may be questionable candidates for some medical treatments because of, the potential for them to cope poorly with the short or long-term effects of treatment, and the lethality of mixing alcohol or drugs with the prescribed regimen they may be given. Psychologists must assess patients past behaviours, current functioning (emotional state, desire or motivation for treatment, coping skills), psychosocial resources (strength in faith or spirituality, social support), and other factors, to evaluate the strengths and potential threats or weaknesses that can impact future behaviour.

Psychologists working in forensic settings are likely to conduct predictive assessments for various reasons. For offender populations, prediction of recidivism is likely required as part of court system procedures relating to sentencing and parole, and defendant and plaintiff initiated evaluations. Family/marital lawyers also frequently hire clinical and forensic psychologists to evaluate clients' current functioning (descriptive assessment or diagnostic assessment) and predict future behaviours. Behaviours of interest in family/marital law might include clients' likelihood of future abusive behaviours; clients' future abilities to manage anger and aggression if rehabilitation is sought; clients' likelihood of complying with child custody mandates and abilities to maintain effective parenting skills, and children's predicted responses to custody arrangements. Numerous other examples exist.

Occupational settings provide rich opportunities for psychological assessment. Questions to be answered in occupational settings may relate to the workforce in a company as a whole, or individuals within a workforce. Prediction assessments might be sought to answer questions such as the following ones:

- What is the likelihood of this employee's occupational success, given the specific accommodations and training available?
- What variables are predictive of burnout in persons with a particular job or position?
- What is the likely psychological impact of a specified corporate change on upper-level management?

Psychologists working in employee assistance programs may conduct more traditional clinical prediction assessments.

Thus far, descriptions and examples of the goals and types of assessments clinical psychologists conduct have remained general. The following section describes several specific types of assessment that are conducted to answer specific questions.

**Q3. Discuss the specific types of assessment.**

*Or*

**Write a short note on cognitive assessment. [June-2020, Q.No.-10]**

**Ans.** To differentiate among the different types of assessment, several key questions are answered within each of the following subsections to address the elements of what, when, who, where, why, and how:

- What are the goals of the assessment?
- When, relative to other life events, will the assessment take place?
- Who requests the evaluation or who refers clients for specific assessments?
- Who is (are) the person(s) to be evaluated?
- Where will the assessment be conducted?
- Why is the assessment necessary?
- How will the information be used?

The answers to these questions vary depending on the assessment prescribed. Some overlap can also be noted as the different applications of assessment are illustrated.

Although classifying an individual as mentally retarded may be useful for communicating a person's general functioning level among professionals, describing the person's strengths, weaknesses, likes and dislikes, will be equally or more important in the development of a behaviour modification plan.

**Cognitive Assessment:** The cognitive assessment focuses on understanding brain-behaviour relationships, information processing, and thinking skills. The following critical aspects of cognition may be targeted for assessment: attention, perception, memory, schemas, learning (intelligence; achievement; aptitude), cognitive development, creativity, language, problem-solving, decision-making, and judgement. Neuropsychological tests, intelligence tests, achievement and aptitude tests, and development tests are specific types of cognitive assessments for evaluating these areas.

Clinicians who conduct or request cognitive assessments are interested in understanding individuals' skills (strengths and deficits), abilities, and limits, and comparing these skills and abilities with clients' own displayed effect and behaviours. Individuals' functioning is usually compared with their own previous or prospective functioning, to normative standards predetermined by research, or both. Some high schools require youth football players and other sports participants) to have cognitive assessments before beginning the football season. These baseline assessments provide individual norms that are later used for comparison with post-injury (concussions) cognitive assessments if football players are hurt during the season. Cognitive assessments may be conducted periodically to evaluate positive or negative change over time, such as yearly achievement testing in language development or mathematics skills.

Intelligence testing exemplifies an assessment done to evaluate individuals' functioning compared with normative standards: parents may request IQ (intelligence quotient testing to determine children's scholastic needs and readiness to begin elementary school, or later in life for psychoeducational planning.

Other reasons cognitive assessments may be indicated are numerous. Cognitive assessments may be required when persons are not reaching expected developmental milestones, such as language skills. Self-recognition or by others of non-normative (non-average) behaviour, either positive (superior intellectual abilities, creativity) or negative (attention problems, extreme emotional ability), often generates referrals for cognitive assessment. Significant changes in cognitive functioning are usually noticed by individuals, family, and friends, and often lead to visits to primary care physicians or emergency rooms; these health professionals may require psychologists? assistance in diagnosing or understanding the cause for the behaviour change (Rozensky, Sweet, & Tovian, 1997).

Such sudden or gradual behaviour changes may have resulted from a known external event (accident), or a known or initially unknown biological change (tumour, medication side effects, ageing process). Thus, cognitive assessments are useful for individuals across the life span, for purposes of diagnosis, understanding, and treatment or future planning.

**Personality Assessment**

- **Definition of Personality:** Various theorists have defined personality in many ways, over the many years that the discipline of psychology has evolved. Most definitions and theorists have agreed that personality refers to stable, enduring characteristics that uniquely define individuals' ways of being or of viewing life situations, the world, and others in it. Furthermore, personality may be defined using the terminology of individuals temperament and traits.

- **Temperament:** This refers to a person's disposition and is often assumed to be largely biologically determined. Much research on temperament has been conducted on infants and children. Equating temperament with personality may be appropriate according to some psychological theories, especially those rooted in the psychodynamic traditions or medical models; other theories might suggest that persons are born with a particular temperament, and stable characteristics develop in addition to this biologically predetermined disposition to result in personality.
- **Traits:** These refer to individuals relatively stable ways of thinking or behaving or their disposition that may develop over time. The term trait implies that the environment and one's interaction with it or others may formatively develop one's personality. Traits differ from persons' behaviours, that is, traits refer to how people are; behaviours describe what people do. If you had to describe your best friend in three sentences, what would you say? Perhaps, you might say that your friend is "fun or funny," "loyal," "kind and compassionate," trustworthy," sociable," "outgoing," or other similar descriptors.

Most people define others in global terms, describing the most characteristic style of the individuals. They attach these global terms based on behaviours they have observed. Your friend may be described as "funny" because she tells jokes and elicits laughter. Some people are described as having "different personalities" depending on the social context (e.g., social versus business). Descriptors, such as those of your friend, are typically representative of the combination of temperament and traits, or his or her "personality."

How did you arrive at the description of your friend? If you are like most people, you have observed your friend in various situations or interactions with you. You observed her behaviour and the emotions she expressed. You also noticed her consistent ways of viewing herself and relating to others and her environment and made inferences based on these observations. In essence, you have conducted a personality assessment, because formal assessment relies on similar processes!

Possible goals and objectives of formal personality assessment are diagnosis and understanding of persons' ways of relating to others and the environment for description, prediction, and treatment in clinical or counselling (career vocational) settings, employment settings, or forensic settings, among others. In your assessment of your friend, you have diagnosed (classified your friend) and attempted to understand him or her. (Don't worry; if you have chosen to pursue a career in clinical psychology, you will often be accused of or asked if you are analysing your friends anyway!)

Substantial training in psychometrics, test theory, test development, diversity variables (ethnicity, race, culture, gender, age, language, disabilities), and supervised experience is required for use of most psychological tests, including personality tests (S. M. Turner, DeMers, Fox, & Reed, 2001).

**Behavioural Assessment:** The behavioural assessment aims to identify the frequency, context, and most importantly, the function of a person's behaviour. The focus of behavioural assessment is on the individual, specific behaviours and comparison of the person's behaviour across situations and in different environments (home, school, work, social situations).

Behavioural assessment developed from the principles of behavioural therapy, and therefore, emphasises the importance of behavioural chains, or the relationships between stimuli and responses, and behaviours and consequences. In the truest sense, behavioural assessments focus only on operationally defined, overt, observable behaviour that can be objectively measured.

The behaviour has been more broadly defined over time with the merging of the cognitive and behavioural theoretical orientations and principles. Behaviours sometimes may refer to cognitive processes such as copying, which has overt and covert components. Behaviourists may accept this leniency in the definition with the caveat that covert processes may be considered internal behaviours. For this discussion, however, the behavioural assessment will be reviewed in its truest form.

In general, psychologists might adopt a behavioural assessment paradigm as a means for evaluating clients and conceptualising their problems (Haynes & O'Brien, 2000; A. M. Nezu et. al., 1997). As a paradigm, clinicians who base all assessments on this model do so because it is usually largely consistent with their theoretical orientation to understanding human behaviour, and their approach to assessment and treatment of patients. Read GPH Book and Save Your Grade.

**Q4. Write short notes on the followings:**

**(i) Psychodiagnostic Assessment of Children**

**Ans.** Dimensional and Categorical Approaches provide comprehensive guidelines for assessing and diagnosing a broad spectrum of childhood disorders. In this groundbreaking new text, Randy Kamphaus (coauthor of the BASC and BASC-II) and Jonathan Campbell discuss both theoretical and practical aspects of the field. Their detailed coverage provides students and professionals with important research findings and practical tools for accurate assessment and informed diagnosis.

This monumental new work begins by explaining dimensional (e.g., classification methods that emphasise quantitative assessment measures such as behaviour rating scales) and categorical (e.g., classification methods that emphasise qualitative assessment measures such as clinical observation and history-taking) methods of assessment and diagnosis. It then highlights assessment interpretation issues related to psychological assessment and diagnosis. The remainder of the text covers constructs and core symptoms of interest, diagnostic standards, assessment methods, interpretations of findings, and case studies for all of the major childhood disorders.

The disorders include:

- Mental retardation Learning disability Autism spectrum disorders
- Depression
- Anxiety disorders
- Traumatic brain injuries
- Eating disorders
- Attention deficit hyperactivity disorder
- Conduct disorder

- Oppositional defiant disorder
- Substance abuse and dependence
- Sub syndromal and hyper syndromal impairments

Psychodiagnostics is understood in two ways:

- In the broadest sense it refers to moving closer to the psychological measurement in general and may refer to any object, verifiable psychodiagnostic analysis, speaking as the identification and measurement of its properties;
- In a narrow sense, a more widespread measuring of the individual psychodiagnostic personality traits.

In psychodiagnostic the data or information gathering can be divided into three main phases:

- Collection of data.
- Processing and interpretation of data.
- Decision-making that is psychodiagnostic and prognosis.

Psychodiagnostics develops methods for detecting and measuring individual psychological characteristics of personality.

As a theoretical discipline, psychodiagnostic deals with variables and constants that characterise the inner world of man.

Psychodiagnostics is a way to verify theoretical constructions. It is a way of moving from abstract theory, generalised to the particular facts.

Theoretical psychodiagnostic relies on the basic principles of psychology:

- Principle of reflection—an adequate reflection of the world provides a person with effective regulation of its activities;
- Principle of development-oriented study of the conditions of psychic phenomena, their trends, qualitative and quantitative characteristics of these changes;
- Principle of the dialectical relation of essence and phenomenon - allows you to see the mutual conditioning of the philosophical categories of the material of psychic reality as long as they non-identical;
- Principle of the unity of consciousness and activity—consciousness and mind are formed in human activity, the activity is regulated by both consciousness and psyche;

- Personal principle—requires psychological analysis of individual to individual, taking into account its specific situation in life, its ontogeny.

These principles underpin the development of psychodiagnostic methods —ways of obtaining reliable data on the content of the variables of mental reality.

The emergence of psycho-diagnostics, as a science and basic stages of its development.

Psychodiagnosis modern history begins with the first quarter of the nineteenth century, that is the beginning of a period of clinical development psychodiagnostic knowledge. Doctor psychiatrists have begun to conduct clinics systematic monitoring of patients, recording and analysing the results of their observations.

At this time there are psychodiagnostic methods such as observation, interviews, analysis of documents. But these methods were qualitative, and therefore on the same data, different doctors often have different conclusions.

Modern methods of psycho diagnostics on the main psychodiagnostic processes, properties and states' rights have appeared in the late nineteenth and early twentieth century. At this time actively developing the theory probability and mathematical statistics, which later became build scientific methods of quantitative psychodiagnosis.

**(ii) Psychological Assessment versus Psychological Testing**

**Ans.** It is important to note the difference between psychological assessment and psychological testing. Testing is a relatively straight forward process wherein a particular test is administered to obtain a specific score. Subsequently, a descriptive meaning can be applied to the score based on normative, nomothetic findings. For example, when conducting psychological testing, an IQ of 100 indicates a person possesses average intelligence.

Psychological assessment, however, is a quite different enterprise. The focus here is not on obtaining a single score, or even a series of test scores. Rather, the focus is on taking a variety of test derived pieces of information obtained from multiple methods of assessment, and placing these data in the context of historical information, referral information, and behavioural observations to generate a cohesive and comprehensive understanding of the person being evaluated. These activities are far from simple. They require a high degree of skill and sophistication to be implemented properly.

Thus, personality assessment is a complex clinical enterprise where the tools of assessment are used in concert with data from referring providers, clients, families, schools, courts, and other influential sources.

Although tests form the cornerstone of the work, personality assessment is the comprehensive interpretation of a person given all relevant data. This is not an easy enterprise and relies on substantial clinical skill, knowledge, and experience. However, if done well, the results can be very fulfilling for both clinicians and clients alike.

**(iii) Monitoring of Treatment**

**Ans.** Personality assessment tests have shown to be sensitive to the changes that clients experience in psychotherapy. Some measures, such as the Beck Depression Inventory were specifically designed to be used as adjuncts to treatment by measuring change.

Personality assessment results can be used as baseline measures, with changes reflected in periodic retesting. Clinicians can use this information to modify or enhance their interventions based on test results.

**(iv) Use of Personality Assessment as Treatment**

**[Dec-2020, Q.No.-10]**

**Ans.** The Therapeutic Assessment model was developed to increase the utility of personality assessment and feedback by making the assessment and feedback a therapeutic endeavour. Based on the principles of self and humanistic psychology, the therapeutic Assessment model views assessment as a collaborative endeavour in which both the client and the assessor work together to arrive at a deeper understanding of the client's personality, interpersonal dynamics, and present difficulties.

The client becomes an active collaborator in a mutual process to better understand the nature of his or her concerns and the assessor discusses (rather than delivers) test results in a manner that is comfortable and understandable to the client. This approach stands in contrast to the more typical information-gathering approach to assessment often used in neuropsychological and/or forensic psychology practice, where clients are less engaged in the process of assessment, and feedback may be provided in only a summary or written format. 

**Q5. Explain the psychodiagnostics assessment.**

**Ans.** Psychodiagnostic assessment is a specialised procedure to identify and differentiate a client's symptoms, enhance diagnostic accuracy, and provide insight into his or her daily experience.

Psychodiagnostics (psychological diagnosis) is a general term covering the process of identifying and emotional or behavioural problem and making a statement about the current status of a client. Psychodiagnostics may also include identifying a syndrome that conforms to a diagnostic system such as the DSM IV-TR. This process involves identifying possible causes of the person's emotional, cognitive, physiological and behavioural difficulties leading to some kind of treatment plan designed to ameliorate the identified problem.

The clinician must carefully assess the client's presenting symptoms and think critically about how this particular conglomeration of symptoms impair the client's ability to function in his daily life. Practitioners often use multiple tools to assist them in this process, including clinical interviewing, observation, psychometric tests and rating scales.

Differential diagnosis is the process of distinguishing one form of mental disorder from another by determining which of two (or more) disorders with similar symptoms the person is suffering from. The DSM IV-TR is the standard reference for distinguishing one form of mental disorder from another. It provides specific criteria for classifying emotional and behavioural disorders and shows the differences among various disorders. In addition to describing cognitive, affective, personality disorders this also deals with a variety of disorders about developmental stages, substance abuse, moods, sexual and gender identity, eating, sleep, impulse control and adjustment.

Unless a thorough picture of the client's past and present functioning is formed, specific counselling goals cannot be formulated. Furthermore, evaluation of progress, change, improvement or success may be difficult without an initial assessment.

**Assessment, Diagnosis and Contemporary Theories of Counselling**

- **Psychoanalytic Theory**: Some psychoanalytically oriented therapists favour psychodiagnostic. This is partly because for a long time in the United States psychoanalytic practise was largely limited to practitioners of medicine. Some of these psychodynamically oriented therapies note that in its effort to be theory-neutral the DSMIV TR eliminated terminology linked to psychoanalytical perspective.

- **Adlerian Theory:** Assessment is a basic part of Adlerian therapy. The initial sessions focus on developing a relationship based on a deeper understanding of the individual's presenting problem. A comprehensive assessment involves examining the client's lifestyle. The therapist seeks to ascertain the faulty, self-defeating beliefs and assumptions about self, others and life that maintains the problematic behavioural patterns the client brings to therapy.
- **Existential Theory**: The main purpose of existent clinical assessment is to understand the personal meanings and assumptions clients use in structuring their existence. This approach is different from the traditional diagnostic framework because it focuses on understanding the client's inner world and not on understanding the individual from an external perspective.
- **Person-centred Theory**: The best vantage point to understand another person is through his subjective world. They believe that the traditional assessment and diagnosis are detrimental because they are external ways of the understanding client.
- **Gestalt Theory:** Gestalt theory gathers certain types of information about their client's perceptions to supplement the assessment and diagnostic work done in the present moment. Gestalt therapists attend to interruptions in the client's contracting functions and the result is a functional diagnosis of how individuals experience satisfaction or blocks in their relationship with the environment.
- **Behaviour Theory**: This begins with a comprehensive assessment of the client's present functioning with questions directed to past learning that is related to current behaviour. Practitioners with a behavioural orientation generally favour a diagnostic stance valuing observation and other objective means of appraising both a client's specific symptoms and the factors that have led up to the client's malfunctioning.

**Q6. What are the stages in psychodiagnostics?**

***Or***

**Discuss the mental status examination in psychodiagnostics. What are the specific areas to cover in mental status examination?**

**[Dec-2019, Q.No.-4]**

*Or*

**Write a short note on Mental Status Examination.**

**[Dec-2020, Q.No.-12]**

**Ans.** Sundberg and Tyler (1962) described the course of clinical assessment as a flow-through four major stages:

**(1) Preparation:** In which the clinician learns of the patient's problem, "negotiates' the referral questions, and plans further steps in assessment;

**(2) Input**: during which data about the patient and his situation are collected;

**(3) Processing**; during which the material collected is organised, analysed and interpreted; and

**(4) Output**: during which the resulting study of the person is communicated and decisions as to further clinical actions made.

Depending on whether the clinician favours a psychometric or clinical orientation there will be greater or lesser use of statistical prediction or clinical interpretation,

Below is the general outline of the stages or phases of clinical assessment found in books of psychological testing and which can provide both a conceptual framework for approaching an evaluation and a summary of some of the points already discussed in blocks. Although the steps in the assessment are isolated for conceptual convenience, in actuality, they often occur simultaneously and interact with one another. Throughout these phases, the clinician should integrate data and serve as an expert on human behaviour rather than merely an interpreter of test scores. This is consistent with the belief that a psychological assessment can be most useful when it addresses specific individual problems and provides guidelines for decision-making regarding these problems.

**Application of Psychodiagnostic Evaluations:** This includes the following areas in which psychodiagnostic assessment is applied.

(1) psychological and emotional injury

(2) psychosomatic disorders

(3) Workers compensation

(4) Industrial injury

(5) Occupational stress

(6) Sexual harassment and discrimination suits

(7) Disability determinations

(8) Maritime stress claims

(9) Workplace violence

(10) Fitness for duty Competence to stand trial

(11) Criminal responsibility

**Evaluating the Referral Question:** Many of the practical limitations of psychological evaluations result from an inadequate clarification of the problem. Because clinicians are aware of the assets and limitations of psychological tests, and because clinicians are responsible for providing useful information, they must clarify the requests they receive. Furthermore, they cannot assume that initial requests for an evaluation are adequately stated. Clinicians may need to uncover hidden agendas, unspoken expectations, and complex interpersonal relationships, as well as explain the specific limitations of psychological tests. One of the most important general requirements is that clinicians understand the vocabulary, conceptual model, dynamics, and expectations of the referral setting in which they will be working (Turner et al., 2001).

Clinicians rarely are asked to give a general or global assessment, but instead are asked to answer specific questions. To address these questions, it is sometimes helpful to contact the referral source at different stages in the assessment process. For example, it is often important in an educational evaluation to observe the student in the classroom environment. The information derived from such an observation might be relayed back to the referral source for further clarification or modification of the referral question. Likewise, an attorney may wish to somewhat alter his or her referral question based on preliminary information derived from the clinician's initial interview with the client.

Psychodiagnostic testing enhances diagnostic accuracy by controlling for subjective opinion because it uses highly reliable, standardised tests that have been validated in clinical trials. For example, the reliability of the Wechsler Adult Intelligence Scale, which measures cognitive abilities and determines intelligence quotients, ranges from impressive .93 to .97. Because it can provide both accurate diagnostics and to grade the severity of impairment, psychodiagnostic testing helps the physician or psychiatrist to make pharmacological or psychotherapeutic treatment recommendations that have the highest likelihood of success. "Differential therapeutics", the prescription of effective treatments and proscription of ineffective ones, is the standard of care in contemporary medicine. Psychodiagnostic testing, because of its standardised and objective qualities, aids the practitioner in developing differential treatment recommendations.

Patients sometimes present confusing clinical pictures. They require sophisticated and extensive work-ups to distinguish the psychological contributions that confound accurate diagnoses and/or treatment of their conditions. Referral for psychodiagnostic testing is a cost-effective and valuable tool in the diagnostic decision-tree,

Examples of appropriate referrals for psychological testing include:

(1) Patients whom you suspect have substance abuse problems

(2) Patients with possible learning disabilities

(3) Patients with suspected mental retardation or poor intellectual functioning

(4) Patients with mood disorders

(5) Patients with anxiety and panic disorders

(6) Patients who have experienced trauma

(7) Children and adolescents who are "acting-out"

(8) Patients with suspected personality disorders

The psychodiagnostic report is designed to answer specific referral questions. These may include questions regarding diagnostic clarification, differentiation between transient "state" disorders and long-standing "trait" disorders (DSM Axis I versus Axis II disorders), intellectual functioning, learning style, current psychosocial stressors, and adaptive ability. Reports also include treatment recommendations that are based on the synthesised results of the clinical interview, mental status exam, patient's personal, family and cultural history, and findings from the standardised tests. Clinicians can use these objective recommendations to develop interventions with the highest likelihood of success.

The information to be gathered in a psychodiagnostic step by step are given below:

(1) State the client's name, age, date of evaluation and examiner. Document the reason for referral. This section captures why a professional psychological assessment was requested and the expected

outcome recommendation type such as special education placement, diagnosis, need for therapeutic intervention and competence

(2) Summarise background information on the client. This report section should be broken up into categories of related information such as medical conditions, test, and medications, clinical history, developmental milestones, education, behaviour, social situation and family. Each subsection should be presented in chronological order.

(3) Provide client information details extracted from interviews with parents or family members that were part of the evaluation procedure. Include facts and professional impressions.

(4) Report on your observations of the client during testing and interviewing. If evaluating a young child, include data on free-play behaviour and interactions with parents or siblings.

(5) List tests used. Because your report may be read by non-professionals, it is helpful to provide a brief description of what each test measures. Report test results. List test and scoring by section, subtest or total score.

(6) Interpret the test results. This critical section of the report can be approached in several ways: you can report the meaning of the results of each test, tie the results to the initial reasons for evaluation, or integrate the results by categories such as intellectual ability, competence, interpersonal skills, neuropsychological factors and mental status.

(7) Write a summary and recommendations. For this section, integrate information from all sections of the report into a capsule of your diagnosis using the DSM IV, your conclusions relative to the reason for evaluation, key findings of the client and recommendations.

(8) Acknowledge the confidentiality of the report information on each page. Print the report on letterhead stationery, sign your name and provide your professional credentials including licence number and licensing authority.

**Mental Status Examination:** The history and Mental Status Examination (MSE) are the most important diagnostic tools a clinical psychologist or a psychiatrist has to obtain information to make an accurate diagnosis. Although these important tools have been standardised in their own right, they remain primarily subjective measures that begin the moment the patient enters the office. The clinician must pay close attention to the patient's presentation, including personal appearance, social interaction with office staff and others in the waiting area, and whether the patient is accompanied by someone (i.e., to help determine if the patient has social support). These first few observations can provide important information about the patient that may not otherwise be revealed through interviewing or one-on-one conversation.

When patients enter the office, pay close attention to their grooming. One should always note things as obvious as hygiene, but, on a deeper level, also note things such as whether the patient is dressed appropriately according to the season. Other behaviours to note may include patients talking to themselves in the waiting area or perhaps pacing outside the office door. Record all observations.

The next step for the interviewer is to establish adequate rapport with the patient by introducing himself or herself. Speak directly to the patient during this introduction, and pay attention to whether the patient is maintaining eye contact. Mental notes such as these may aid in guiding the interview later. If patients appear uneasy as they enter the office, attempt to ease the situation by offering small talk or even a cup of water. Many people feel more at ease if they can have something in their hands. This reflects an image of genuine concern to patients and may make the interview process much more relaxing for them.

Beginning with open-ended questions is desirable to put the patient further at ease and to observe the patient's stream of thought (content) and thought process. Begin with questions such as "What brings you here today?" or "Tell me about yourself." These types of questions elicit responses that provide the basis of the interview. Keep in mind throughout the interview to look for nonverbal cues from patients. As they speak, for example, note if they are avoiding eye contact, acting nervous, playing with their hair, or tapping their foot repeatedly. In addition to the patient's responses to questions, all of these observations should be noted during the interview process.

As the interview progresses, more specific or close-ended questions can be asked to obtain specific information needed to complete the interview.

At some point during the initial interview, a detailed patient history should be taken. Every component of the patient history is crucial to the treatment and care of the patient it identifies. The patient history should begin with identifying patient data and the patient's chief complaint or reason for coming to the clinic. The patient's chief complaint should be a quote recorded just as it was spoken, in quotation marks, in the patient's record. This also is where all history of illness is recorded, including psychiatric history, medical history, surgical history, and medications and allergies. Of interest, it is important to make a direct inquiry to items such a family history of members being murdered, etc.

Obtain a complete social history. This addition to patient history can be most crucial when discharge planning begins. Inquire if the patient has a home. Also ask if the patient has a family, and, if so if the patient maintains contact with them. This also is the area in which any history of drug and alcohol abuse, legal problems, and history of abuse should be recorded.

Following the completion of the patient's history, perform the MSE to test specific areas of the patient's spheres of consciousness. To begin the MSE, once again evaluate the patient's appearance. Document if eye contact has been maintained throughout the interview and how the patient's attitude has been towards the interviewer. Next, to describe the mood aspect of the examination, ask patients how they feel. Normally, this is a one-word response, such as "good" or "sad."

Next, the interviewer's task is to define the patient's affect, which will range from expansive (fully animated) to flat (no variation). The patient's speech then is evaluated. Note if the patient is speaking at a fast pace or is talking very quietly, almost in a whisper. Thought process and content are evaluated next, including hallucinations or delusions, obsessions or compulsions, phobias, and suicidal or homicidal ideation or intent.

Then, the patient's sensorium and cognition are examined, most commonly using the Mini-Mental State Examination. The interviewer should ask patients if they know the current date and their current location to determine their level of orientation. Patients' concentration is tested by spelling the word "world" forward and backwards. Reading and writing are evaluated, as is visuospatial ability. To examine patients' abstract thought process, have them identify similarities between 2 objects and give the meaning of proverbs, such as "Don't cry over spilt milk." Once this is completed, perform the physical examination and needed laboratory tests to help exclude medical causes of presenting symptoms.

A compilation of all information gathered throughout the interview and MSE leads to the differential diagnosis of the patient. Once this diagnosis is established, a treatment plan is formulated. At this point, involving the treatment team (e.g., social workers, nurses, others) is important to help carefully explain to patients what their treatment will entail.

Once the history and MSE are complete, documenting this event accurately and efficiently is important.

Specifically, the Mental Status Examination Should Cover the Following:

- Appearance, attitude and motor activity–dress, grooming, signs of illness and behaviour
- Mood and affect–a range, liability appropriateness
- Speech - quality
- Thought-Content (Delusion, suicidal & homicidal ideations, obsessions)
- Thought-Form (Circumstantiality, tangentiality, loosening of associations, flight of ideas, derealisation, depersonalisation, dissociative events, concreteness, grandiosity)
- Perception-Hallucinations and illusions

  Alertness

  Orientation to time, place, and person

  Concentration

  Recent and remote memory

  Language (e.g., naming objects, repeating phrases, the performance of commands)

  Calculations

  Construction

  Insight and judgement
- Hallucinations and illusions
- Onset of illness

**Symptoms of Depression**

- Sleep (hypersomnia or insomnia)
- Interest (loss of interest in activities once enjoyed)
- Guilt (inappropriate guilt, feelings of worthlessness)

- Energy (decreased)
- Concentration (decreased)
- Appetite (increased or decreased)
- Psychomotor agitation/retardation
- Suicidal ideation

**Acquiring Knowledge Relating to the Content of the Problem:** Before beginning the actual testing procedure, examiners should carefully consider the problem, the adequacy of the tests they will use, and the specific applicability of that test to an individual's unique situation. This preparation may require referring both to the test manual and additional outside sources. Clinicians should be familiar with operational definitions for problems such as anxiety disorders, psychoses, personality disorders, or organic impairment so that they can be alert to their possible expression during the assessment procedure. Competence in merely administering and scoring tests is insufficient to conduct an effective assessment. For example, the development of an IQ score does not necessarily indicate that an examiner is aware of different cultural expressions of intelligence or the limitations of the assessment device. Clinicians must have in-depth knowledge about the variables they are measuring or their evaluations are likely to be extremely limited.

Related to this is the relative adequacy of the test in measuring the variable being considered. This includes evaluating certain practical considerations, the standardisation sample, and reliability and validity. It is important that the examiner also consider the problem about the adequacy of the test and decide whether a specific test or tests can be appropriately used on an individual or group. This demands knowledge in such areas as the client's age, sex, ethnicity, race, and educational background, motivation for testing, anticipated level of resistance, social environment, and interpersonal relationships. Finally, clinicians need to assess the effectiveness or utility of the test in aiding the treatment process.

**Data Collection:** After clarifying the referral question and obtaining knowledge relating to the problem, clinicians can then proceed with the actual collection of information. This may come from a wide variety of sources, the most frequent of which are test scores, personal history, behavioural observations, and interview data. Clinicians may also find it useful to obtain school records, previous psychological observations, medical records, police reports, or discuss the client with parents or teachers. It is important to realise that the tests themselves are merely a single tool, or source, for obtaining data.

The case history is of equal importance because it provides a context for understanding the client's current problems and, through this understanding, renders the test scores meaningful. In many cases, a client's history is of even more significance in making predictions and in assessing the seriousness of his or her condition than his or her test scores. For example, a high score on depression on the MMPI-2 is not as helpful in assessing suicide risk as are historical factors such as the number of previous attempts, age, sex, details regarding any previous attempts, and length of time the client has been depressed. Of equal importance is that the test scores themselves are usually not sufficient to answer the referral question.

For specific problem solving and decision-making, clinicians must rely on multiple sources and, using these sources, check to assess the consistency of the observations they make.

**Interpreting the Data:** The end product of the assessment should be a description of the client's present level of functioning, considerations relating to a etiology, prognosis, and treatment recommendations. Etiologic descriptions should avoid simplistic formulas and should instead focus on the influence exerted by several interacting factors. These factors can be divided into primary, predisposing, precipitating, and reinforcing causes, and a complete description of a etiology should take all of these into account. Further elaborations may also attempt to assess the person from a systems perspective in which the clinician evaluates patterns of interaction, mutual two-way influences, and the specifics of circular information feedback. An additional crucial area is to use the data to develop an effective intervention plan.

Clinicians should also pay careful attention to research on, and the implications of, incremental validity and continually be aware of the limitations and possible inaccuracies involved in clinical judgement. If actuarial formulas are available, they should be used when possible. These considerations indicate that the description of a client should not be mere labelling or classification, but should rather provide a deeper and more accurate understanding of the person. This understanding should allow the examiner to perceive new facets of the person in terms of both his or her internal experience and his or her relationships with others.

To develop these descriptions, clinicians must make inferences from their test data. Although such data is objective and empirical, the process of developing hypotheses, obtaining support for these hypotheses, and integrating the conclusions is dependent on the experience and training of the clinician. This process generally follows a sequence of developing impressions, identifying relevant facts, making inferences, and supporting these inferences with relevant and consistent data. Maloney and Ward (1976) have conceptualised a seven-phase approach to evaluating data.

They note that, in actual practice, these phases are not as clearly defined but often occur simultaneously. For example, when a clinician reads a referral question or initially observes a client, he or she is already developing hypotheses about that person and checking to assess the validity of these observations,

***Phase 1:*** The first phase involves collecting data about the client. It begins with the referral question and is followed by a review of the client's previous history and records. At this point, the clinician is already beginning to develop tentative hypotheses and to clarify questions for investigation in more detail. The next step is actual client contact, in which the clinician conducts an interview and administers a variety of psychological tests.

The client's behaviour during the interview, as well as the content or factual data, is noted. Out of this data, the clinician begins to make his or her inferences.

***Phase 2:*** Phase 2 focuses on the development of a wide variety of inferences about the client. These inferences serve both a summary and explanatory function. For example, an examiner may infer that a client is depressed, which also may explain his or her slow performance, distractibility, flattened affect, and withdrawn behaviour. The examiner may then wish to evaluate whether this depression is a deeply ingrained trait or more a reaction to a current situational difficulty. This may be determined by referring to test scores, interview data, or any additional sources of available information. The emphasis in the second phase is on developing multiple inferences that should initially be tentative. They serve the purpose of guiding future investigation to obtain additional information that is then used to confirm, modify, or negate later hypotheses.

***Phase 3:*** Because the third phase is concerned with either accepting or rejecting the inferences developed in Phase 2, there is a constant and active interaction between these phases. Often, in investigating the validity of an inference, a clinician alters either the meaning or the emphasis of inference or develops entirely new ones. Rarely is an inference entirely substantiated, but rather the validity of that inference is progressively strengthened as the clinician evaluates the degree of consistency and the strength of data that support a particular inference. For example, the inference that a client is anxious may be supported by WAIS-III subscale performance, MMPI-2 scores, and behavioural observations, or it may only be suggested by one of these sources. The amount of evidence to support an inference directly affects the amount of confidence a clinician can place in this inference.

***Phase 4:*** As a result of inferences developed in the previous three phases, the clinician can move in Phase 4 from specific inferences to general statements about the client. This involves elaborating each inference to describe trends or patterns of the client. For example, the inference that a client is depressed may result from self verbalisations in which the client continually criticises and judges his or her behaviour. This may also be expanded to give information regarding the ease or frequency with which a person might enter into the depressive state. The central task in Phase 4 is to develop and begin to elaborate on statements relating to the client.

***Phases 5, 6, 7:*** The fifth phase involves a further elaboration of a wide variety of the personality traits of the individual. It represents the integration and correlation of the client's characteristics. This may include describing and discussing general factors such as cognitive functioning, affect and mood, and interpersonal-intrapersonal level of functioning.

Although Phases 4 and 5 are similar, Phase 5 provides a more comprehensive and integrated description of the client than Phase 4. Finally, Phase 6 places this comprehensive description of the person into a situational context and Phase 7 makes specific predictions regarding his or her behaviour. Phase 7 is the most crucial element involved in decision-making and requires that the clinician takes into account the interaction between personal and situational variables.

Establishing the validity of these inferences presents a difficult challenge for clinicians because, unlike many medical diagnoses, psychological inferences cannot usually be physically documented. Furthermore, clinicians are rarely confronted with feedback about the validity of these inferences. Despite these difficulties, psychological descriptions should strive to be reliable, have adequate descriptive breadth, and possess both descriptive and predictive validity. Reliability of descriptions refers to whether the description or classification can be replicated by other clinicians (inter-diagnostician agreement) as well as by the same clinician on different occasions (intra-diagnostician agreement).

The next criterion is the breadth of coverage encompassed in the classification. Any classification should be broad enough to encompass a wide range of individuals, yet specific enough to provide useful information regarding the individual being evaluated. To be a top scorer– Read only GPH book.

**Q7. How test batteries can be used?**

*Or*

**What is a test battery? Discuss its uses. [June-2020, Q.No.-6]**

**Ans.** A group, series, or set of several tests designed to be administered as a unit in order to obtain a comprehensive assessment of a particular factor or phenomenon.

Several examples of this usage occur in neuropsychological instruments (such as the Halstead-Reitan Neuropsychological Battery) where many cognitive functions need to be evaluated, using separate tests, to detect possible brain impairment. The term battery is also used to designate any group of individual tests specifically selected by a psychologist for use with a given client to answer a specific referral question, usually of a diagnostic nature.

Although tests are used for a variety of purposes in the area of psychopathology, their use often falls into one of two categories as given below:

- a need to answer a very specific and focussed diagnostic question (e.g., does this patient represents a suicide risk?);
- a need to portray in a very broad way the client's psychodynamics, psychological functioning, and personality structure.

The answer to the first category can sometimes be given by using a very specific, focussed test. In the example given above, The typical scale of suicidal ideation is the answer to the diagnostic question. For the second category, the answer is provided either by a multivariate instrument like the MMPI, or a test battery, a group of tests chosen by the clinician to provide potential answers.

A test battery gives a broader and firmer base for assessment than is possible with individual tests. The battery should be chosen to be as representative as possible to the particular needs of the individual patient. In the psychodynamic tradition, a common battery for testing adults for therapy planning includes, as a rule, the Wechsler Adult Intelligence scale, Rorschach, and TAT. Although the same basic battery may be used, such procedures are interpretable towards different ends. Thus, the individualisation of a psychological examination involves varying one's orientation towards the analysis and interpretation of data yielded by the same battery of broad-gauged tests as well as putting together a unique package of different procedures for each patient.

In practice, the two alternatives are often combined and a common nucleus is used with procedures added to answer specific questions.

Sometimes test batteries are routinely administered to new clients in a setting for research purposes, for evaluation of the effectiveness of specific therapeutic programs, or to have a uniform set of data on all clients so that base rates, diagnostic questions, and other aspects can be determined. The use of a test battery has several advantages other than simply an increased number of tests. For one, differences in performance on different tests may have diagnostic significance. If we consider test results as indicators of potential hypotheses (e.g., this client seems to have difficulties solving problems that require spatial reasoning), then the clinician can look for supporting evidence among the variety of test results obtained.

**Q8. Explain the concept of assessment interview.**

***Or***

**Explain the skills and techniques of an assessment interview.**

**Ans.** The assessment interview is very similar to a regular job interview but focuses more directly on your personality. Its nature is more psychological than a job interview and usually will 'plunge deeper'. An assessment interview is therefore often conducted by a psychologist, but your conversation partner could also be an HR staff member or a member of the board.

Most helping professionals use interviewing as a standard approach to assessing problems and formulating hypotheses and conclusions. Talking with appropriate, interested, and knowledgeable parties (the patient, family members, school teachers, physicians) is usually an important early step in conducting an assessment. Interviewing in clinical psychology entails much more than posing a series of questions to collect data about a case. Asking critical questions, carefully listening to answers, attending to missing or inconsistent information, observing nonverbal behaviour, developing hypotheses, and ruling out alternative hypotheses are all part of the interviewing process.

The interview is a thoughtful, well planned, and deliberate conversation designed to acquire important information (facts, attitudes, beliefs) that enables the psychologist to develop a working hypothesis of the problem(s) and its best solution. Although a great deal of research has been conducted on interviewing skills, the psychologist does not read a manual on how to conduct an interview and then become an expert. Effective interviewing is developed over time, practice, supervision, experience, and natural skill. While the actual information obtained might vary greatly depending on the specific purpose of the interview, generally a list of standard data is collected and discussed.

This includes demographic information such as name, address, telephone number, age, gender, or grade in school, occupation, ethnicity, marital status, and living arrangements. Information about current and past medical and psychiatric problems and treatments are also usually obtained. The chief complaint or a list of symptoms experienced by the patient has discussed as well as the patient's hypotheses regarding the contributing factors associated with the development and maintenance of the problem(s). The interviewer often wants to know how the person has tried to cope with the problem(s) and why he or she wishes to obtain professional services now.

**Skills and Techniques:** An interview is generally conducted as part of any psychological evaluation. Although numerous different interviewing situations exist, certain techniques and skills are necessary for nearly all types of interviews. These include developing rapport, effective listening skills, effective communication, observation of behaviour, and asking the right questions.

**(1) Rapport:** When patients talk with a psychologist about problems they are experiencing, they are often uncomfortable sharing their intimate concerns with a stranger. They may have never discussed these concerns with anyone before, including their best friends, parents, or spouse. They may worry that the psychologist might make negative judgements about their problems. They may feel embarrassed, silly, worried, angry, or uncomfortable in a variety of ways. An individual from an ethnic, racial, or sexual minority may fear being misunderstood or maltreated. To develop a helpful, productive, and effective interview, the psychologist must develop a rapport with the person he or she is interviewing. Rapport is a term used to describe the comfortable working relationship that develops between the professional and the interviewee. The psychologist seeks to develop an atmosphere and relationship that is positive, trusting, accepting, respectful, and helpful.

Although there is no specific formula for developing rapport, several principles are generally followed. These are given below:

- **(i) Principle of Attention:** First, the professional must be attentive. He or she must focus complete attention on the patient without interruption from distractions such as telephone calls or personal concerns.
- **(ii) Principle of Friendly Posture:** Second, the professional must maintain a rapport building posture, for example, by maintaining eye contact and facing the patient with an open posture without a physical barrier such as a large desk impeding. communication.
- **(iii) Principle of Listening:** Third, the psychologist actively and carefully listens to the patient, allowing him or her to answer questions without constant interruption.
- **(iv) Principle of being Non-judgemental:** Fourth, the psychologist is non-judgemental and non-critical when interacting with the patient, especially regarding personal disclosures.
- **(v) Principle of Empathy and Respect for the Patient:** Fifth, the professional also strives towards genuine respect, empathy, sincerity, and acceptance, without acting as a friend or a know it all type of person.

(vi) **Principle of Creating a Supportive Professional Atmosphere:** Sixth, the professional tries to create a supportive, professional, and respectful environment that will help the patient feel as comfortable and as well understood as possible during the interview.

**(2) Effective Listening Skills:** In addition to the development of rapport, an effective interviewer must be a good listener.

While this may appear obvious, good listening skills are important to develop and generally do not come naturally for most people. People often find it challenging to fully listen to another without being distracted by their thoughts and concerns. Many are too focussed on what they are thinking or want to say rather than on listening to someone else. Furthermore, careful listening must occur at many different levels. This includes the content of what is being said as well as the feelings behind what is being said.

Listening also involves paying attention to not only what is being said but how it is presented. For example, someone may deny that he or she is angry yet have their arms crossed and teeth clenched, thus suggesting otherwise. Listening also includes paying attention to what is not being said. Thus, listening involves a great deal of attention and skill including the ability to read between the lines.

Effective interviewers must learn to use and develop active listening skills, which include paraphrasing, reflection, summarisation, and clarification techniques (Cormier & Cormier, 1991). Paraphrasing involves rephrasing the content of what is being said. It means careful listening to another's story and then attempting to put the content of the story into a summary. The purpose of paraphrasing is to help the person focus and attend to the content of his or her message. In contrast, reflection involves rephrasing the feelings of what is being said to encourage the person to express and understand his or her to feel better.

Summarisation involves both paraphrasing and reflection in attempting to pull together several points into a coherent brief review of the message. Summarisation is used to highlight a common overall theme of the message.

Finally, clarification includes asking questions to ensure that the message is being fully understood. Clarification is needed to ensure that the interviewer understands the message as well as helping the person elaborate on his or her message.

Examples of these techniques are provided in the following example of a couple trying to decide if they should get married.

Edward is a 32-year-old man who has been dating Jenny, a 29-year-old woman, for several years. He feels that he cannot commit to marriage because he feels unsure if Jenny is the right one" for him. Jenny wants to marry Edward and reports feeling frustrated that he has so many doubts. Edward further reports that he is unsure if he could stay faithful to one person for the rest of his life.

*EDWARD:* "I'm not much of a believer in the institution of marriage. It seems to me that it made sense when the average life span was only 30 years or so. How can someone decide this during their 20s or 30s and have it be a good decision for 50 years or more? My parents are still married after 50 years but they hate each other. I don't know why they stay together. Jenny is nice and I like being with her but who knows what the future will hold for us. She has a lot of great qualities but some characteristics drive me nuts. For example, I don't like some of her friends. They are boring. She is a practical person, which I like, but sometimes there is not a lot of excitement in our relationship."

Examples of active listening techniques offered by the therapist follow:

*PARAPHRASE:* "So you seem to be unsure if marriage to Jenny or anyone for that matter is right for you."

*REFLECTION:* "To some degree, you feel bored in your relationship."

*SUMMARISATION:* "You are unsure if marriage is right for you and you are concerned that Jenny may not be the right person for you regardless of your views on marriage."

*CLARIFICATION:* "When you say that your relationship lacks excitement are you also referring to your sexual relationship?"

**(3) Effective Communication:** To conduct a successful interview, effective communication is a requirement. The professional must use language appropriate to the patient, whether a young child, an adolescent, or a highly educated adult. The interviewer generally avoids the use of professional jargon, or psychobabble, and speaks in terms that are easily understood. The interviewer tries to fully understand what the patient is trying to communicate and asks for clarification when he or she is unsure.

**(4) Observation of Behaviour**: The interviewer pays attention not only to what is being said during a clinical interview but also to how it is being said. Observation of nonverbal communication (e.g., body posture or body language, eye contact, voice tone, attire) provides potentially useful information. For example, a patient may describe severe depressive symptoms and suicidal thoughts, yet smile a great deal and appear energised and in good spirits during the interview.

Another patient might state that he or she feels completely comfortable, yet sits with arms and legs tightly crossed while avoiding eye contact. Inappropriate dress (e.g., T-shirt and shorts on a very cold winter day or for a job interview) or a dishevelled appearance may provide further insight into the nature of the patient's difficulties.

**(5) Asking the Right Questions:** A good interviewer must ask the right questions. All too often, inexperienced interviewers forget to ask a critical question only to remember it after the patient has left. Experience with interviewing and a solid understanding of psychopathology and human behaviour are needed to ask the right questions. Typical questions deal with issues such as the frequency, duration, severity, and patient's perception of the etiology of the presenting problem. A careful understanding of the symptoms as well as the patient's efforts to cope with the problem is usually important.

**Q9. Discuss the formats and types of interviews.**

**[Dec-2020, Q.No.-4]**

*Or*

**Write a short note on computer assisted interviews.**

**[June-2021, Q.No.-11]**

**Ans.** The most common types of interviews include initial intake interviews (first meeting overview), exit interviews(closure to a clinical relationship), mental status interviews, crisis interviews, and diagnostic interviews. The goals and purposes of these interviews are the same as the overall goals of assessment. Among these types of interview, there' are three major formats: structured, semi structured, and unstructured.

**(1) Structured Interviews:** Structured interviews are usually published or pre-established and standardised lists of questions with specific directions or flowcharts of questions to ask following certain responses. These interview outlines (similar to scripts or questionnaires) are used for predetermined purposes (diagnosis, symptom, or behaviour description) and allow for comparison of responses across individuals or therapists. Since the interviews require little clinical judgement or inference, persons without graduate training in psychology can be trained to use structured interviews under supervision.

The Diagnostic Interview for Children and Adolescents (DICA-R; Reich, Joseph, & Shayk, 1991) and the Structured Clinical Interview for DSM-IV (SCID-I; First, Gibbon, Spitzer, Williams& Benjamin 1997) are two examples of such interviews.

**(2) Semi-Structured Interviews:** Semi-structured interviews require more clinical skill and judgement. These interviews, such as the Hamilton Rating Scale for Depression (Hamilton, 1960), provide a list of questions or content areas that need to be covered. The exact wordings of the questions or order in which they are asked are determined by the clinicians. Often, the flow of a semi-structured interview seems like a more natural dialogue between the clinician and client compared with a structured interview, which provides little opportunity for tangential patient self-disclosure or input into the direction of the interview. Much like structured interviews, many semi-structured interviews are published in manuals and provide scoring instructions and normative or comparison scores. Semi-structured interviews are commonly used in qualitative research and clinical assessments.

**(3) Unstructured Interviews:** Unstructured interviews are clinician driven and are usually individualised to the purpose of the assessment. Since they are not manualised and are not accompanied by administration or scoring instructions, unstructured interviews are rarely, if ever, used in research settings. The quality of data gathered by clinicians using unstructured interviews is entirely dependent on the clinicians' interviewing skills, clinical judgement, and insight. This type of interview structure is most susceptible to individual biases and requires the greatest amount of training and skill for maximum results.

**Types of Interviews:** There are many different types of interviews conducted by psychologists. Some interviews are conducted prior to admission to a clinic or hospital, some are conducted to determine if a patient is in danger of injuring herself or someone else, some are conducted to determine a diagnosis. Whereas some interviews are highly structured with specific questions asked of all patients, others are unstructured and spontaneous.

While not an exhaustive list, this section briefly reviews examples of the major types of interviews conducted by clinical psychologists.

**(1) Initial intake Interviews:** Initial intake interviews are designed to gain an overview of a patient's problems, strengths, and resources, and reasons for seeking assessment, treatment, or hospital admission. In some ways, it can be viewed as a needs assessment of the patient, and an opportunity for the clinician's observation, diagnosis, and short-term and/or long-term clinical pathway goal planning. Intake interviews often include a combination of mental status interviews and diagnostic interviews.

**(2) Mental Status Assessment:** Mental status interviews focus on a client's current psychological functioning. The goal of a mental status interview is to gain an overview of client mental health, and identify normal versus abnormal or unusual thinking, thought processing, behaviours, or other characteristics. This type of interview has specific components and is mostly factual and data-based.

Clinicians make little to no interpretations of data collected in this type of interview, with the exception of some estimation of judgement, insight, and intellectual functioning, which may be largely based on clinical impression.

The mental status interview goes beyond the exchange of questions and answers and incorporates many behavioural observations. Behavioural observations include evaluation of the client's hygiene based on presentation, gait, speech (normal, pressured, slowed, slurred), eye contact, posture, behavioural manifestations of mood disorder (e.g., anxiety as represented by excessive fidgetiness or handwringing), and other observations.

Traditional questioning is used to inquire about a client's orientation to Persons (Who are you? Who brought you here? Who am I? Who is the President of India?) Places (Where are you now? What city and state do you live in? Where were you born?), and Time (What time of day is it? What day of the week is it? What year are we in? What holiday is coming up next?), thoughts, mood, affect, behaviours, short-term memory (e.g., remember this list of three objects, and I will ask you about them again later) and cognitive functioning (attention, concentration), medical status (e.g., use of medications), illicit and legal substance use, an estimate of intellectual functioning, suicidal and homicidal history or current thoughts or plans, insight, and judgement. Assessment of delusions and hallucinations is typically included in this evaluation.

As mentioned, most mental status interviews are conducted as part of an intake or subsequent evaluation. Because this interview is a standard clinical method of assessment and not typically used for comparative purposes, formalised rating scales are rarely if ever used.

**(3) Crisis Interviews:** Psychologists who work in acute psychiatric services, emergency rooms, or outpatient mental health clinics are most likely to conduct crisis interviews. However, most clinical psychologists need to conduct crisis interviews periodically, regardless of their setting of employment. Crisis interviews are directed towards clients who are in acute distress due to an exacerbation or increase in psychological disturbance, or who have suffered a traumatic or life-threatening incident.

Because these situations can arise in any setting (psychiatric, medical, school, research, etc.), all therapists must be prepared for the responsibility of determining clients' imminent risk for harming themselves or someone else, or inability to care for themselves, given a heightened state of psychological arousal or psychotic episode.

Crisis interviews are more focussed than intake interviews, and diagnostic interviews. Often, portions of a mental status exam, if not an entire exam, will be incorporated into this type of interview. Crisis interviews have the specific purpose of informing therapists' decisions about patients' safety, placement (psychiatric or medical hospital admission), or immediate intervention (crisis hotline leading to police outreach). Questions are typically focussed on gaining information about crisis situations, chief symptom complaints, symptom duration and severity, clients' safety, resources and supports, risks, and overall client functioning. Rational and systematic clinical decision-making, and knowledge and facility with procedures for individual settings (e.g., emergency help contacts, involuntary commitment procedures, steps for assisting women to leave homes of domestic violence) are two of the most important therapist attributes necessary for the management of crisis situations and crisis interviews.

**(4) Diagnostic Interview:** The purpose of a diagnostic interview is to obtain a clear understanding of the patient's particular diagnosis. Thus patient-reported symptoms and problems are examined in order to classify the concerns into a diagnosis. Typically, the Diagnostic and Statistical Manual-IV (DSM IV; American Psychiatric Association, 2000) is used to develop a diagnosis based on five categories or axes.

The DSM IV is used by hospitals, clinics, insurance companies, and the vast majority of mental health professionals to classify and diagnose psychiatric problems. While this is the most widely used diagnostic classification of psychiatric disorders in the United States, other classification systems exist and have both advantages and disadvantages.

The five axes for each diagnosis provide information concerning the clinical syndromes, the influence of potential personality disorders, medical problems, psychosocial stressors, and level of functioning. Specifically,

Axis I includes the presence of clinical syndromes (e.g., depression, panic disorder, schizophrenia).

Axis II includes potential personality disorders (e.g., paranoid, antisocial, borderline).

Axis III includes physical and medical problems (e.g., heart disease, diabetes, cancer).

Axis IV includes psychosocial stressors currently experienced by the patient (e.g., fired from job, marital discord, financial hardship).

Axis V (Global Assessment of Functioning or GAF) includes a clinician rating of how well the patient is coping with his or her problems (1 = poor coping, 100 = excellent coping). The interview is conducted to rule out inapplicable diagnoses and rule inapplicable ones. Thus, the goal of the interview is to determine whether the patient meets the diagnostic criteria of a particular disorder.

Diagnostic interviewing can be challenging. It is frequently difficult to ascertain the precise diagnosis through interview alone. Also, co morbidity may complicate the clinical picture. For instance, a patient who has been losing a lot of weight might be interviewed to determine whether he or she has anorexia nervosa, a disorder that results in self-starvation. Anorexia nervosa is especially prevalent in adolescent girls. Significant weight loss may also be associated with a number of medical problems (e.g., brain tumour) or other psychiatric problems (e.g., depression).

To determine whether the weight loss symptoms might be associated with anorexia nervosa, the clinician may wish to conduct a diagnostic interview to see if the patient meets the DSM-IV diagnostic criteria for anorexia nervosa. Furthermore, additional possible diagnoses may need to be considered as well (e.g., depression, phobia, borderline personality). While some clinicians might choose to use a structured clinical interview, most would conduct their own clinical interview.

**(5) Computer Assisted Interviews:** A next step in the evolution of structured interviews involves computer interviewing. As computers become more sophisticated and less expensive, programs can be developed to administer highly complex, efficient, and effective interviews. Computers can be used to ask patients questions and record their responses in a very objective manner. Numerous decision trees can be employed for appropriate follow up questions to the patient's answers.

Furthermore, some patients feel more comfortable answering sensitive and potentially embarrassing questions via computer rather than talking face to face with a human interviewer. However, some people are uncomfortable with using computers in this way and prefer to talk with a professional person about problems. Computer-assisted interviews have been used in clinical settings where patients can answer a variety of questions about their concerns while in a waiting area prior to their face to face meeting with a counsellor. Results from the computer interview can be provided to the counsellor to help in the treatment process.

Confidentiality concerns must be addressed when sensitive material is being requested in a public area (e.g., waiting room) and when access to computer files is not closely controlled.

**(6) Exit Interviews:** Exit interviews are conducted at the end of an inpatient or outpatient treatment, medical inpatient visit, or occupational tenure. These interviews provide therapists or another designated professional or paraprofessional with an opportunity to review assessment or therapy content with clients, provide feedback on progress; help clients engage in the future thinking about maintenance of treatment gains or managing future problems; create plans for future crises, relapses, or booster sessions; and gain clients' feedback on the usefulness of various aspects of the treatment. When exit interviews are conducted by the therapist at the end of treatment, these interviews are often called "termination sessions," although one could argue that ending treatment marks a new beginning for clients, rather than an ending. A termination interview provides a forum for clients to appropriately express their feelings and emotions about ending therapy.

**Q10. What do you mean by psychological report and communicating assessment results?**

**Ans. The Psychological Report:** A psychological assessment can include numerous components such as norm-referenced psychological tests, informal tests and surveys, interview information, school or medical records, medical evaluation and observational data. A psychologist determines what information to use based on the specific questions being asked. Its major purpose is to help the referral source make decisions related to the client. It thus represents the end product of the assessment. An ideal report will be written according to general guidelines and in a flexible but predictable format.

The most frequent categories of reports are centred around questions related to intelligence/achievement, personality/psychopathology, and neuropsychology areas. Additional, less frequent categories include adaptive/functional, developmental, neuro behavioural, aphasia, and behavioural medicine/rehabilitation. The most frequent general issues related to diagnosis and answering which type of treatment would be most effective for a given client. Each of the various categories of assessment requires different types of assessment instruments, knowledge related to the type of difficulty, awareness of the context (educational, legal, medical, rehabilitation, forensic), and knowledge of the various resources available in the community.

**Communicating Assessment Results:** Clients' recall and understanding of test interpretations are frequently incomplete. It has been shown that clients who receive test interpretations generally make greater gains in incorporating the results. This document presents a client cantered approach to testing and interpretation. It explains how the client first participates in the selection of the general type of tests to be administered, and then with the help of the guidance counsellor, learns how to interpret the test. This process helps reduce the chance of a client misunderstanding the test results or recalling them inaccurately. Test results in counselling constitute interventions that can facilitate change and lead to greater awareness, knowledge, and self understanding. This ultimately can lead clients to make more effective decisions.

After a psychological evaluation, the psychologist will often schedule a feedback session to show the patient the results, explain the findings in understandable language, and answer all questions. Often psychologists must also explain their assessment results to other interested parties such as parents, teachers, attorneys, and physicians.

In addition to oral feedback, the psychologist typically prepares a written report to communicate test findings. Most testing reports include the reason for the referral and the identification of the referring party, the list of assessment instruments used, actual test scores (such as percentile ranks), the psychologist's interpretation of the scores and findings, a diagnostic impression, and recommendations. It is important to ascertain the audience for whom the report is being written.

A report directed to another mental health professional may be very different from one to a school teacher or a parent. Most psychologists avoid professional jargon so that their reports will be understandable to non-psychologists. Psychologists also must handle reports confidentially and send them only to appropriate persons.

**Q11. Write general guidelines for writing a report.**

**Ans.** General Guidelines for Writing a Report:

- **Length of the Report:** The length of the report varies considerably across various referral settings. Traditionally, psychological reports have been between four and seven single-spaced pages. In medical contexts where time efficiency is crucial, psychological reports rarely exceed two pages. However, psychological reports in a wider number of contexts also appear to be getting shorter due to the cost containment and time efficiency demands of managed healthcare. In contrast, legal contexts demand far more detail, require greater accountability, typically have more complex referral questions, and involve more flexible, ample methods of reimbursement. As a result, reports tend to be 7-10 pages and sometimes even longer.

Reports are therefore influenced by and formatted according to the conventions of other health professionals working within the contexts psychologists write for.

- **Degree of Emphasis:** A well-written report also pays particular attention to the degree of emphasis given to various points. Sometimes, the evidence for a conclusion will be consistent, strong, and clear and this can then be stated accordingly in the report. Other information might be more speculative and should be written with an appropriate degree of tentativeness.
- **Domains:** Test interpretations are ideally presented and organised around specific domains. The selection of which domains to include should be driven by the types of questions the **referral source is re**questing. These questions largely determine the types of assessment tools used and types of questions asked of the resulting data. Since each client is different and lives within a different context, the number of domains will vary considerably. Within a psychoeducational context, relevant domains might revolve around cognitive ability, level of achievement, presence of a learning disability, or learning style. In contrast, a report written to assess personality/psychopathology might focus more on such areas as coping style, level of emotional functioning, suicide potential, characteristics relevant to psychotherapeutic intervention, or diagnosis.

  Sometimes test results are presented in a test by test fashion. This has the advantage of making it clear where the data came from. However, it runs the risk of being overly data/test-oriented rather than person-oriented. Research has consistently indicated that readers of reports do not feel this style is 'user friendly'. Also, it indicates a failure to integrate data from a wide number of sources and suggests that the practitioner has not adequately conceptualised the case. It also encourages a technician oriented role rather than one in which a knowledgeable clinician integrates a wide array of information to help solve a client's problem.
- **Deciding What to Include:** Consistent with the above themes, deciding what include is largely determined by the referral

source. One general principle is that material should only be included if it helps to further understand the client. In this respect, what is unique rather than what is average is usually more important. For example, describing a client's appearance is typically not useful if they made modal responses to the test material and were dressed in average appropriate clothes. In contrast, a client who was obsessively concerned with accuracy (ignoring time concerns) and dressed in an unusually formal fashion does provide useful behavioural observations. These observations also help to place test scores in a wider context, give information related to coping style, and an indication of their personality type.

- **Raw Data and Quantitative Scores:** Generally, raw data and quantitative scores should be avoided in the impressions/ interpretations section of the report. They can potentially make the report seem overly technical and cluttered. Sometimes, however, providing concrete behavioural observations or actual responses to selected items (i.e. MMPI-2 critical items) can make abstract points seem more immediate and insightful into the content of the person's thought processes. This can serve to balance out more high-level abstractions. Also, providing a clear statistic such as a percentile can sometimes make a description seem more clear and accessible. For example, a report might describe how a client with an average IQ had a quite low auditory memory. Stating they only scored in the '5th percentile' (or 'only five people out of a hundred scored in this range') can provide some precision into the magnitude of their difficulties.
- **Client Feedback:** One of the crucial roles of a psychological report is to assist in providing client feedback. This is by client advocacy legislation and the American Psychological Association's ethical guidelines in that clients should know the types of information and recommendations being made about and for them. Such feedback is expected to be clear, accurate, direct, and understandable. This means the results need to be phrased in everyday language rather than formal psychological terminology. There has also been increasing evidence that well-

integrated client feedback has clear therapeutic benefits. Thus the report and related feedback) can potentially become an integral part of therapy itself. While feedback is typically verbal, an important option is to design the written report, or at least an edited version of the report, in such a way as to be of optimal benefit to the client.

**Q12. State the models of psychological reports.**

**Ans.** The three models for psychological reports to be discussed are the Test Oriented Model, the Domain Oriented Model, and the Hypothesis Oriented Model. In the Test Oriented Model, results are discussed on a test-by-test basis. Each test is listed by name and significant results for that test are presented.

In the Test Oriented Model, results are discussed on a test-by-test basis. Each test is listed by name and significant results for that test are presented. Each test is generally discussed in a separate paragraph. Little or no effort is made to compare and contrast data between the various tests (at least not in the "Results of Assessment" section). The strength of this approach is that it makes clear the source of each piece of data. This could be important in certain settings, such as forensic reports. The weakness of this model is that the reader's attention becomes focussed on the tests, rather than on the client's adaptive functioning.

It also communicates to the reader that psychological assessment is a low-level, technical skill which involves little more than giving the test and copying some interpretive statements out of a manual. It ignores the role of the psychologist as the integrator of the test data; a professional who brings to bear his knowledge of how the test was constructed, how it was normed, limits to generalisability of test data, and how to use the data in a theoretical/conceptual manner to better understand the client. The Test Oriented Model was used extensively in past but has become increasingly unpopular in recent years.

In the Domain Oriented Model, results are grouped according to abilities or "functional domains". Separate paragraphs are usually devoted to such topics as intellectual ability, interpersonal skills, psychosocial stressors, coping techniques, intrapersonal needs, motivational factors, depression, psychotic features, etc. This model is useful when there is no specific referral question and you're not certain what use will be made of your data. For example, little background information may be available on a newly admitted patient. You're not sure why he was admitted or what factors precipitated the admission. Therefore, it is hard to know which portions of your data will be useful to the treatment team. The Domain Oriented Model is also common in neuropsychological reports, where a variety of providers may eventually become involved in the case. Each provider will focus on separate parts of the report to assist in a specific aspect of the intervention. This approach is also helpful when the assessment is being used to monitor treatment progress. It allows you to monitor changes in the client's functioning across a wide variety of areas. The weakness of the Domain Oriented approach is that the reader may be presented with a lot of information that has little relevance to his intended intervention. He may become so distracted by parts of the report he doesn't understand, that he fails to focus on information which could be helpful sometimes pejoratively referred to as a "shotgun" approach, referring to its apparent effort to hit all the possible target issues.

In the Hypothesis Testing Model, results are focussed on possible answers to the referral question(s). The idea is to present a hypothesis in the "Purpose for Evaluation" section, then present data systematically to support or refute the hypothesis. Separate paragraphs in the "Results of Evaluation" section address theoretical/conceptual issues by integrating data from the history, mental status exam and behavioural observations with data from all the tests. Tests are rarely mentioned by name. For example, information from scale 2 on the MMPI-2 may be combined with interpretive data from the MCMI dysthymia scale. If the integration of this information is consistent with the history and the mental status exam, it is included in a paragraph dealing with depression. The strength of this model lies in its efficiency and concise focus on the referral problem. The reader isn't distracted by unrelated details. The primary weakness of the model is that you don't report some of the information which is unrelated to the purpose of the evaluation" but which could potentially be useful to other disciplines.

**Levels of Reports:** Having covered the issue of report Models, this discussion will now turn to "levels" of reports. Three levels of reports, viz., level 1, level 2and level 3 will be covered.

A "Level One" report is the copied out of the manual level. The interpretive data come directly from the manual (or computer print out) and usually follow the format. This makes for a conceptually weak report and may actually do more harm than good for the client. Keep in mind that many of the referral agents will have little understanding of the limits to generalisability and external validity of "raw" test data. This level of report is only appropriate when there are extenuating circumstances which make it impossible to interview the patient or to obtain background information. In those cases, the report should be clearly qualified with a statement to the effect that...."These results represent a blind interpretation of test data and should be considered tentative until confirmed by subsequent clinical data or background information".

A "Level Two" report represents the minimum level of conceptual input which should be used for most purposes. Of all the possible interpretive hypotheses generated by the test, the only ones included in the "Results of Evaluation" are those that have been confirmed (either by the history or in the clinical interview).

A "Level Three" report represents the highest level of conceptualisation. Its format is similar to a Level Two report. However, it also presents a theoretical conceptualisation of the problem. Ideally, this report will integrate all available information to:

- describe the nature of the problem and how it developed over time
- describe factors which influence and reinforce the problem
- describe any recent exacerbating factors which led to the referral
- provide suggestions for intervention based on the client's strengths, weaknesses, and coping skills.

**Q13. Write the format for psychological reports.**

*Or*

**Discuss the format for writing psychological report.**

**[June-2019, Q.No.-9]**

*Or*

**Discuss the general guidelines for writing a psychological report.**

**[Dec-2019, Q.No.-3][Dec-2020, Q.No.-5]**

**Ans.** The tests have been conducted and the observations compiled. For some psychologist practitioners, the most daunting step still awaits:

how best to convey the complexities of what's been learned about an individual in a single report.

Developing and honing psychological assessment report writing skills is not easy, says Hadas Pade, PsyD, an assistant professor at Alliant International University's California School of Professional Psychology in San Francisco, who co-leads workshops on writing meaningful reports. Report writing is sometimes given short shrift in psychology training programs, she says, which focus more on teaching test administration, scoring and interpretations.

'Test results', 'Summary and recommendations'). Some reports might demand (and practitioners prefer to include) an extensive history whereas others might minimise the history in favour of spending relatively greater time elaborating on impressions and interpretations. Given the recent trends towards treatment planning and demonstrating the practical, everyday relevance of assessment, some reports might place relatively greater emphasis and length into providing concrete, specific recommendations for psychotherapy planning, vocational training, educational intervention, or neuropsychological rehabilitation.

Even if reports do not formally designate specific headings and subheadings, they still typically include a predictable series of content areas. The following listing provides an outline of typical areas (from Groth Marnat, 1999; Williams & Boll, 2000):

Name:

Age (date of birth):

Sex:

Ethnicity:

Date of report:

Name of examiner:

Referred by:

(1) Referral question

(2) Evaluation procedures

(3) Behavioural observations

(4) Background information

(5) Test results

(6) Impressions and interpretations

(7) Summary and recommendations

An additional feature is an indication at the top of the report that the report is 'Confidential'. The report should conclude with the signature, name, and title of the author. This is crucial since it indicates that responsibility for the contents of the report is being formally accepted by the author. Identifying information is fairly straight forward (name, age, sex, etc.) but the additional features (I-VII) require elaboration.

**(1) Referral Question:** The referral question sets the stage for the rest of the report. It is therefore especially important to make sure it is as clear and specific as possible (i.e. 'My understanding is that you would like me to evaluate Mr X with particular reference to the nature and severity of his deficits, the extent of care he would require, ability to work, personality functioning, and the likelihood of any further improvement). Often clarifying the referral question will require discussions with the referral source since it is not unusual to have an initially poorly articulated (or at least partially developed) referral question. One means of assisting with this is to ask the referral source what decisions they need to make related to the client. 'Sometimes discussions with the referral source will mean indicating the sorts of questions that can and cannot be answered through formal assessment. Such discussions may even result in a mutual decision that formal assessment is not appropriate for the case. An articulated referral question will carry through to the rest of the report in that it provides a frame of reference for this material as well as a rationale for what is relevant to include in the sections on background information (history), impressions/interpretation, and especially the summary/recommendations section.

One effective technique is to create bulleted points in the summary, each of which provides a clear answer to each of the referral questions. However, the points need to be consistent with material presented previously in the impressions/interpretation section. A nice beginning to the referral question section (and the report in general) is to make a brief, succinct, orienting, statement related to the client (i.e. 'Mr X is a 36 year old, white, right-handed, married male with a high school education who sustained a severe, diffuse closed head injury on April 12, 1998).

**(2) Evaluation Procedures:** The evaluation procedures section is simply a listing of the various instruments used. Sometimes, particularly in legal settings, this includes the date when administered and the length of time they took to complete the test. It is sometimes useful to include the total time involved in the entire evaluation. If the report relied on previous records (academic, vocational, legal, medical), then the dates and, if relevant, the authors of the reports should be given (i.e. 'Also, I reviewed the following reports by ...).

**(3) Behavioural Observations:** Often behavioural observations can provide a useful context for understanding test data. For example, low scores on cognitive tests may be the result of low motivation or perhaps a problem-solving style that sacrifices speed for accuracy. These and related behavioural observations can be noted in the behavioural observations section. Behavioural observations should generally be kept concise and relevant. They should also refer to concrete, observable behaviours rather than either high-level abstractions or conclusions about the client. Thus, it would be preferable to state that the client moved slowly and they were self-critical (i.e. "the client continually commented that they weren't able to do very well') rather than to make inferences (i.e. 'the client appeared depressed'). Inconsistencies in the client's behaviour might also be useful to note. These might include a young person who acts older than their stated age or a person who says they feel fine but appear anxious and defensive. Additional domains of behavioural observations include attitude towards the examiner and test situation, attitudes towards self, reaction to praise, reaction to failure, motor co-ordination, reaction time, and behaviours related to speech and language.

**(4) Background Information:** One of the potentially most useful functions of the professional psychologist is to provide descriptions of relevant background information. This might be particularly important in a medical context where physicians neither have the time nor the appropriate training to access important client information.

**(5) Summary and Recommendations:** The most valuable section is usually the summary and recommendations. The importance of this section is that sometimes it is the only section read by allied health professionals concerned with time efficiency. The summary provides an opportunity for the practitioner to succinctly state the main conclusions of the report. As indicated previously, the summary section also provides an opportunity to make sure each one of the referral questions has been addressed. The recommendations are an opportunity to provide person-focussed suggestions for solving specific problems. A clear research finding is that reports are typically rated as most useful if the recommendations are highly specific rather than general. Thus a statement such as a client should begin individual psychotherapy' is not as useful as one that states the 'client is likely to benefit most from weekly sessions of individual psychotherapy using strategies to decrease their level of subjective distress, enhance social supports, and increase their level of awareness related to self-defeating patterns in interpersonal relationships'. Once a report has been submitted, follow up contact with the referral source is advisable to provide ongoing feedback related to the accuracy and usefulness of the report as well as help facilitate the actual implementation of the recommendations.

❑❑❑

# 3 TESTS OF COGNITIVE FUNCTIONS

## INTRODUCTION

In this chapter, the assessment of intelligence has tremendous potential for great use and great abuse. IQ tests can be used to categorise people into oblivion and misinterpreted to support a wide variety of racist and sexist ideologies. It will briefly touch on the history of intelligence assessment and then focus on the Wechsler Scales, the Stanford Binet V, and then describe more recent tests of cognitive development, such as the Kaufman tests, the Woodcock-Johnson, the Differential Ability Scales, and the Cognitive Assessment System. After that, we will be dealing with conceptual thinking and measurement. We will present the various tests that could be used for the purpose and then discuss the applicability and limitations of these tests. A number of authors have alluded to the range of possible human memory systems but in the present context we will mainly be concerned with the more customary use of the term, that is the retention of specific information which has been acquired in the recent past. It is this aspect of memory which forms the basis of most of the memory symptoms reported by brain-damaged patients and which is the main focus. It expands the discussion of assessment in clinical psychology at last.

**Q1. Write a note on history of intelligence assessment.**

**Ans.** The first modern intelligence test in IQ history was developed in 1904, by Alfred Binet (1857-1911) and Theodore Simon (1873-1961). The French Ministry of Education asked these researchers to develop a test that would allow for distinguishing mentally retarded children from normally intelligent, but lazy children.

Alfred Binet, with the assistance of the Minister of Public Instruction in Paris (who was eager to separate mentally retarded from normal children in the classroom), published the first 'real' intelligence test in 1905. Like Galton's test, Binet's instrument had only a vague tie to theory (in this case, the notion that intelligence was a single, global ability that people possessed in different amounts). In a stance antithetical to Galton's, Binet declared that because intelligence is complex, so, too, must be its measurement. He conceptualised intelligence as one's ability to demonstrate memory, judgement, reasoning, and social comprehension, and he and his colleagues developed tasks to measure these aspects of global intelligence.

Binet's contributions included his focus on language abilities (rather than the non-verbal skills measured by Galton) and his introduction of the mental age concept, derived from his use of age levels, ranging from 3 to 13 years, in his revised 1908 scale (mental age was the highest age level at which the child had success; the Intelligence Quotient, or IQ, became the ratio of the child's mental age to chronological age, multiplied by 100). In 1916, Lewis Terman of Stanford University translated and adapted the Binet-Simon scales in the US to produce the Stanford Binet (Terman, 1916).

Nearly coinciding with the Stanford Binet's birth was a second great influence on the development of IQ tests in the US: America's entry into World War I in 1917. Practical concerns superseded theoretical issues. Large numbers of recruits needed to be tested quickly, leading to the development of a group IQ test, the Army Alpha. Immigrants who spoke English poorly or not at all had to be evaluated with nonverbal measures, spearheading the construction of the nonverbal group test, the Army Beta.

The next great contributor to IQ test development was David Wechsler. While awaiting induction into the US Army in 1917, Wechsler obtained a job with, e.g. Boring that required him to score thousands of

Army Alpha exams. After induction, he was trained to administer individual tests of intelligence such as the new Stanford Binet. These clinical experiences paved the way for his Wechsler series of scales. Wechsler borrowed liberally from the Stanford Binet and Army Alpha to develop his Verbal Scale and from the Army Beta and Army Performance Scale Examination to develop his non-verbal Performance Scale. His creativity came not from his choice of tasks, all of which were already developed and validated, but from his insistence that everyone should be evaluated on both verbal and non-verbal scales, and that profiles of scores on a variety of mental tasks should be provided for each individual to supplement the global or aggregate measure of intelligence.

**Q2. Explain the measures of intelligence.**

*Or*

**Describe Wechsler's scales for children. [Dec-2019, Q.No.-7]**

*Or*

**Describe Wechsler scales for adults (WAIS III), its administration and scoring. [June-2021, Q.No.-2]**

**Ans.** The intelligence quotient (IQ) is a measure of intelligence that is adjusted for age. The Wechsler Adult Intelligence Scale (WAIS) is the most widely used IQ test for adults. Brain volume, speed of neural transmission, and working memory capacity are related to IQ.

**(1) Wechsler Scales:** While Wechsler (1974) defined intelligence as being a person's capacity to understand and cope with his or her environment, his tests were not predicated on this definition. Tasks developed were not designed from well-researched concepts exemplifying his definition. Virtually all of his tasks were adapted from other existing tests. Wechsler did not give credence to one task above another but believed that this global entity called intelligence could be ferreted out by probing a person with as many different kinds of mental tasks as one can conjure up. Wechsler did not believe in a cognitive hierarchy for his tasks, and he did not believe that each task was equally effective. He felt that each task was necessary for the fuller appraisal of intelligence. All of his scales yields IQs with a mean of 100 and standard deviation (SD) of 15, as well as subtest scaled scores with mean =10 and SD= 3.

**(2) Wechsler Scales for Adults:** The Wechsler-Bellevue Intelligence Scale was developed and published by David Wechsler (1896–1981) in

1939. The test was revised in 1955 and renamed the Wechsler Adult Intelligence Scale (WAIS) and revised again in 1981 as the Wechsler Adult Intelligence Scale-Revised (WAIS-R; Wechsler, 1981). The third edition was published in 1997 (WAIS-III; Wechsler, 1997) and the most recent edition is the scale of the fourth edition published in 2008 (WAIS-IV; Wechsler, 2008) thus the WAIS-IV is the current version of the test in use today.

**(3) WAIS-III:** The WAIS-III consists of seven individual verbal subtests (Information, Similarities, Arithmetic, Vocabulary, Comprehension, Digit Span, and Letter-Numbering Sequencing) and seven Performance (or nonverbal) subtests (Picture Completion, Picture Arrangement, Block Design, Object Assembly, Matrix Reasoning, Digit Symbol, and Symbol Search). Each subtest includes a variety of items that assess a particular intellectual skill of interest (e.g., the vocabulary subtest includes a list of words that the respondent must define). The WAIS-III generally takes about one to one-and-a-half hours to individually administer to someone between the ages of 16 and 74. Three IQ scores are determined using the WAIS-III: a Verbal IQ, a Performance IQ, and a Full Scale (combining both Verbal and Performance) IQ score. The mean IQ score for each of these three categories is 100 with a standard deviation of 15. Scores between 90 and 110 are considered within the average range of intellectual functioning. Scores below 70 are considered to be in the mentally deficient range, while scores above 130 are considered to be in the very superior range. The individual subtests (e.g., Vocabulary, Block Design) have a mean of 10 and a standard deviation of 3. These subtests form the basis for subtle observations about the relative strengths and weaknesses possessed by each individual. The table below gives the details of the subtests of WAIS-III.

***Administration and Scoring of the WAIS-III:*** WAIS-III must be administered on an individual basis by a specially trained psychologist. Although the administration and scoring of some subtests (e.g., arithmetic) is a relatively simple matter, many of the subtests, especially those comprising open-ended questions, call for informed professional judgement in scoring responses. A large part of the examiner's job is to establish and maintain rapport with the person taking the test. The subtests of the WAIS-III are given separately, alternating the verbal and performance subtests. The examinee first completes the picture completion subtest, which is simple and nonthreatening (this helps to capture the examinee's interest), then the vocabulary subtest, then the digit-symbol coding subtest, and so on. In each subtest, items are arranged in order of difficulty, with the easier items at the beginning of each subtest and the more difficult items given later. For most subtests, it is neither necessary nor useful to administer all test items to every subject. Instead, a fairly easy item is given first, and a subject who answers that item correctly receives credit for that item and all the easier items of the subtest. If the subject fails the first item, the examiner administers all the easier items to determine what types of problems the subject can or cannot solve. Similarly, if a subject consecutively fails a number of the moderately difficult items, the examiner concludes the subtest, rather than administering the most difficult items. The rationale for this procedure is that subjects tend to lose interest in testing if they are forced to respond to several items that are either insultingly easy or impossibly difficult for them.

The WAIS-III manual includes tables that are used to transform raw scores on each of the subtests to standard scores with a mean of 10 and a standard deviation of 3 (the same scale as used by the Stanford-Binet Fifth Edition). These standardised subtest scores provide a uniform frame of reference for comparing scores on the different sections of the WAIS-II. For example, if a person receives a score of 16 on the digit span test and 9 on the block design test, one might reasonably infer that this person is relatively better at the functions measured by the digit span test than at those measured by the block design test.

Traditionally, interpretation of the WAIS focussed on Verbal, Performance, and Full-Scale IQ. These scores are still reported in WAIS-III, but there is growing consensus that the Verbal-Performance dichotomy is not sufficient for understanding individuals' intelligence. The WAIS-III provides scores for four empirically supported indices: Verbal Comprehension (Vocabulary, Similarities, Information), Perceptual Organisation (Picture Completion, Block Design, Matrix Reasoning), Working Memory (Arithmetic, Digit Span, Letter-Number Sequencing), and Processing Speed (Digit-Symbol Coding, Symbol Search). The Picture Arrangement, Comprehension, and Object Assembly subtests do not contribute to these index scores. The WAIS-III manual provides tables for converting verbal, performance, and full-scale scores into deviation IQs based on a mean of 100 and a standard deviation of 15.

**(4) WAIS-IV:** The current version of the test, the WAIS-IV, which was released in 2008, is composed of 10 core subtests and five supplemental subtests, with the 10 core subtests comprising the Full-Scale IQ. With the new WAIS-IV, the verbal/performance subscales from previous versions were removed and replaced by the index scores. The General Ability Index (GAI) was included, which consists of the Similarities, Vocabulary, Information, the Block Design, Matrix Reasoning and Visual Puzzles subtests. The GAI is clinically useful because it can be used as a measure of cognitive abilities that are less vulnerable to impairment.

Four index scores are representing major components of intelligence:

(i) Verbal Comprehension Index (VCI)

(ii) Perceptual Reasoning Index (PRI)

(iii) Working Memory Index (WMI)

(iv) Processing Speed Index (PSI)

The Verbal Comprehension Index includes four tests:

**(i) Similarities:** Abstract verbal reasoning (e.g., "In what way are an apple and a pear alike?")

**(ii) Vocabulary:** The degree to which one has learned, been able to comprehend and verbally express vocabulary (e.g., "What is a guitar?")

**(iii) Information:** Degree of general information acquired from culture (e.g., "Who is the president of Russia?")

**(iv) Comprehension (supplemental):** Ability to deal with abstract social conventions, rules and expressions (e.g., "What do Kill 2 birds with 1 stone metaphorically mean?")

The Perceptual Reasoning Index comprises five tests

**(i) Bock Design:** Spatial perception, visual abstract processing & problem-solving.

**(ii) Matrix Reasoning:** Nonverbal abstract problem solving, inductive reasoning, spatial reasoning.

**(iii) Visual Puzzles:** non-verbal reasoning.

**(iv) Picture Completion** (supplemental). Ability to quickly perceive visual details.

**(v) Figure Weights (supplemental):** quantitative and analogical reasoning

The Working Memory Index is obtained from three tests:

(i) **Digit span:** attention, concentration, mental control (e.g., Repeat the numbers 1-2-3 in reverse sequence)

(ii) **Arithmetic:** Concentration while manipulating mental mathematical problems (e.g., "How many 45-cent stamps can you buy for a dollar?")

(iii) **Letter Number Sequencing (supplemental):** attention and working memory (e.g., Repeat the sequence Q-1-B-3-1-2, but place the numbers in numerical order and then the letters in alphabetical order)

The Processing Speed Index includes three tests:

(i) **Symbol Search:** Visual perception, speed

(ii) **Coding:** Visual-motor co-ordination, motor and mental speed

(iii) **Cancellation (supplemental):** visual-perceptual speed

Two broad scores are also generated, which can be used to summarise general intellectual abilities:

(i) Full-Scale IQ (FSIQ), based on the total combined performance of the VCI, PRI, WMI, and PSI

(ii) General Ability Index (GAI), based only on the six subtests that comprise the VCI and PRI

The WAIS-IV was standardised on a sample of 2,200 people in the United States ranging in age from 16 to 90. An extension of the standardisation has been conducted with 688 Canadians in the same age range. The median Full-Scale IQ is centred at 100, with a standard deviation of 15. In a normal distribution, the IQ range of one standard deviation above and below the mean (i.e., between 85 and 115) is where approximately 68 per cent of all adults would fall.

**(5) The Wechsler Scales for Children:** The Wechsler Intelligence Scale for Children(WISC) was first published in 1949 and was revised in 1974 (and renamed the Wechsler Intelligence Scale for Children Revised; WISC-R) and revised again in 1991(renamed the Wechsler Intelligence Scale for Children-Third Edition; WISC-III) and again in 2003 (now named the Wechsler Intelligence Scale for Children-Fourth Edition).

The WISC-IV is the version currently used today. The WISC-IV has both verbal and nonverbal subscales similar to those used in the WAIS-III. However, WISC IV questions are generally simpler because they were developed for children aged 6 to 16 rather than for adults. Furthermore, they are clustered into four categories that represent different areas of intellectual functioning.

These include; (i) Verbal Comprehension, (ii) Perceptual Reasoning, (iii) Working Memory, and (iv) Processing Speed.

Each of these four areas of intellectual functioning includes both "core" or mandatory subtests that must be administered to derive an index or IQ score as well as at least one "supplementary or optional subtest that is not included in the index or IQ score. The Verbal Comprehension category consists of three core subtests including Similarities, Vocabulary, and Comprehension as well as two supplementary subtests that include Information and Word Reasoning. The Perceptual Reasoning category. also consists of three core subtests, including Block Design, Picture Concepts, and Matrix Reasoning as well as one supplementary subtest called Picture Completion. The working memory category consists of two core subtests including Digit Span and Letter-Number Sequencing as well as one supplementary subtest entitled Arithmetic. Finally, the Processing Speed category consists of two core subtests including coding and Symbol Search as well as one supplementary subtest entitled Cancellation.

The WISC-IV provides four index score IQs as well as an overall or full-scale IQ based on the scores from all of the four index scores. These IQ scores all are set with a mean of 100and a standard deviation of 15. The four-factor scores (i.e., Verbal Comprehension, Perceptual Reasoning, Working Memory, and Processing Speed) were developed using factor analytic techniques and numerous research studies to reflect human intellectual functioning. Each of the subtests uses a mean of 10 and standard deviation of 3. The WISC-IV has been shown to have excellent reliability, validity, and stability (Wechsler, 2003).

**(6) The Wechsler Preschool and Primary Scale of Intelligence (WPPSI):** WPPSI was developed and published in 1967 for use with children aged 4 to6. The test was revised in 1989 and became known as the Wechsler Preschool and Primary Scale of Intelligence-Revised (WPPSI-R) and revised again in 2002 as the WPPSI-III. The WPPSI-III is the current version of the test being used today. The WPPSI-III is used for children ranging in age from 2 to 7. Like the other Wechsler scales (WAIS-III, WAIS-III NI, and WISC-IV), the WPPSI-III has both Verbal and Performance scales resulting in four IQ scores: Verbal IQ, Performance IQ,

Processing Speed IQ, and Full-Scale IQ. Similar to the other Wechsler scales, IQ scores have a mean of 100 and a standard deviation of 15, while the subtest scores have a mean of 10 and a standard deviation of 3. The Verbal IQ score consists of the Information, Vocabulary, and Word Reasoning subtest while the Comprehension and Similarities subtests are not included in the calculation of the Verbal IQ score. The Performance IQ consists of the Block Design, Matrix Reasoning, and Picture Concept subtests while the Picture Completion and Object Assembly are not included in the calculation of the Performance IQ score.

The Processing Speed IQ score consists of the Symbol Search and Coding Subtest. The WPPSI-III has been shown to have satisfaction, reliability, validity, and stability (Wechsler, 2002).

**Q3. Explain Stanford-binet scale.**

**Ans.** The Stanford–Binet Intelligence Scales (or more commonly the Stanford–Binet) is an individually administered intelligence test that was revised from the original Binet–Simon Scale by Lewis Terman, a psychologist at Stanford University. The Stanford–Binet Intelligence Scale is now in its fifth edition (SB5) and was released in 2003. It is a cognitive ability and intelligence test that is used to diagnose developmental or intellectual deficiencies in young children. The test measures five weighted factors and consists of both verbal and nonverbal subtests. The five factors being tested are knowledge, quantitative reasoning, visual-spatial processing, working memory, and fluid reasoning.

The scale developed by Binet and Simon in 1905 consisted of a set of 30 problems, varying from extremely simple sensory-motor tasks to problems involving judgement and reasoning. The basic strategy followed in this test and its many revisions were to observe the subject's reactions to a variety of somewhat familiar, yet challenging tasks. Terman and Merrill (1937) neatly summarise Binet's procedures, noting that this type of test is "not merely an intelligence test; it is a method of the standardised interview which is highly interesting to the subject and calls forth his natural responses to an extraordinary variety of situations".

Binet's original scales have undergone several major revisions. The fifth edition of the Stanford-Binet (Roid, 2003) represents the cumulative outcome of a continuing process of refining and improving the tests. Following a model adopted with the release of the fourth edition of this test in 1986, the selection and design of the tests included in the Stanford-

Binet are based on an increasingly well-articulated theory of intelligence. The fifth edition of the Stanford-Binet leans less heavily on verbal tests than in the past; the current version of the test includes equal representation of verbal and nonverbal subtests. In this edition, both verbal and nonverbal routing tests are used to quickly and accurately adapt test content and testing procedures to the capabilities of th individual examinee.

Each subtest of the Stanford-Binet is made up of open-ended questions or tasks that become progressively more difficult.

**Characteristics of the Stanford Binet Scale:** Like many other tests of general mental ability, the Stanford-Binet samples a wide variety of tasks that involve the processing of information and measures an individual's intelligence by comparing his or hers performance on these tests; the Stanford-Binet has employed a well-developed theory of intelligence to guide the selection and development of subtests. Drawing on the work of Vernon (1965), R. B. Cattell (1963), Sternberg (1977, 1981), and others, the authors of the Stanford-Binet have formulated a hierarchical model of cognitive abilities and have used this model in selecting subtests and in scoring the Stanford-Binet.

The theoretical model used in developing and interpreting the Stanford-Binet. The current version of the Stanford-Binet measures five general factors (Fluid Reasoning, Knowledge, Quantitative Reasoning, Visual-Spatial Processing and Working Memory), using both verbal and nonverbal tasks. In several cases, there are different sets of tasks that are appropriate at varying developmental levels. So, for example, in evaluating the Verbal Fluid Reasoning of a young examinee (or an examinee who finds age-appropriate questions too difficult), you might use simple reasoning tasks, whereas verbal absurdities tasks might be used for more advanced examinees and verbal analogies tasks might be appropriate for the oldest and most advanced examinees.

Examinees receive scores on each of the ten subscales (scales with a mean of 10 and standard deviation of 3), as well as composite scores for Full Scale, Verbal and Nonverbal IQ, reported on a score scale with a mean of 100 and a standard deviation of 15. Historically, the IQ scale based on a mean of 100 and a standard deviation of 15 had been the norm for almost every other major test, but the Stanford-Binet had used a score scale with a standard deviation of 16. This might strike you as a small difference, but what it meant was that scores on the Stanford Binet were hard to compare with scores on all other tests; a score of 130 on previous versions of the Stanford-Binet was not quite as high a score as a 130 on any other major test (if the standard deviation is 16, 130 is 1.87 standard deviations above the mean, whereas, on tests with a standard deviation of 15, it is 2 standard deviations above the mean). The current edition of the Stanford Binet yields IQ scores that are comparable to those on other major tests.

**Administration and Scoring of the Stanford-Binet:** Throughout its history, the Stanford-Binet has been an adaptive test in which an individual responds to only that part of the test that is appropriate for his or her developmental level. Thus, a young child is not given difficult problems that would lead only to frustration (e.g., asking a 5-year-old why we have a Constitution). Similarly, an older examinee is not bored with questions that are well beneath his or her age level (e.g., asking a 10-year-old to add 4+5). Subtests in the Stanford Binet are made up of groups of items that are progressively more difficult. A child taking the test may respond to only a few sets of items on each subtest.

One of the examiner's major tasks has been to estimate each examinee's mental age to determine the level at which he or she should be tested. The recent revisions of the Stanford-Binet include objective methods of determining each appropriate level for each examinee through the use of routine tests; the current edition uses both verbal (Vocabulary) and nonverbal (Matrices) routing tests.

Historically, the Stanford-Binet has been regarded as one of the best individual tests of a child's intelligence available. The recent revisions of the Stanford-Binet may increase its relevance in adult testing.

**Q4. Write a short note on the following:**

**(a) Woodcock-Jhonson psycho educational battery**

**Ans.** An assessment, now in its third edition, that measures cognitive ability and academic achievement in children, young people, or adults. The tests of cognitive ability produce a full-scale intelligence score and determine strengths and weaknesses of information processing. The tests of academic achievement assess abilities in reading, written language, mathematics, and knowledge. They also assess basic skills in each of these areas and the level of application of those skills by the person being assessed. This battery is one of the main diagnostic tools used to evaluate a student for specific learning disabilities. Test results on the cognitive portion, when combined and compared with the results of the achievement portion, reveal the learning style of a student who may have a learning disability, documented by a statistically significant numerical difference between actual performance and cognitive potential. [developed in 1977 by Richard W. Woodcock (1928), US psychologist, and his business partner Mary E. Bonner Johnson].

The WJ III, for ages 2 to 90+ years and composed of Cognitive and Achievement sections, is undoubtedly the most comprehensive test battery available for clinical assessment. The WJ HI Cognitive battery (like the WJ-R) is based on Hom's (1989) expansion of the fluid/crystallised model of intelligence and measures seven separate abilities: Long-Term Retrieval, Short-Term Memory, Processing Speed, Auditory Processing, Visual Processing, Comprehension-Knowledge and Fluid Reasoning. An eighth ability, Quantitative Ability, is measured by several subtests on the Achievement portion of the WJ III.

**(b) Raven's progressive matrices**

**Ans.** The Raven's Progressive Matrices is administered as a nonverbal group test. It is typically a 60-item test used in measuring abstract reasoning and regarded as a non-verbal estimate of fluid intelligence. Many patterns are presented in the form of a 6×6, 4×4, 3×3, or 2×2 matrix, giving the test its an Raven's Progressive Matrices (available in both paper and computer-administered forms) are made up of a series of multiple-choice items, all of which follow the same basic principle. Each item represents a perceptual analogy in the form of a matrix. Some valid relationship connects items in each row in the matrix, and some valid relationship connects items in each column of the matrix. Each matrix is presented in such a way that a piece of the matrix, located in the lower-right comer, is missing. The subject must choose from among six or eight alternatives the piece that best completes each matrix.

There are three forms of Raven's Progressive Matrices. The most widely used form, the Standard Progressive Matrices, consists of 60 matrices grouped into 5 sets. Each of the 5 sets involves 12 matrices whose solutions involve similar principles but vary in difficulty. The principles involved in solving the 5 sets of matrices include perceptual discrimination, rotation, and permutations of patterns. The first few items in each set are comparatively easy, but the latter matrices may involve very subtle and complex relationships.

The Standard Progressive Matrices are appropriate both for children above 5 years of age and adults; because of the low floor and fairly high ceiling of this test, the Standard Matrices are also appropriate for most ability levels. For younger children (ages 4 to 10), and for somewhat older children and adults who show signs of retardation, the Coloured Progressive Matrices seem to be more appropriate. This test consists of three sets of 12 matrices that employ colour and are considerably less difficult than those that make up the Standard Progressive Matrices.

Finally, the Advanced Progressive Matrices are appropriate for intellectually advanced subjects who find the Standard Matrices too easy. The Advanced Matrices are made up of 3 sets of 12 matrices, many of which involve extremely subtle principles in their solutions. The test effectively discriminates among those who receive extremely high scores on the Standard Progressive Matrices.

**(c) Kaufman assessment battery for children**

**Ans.** The K-ABC-II (Kaufman & Kaufman, 2004) is administered to children between the ages of 3 and 13 and has five global scales including Sequential Processing, Simultaneous Processing, Learning Ability, Planning Ability, and Crystallised Ability. Scores are then combined to create a Mental Processing Index (MPI) and a nonverbal index. The development of the K-ABC reflects a different theoretical approach to intellectual assessment relative to the Wechsler scales. The K-ABC-II was developed from research and theory in neuropsychology and, unlike both the Wechsler and Stanford-Binet scales, has achievement scores to measure skills such as reading ability. Many clinicians feel that the K-ABC-I is more enjoyable and engaging for children than the Wechsler scales and Stanford Binet, as well as a less verbally dependent test. Furthermore, the K-ABC-II generally takes less time to administer than the Wechsler and Stanford-Binet.

The Sequential Processing/Short-Term Memory Scale is designed to measure the ability to solve problems by remembering and using an ordered series of images or ideas. The Simultaneous/Visual Processing Scale measures the ability to solve spatial, analogical, or organisational problems that require the processing of many stimuli at one time. The Learning Ability/Long-Term Storage and Retrieval Scale measures the ability to complete different types of learning tasks. Immediate recall and delayed recall tasks are included in this scale. The Planning Fluid Reasoning Scale measures the ability to solve nonverbal problems that are different from the kinds taught in school. Verbally mediated reasoning must be used to solve the problems. The Knowledge/Crystallised Ability Scale measures knowledge of words and facts using both verbal and pictorial stimuli and requiring either a verbal or pointing response. Means are set at 100 with standard deviations of 15.

**Kaufman Adolescent and Adult Intelligence Test (KAIT):** The Kaufman Adolescent and Adult Intelligence Test (KAIT) (Kaufman & Kaufman, 1993) is an individually administered intelligence test for individuals between the ages of 11 and more than 85 years. It provides Fluid, Crystallised, and Composite IQs. It includes a Core Battery of six subtests (three Fluid and three Crystallised) and an Expanded Battery that also includes alternate Fluid and Crystallised subtests plus measures of delayed recall of information learned earlier in the evaluation during two of the Core subtests. The book you can believe most–GPH book.

**(d) Differential abilities scale**

**Ans.** The DAS was developed by Elliott (1990) and is an individually administered battery of 17 cognitive and achievement tests for use with individuals aged 2 through to 17 years. The DAS Cognitive Battery has a preschool level and a school-age level. The school-age level includes reading, mathematics, and spelling achievement tests that are referred to as 'screeners'. The same sample of subjects was used to develop the norms for the Cognitive and Achievement Batteries; therefore, intra- and inter-comparisons of the two domains are possible. The DAS is not based on a specific theory of intelligence. Instead, the test's structure is based on tradition and statistical analysis. Elliott (1990) described his approach to the development of the DAS as 'eclectic and credited the work of researchers such as Cattell Horn, Das, Jensen, Thurstone, Vernon, and Spearman.

**Q5. Discuss some of the questions and controversies concerning IQ testing.**

***Or***

**Discuss the various controversies with regard to IQ testing.**

**[June-2019, Q.No.-7]**

***Or***

**Discuss the questions and controversies connecting the IQ testing.**
**[June-2020, Q.No.-7]**

**Ans.** Some of the questions and controversies concerning IQ testing are as follows:

**(1) Are We Born With A Certain IQ?:** Often people assume that we are born with an innately determined level of intellectual ability that is not influenced by social, emotional, and environmental factors. Some suggest that IQ differences found among different racial groups might be due to inborn differences in intelligence. A great deal of controversy has raged in this debate for many years. The publication of the book The Bell Curve (Herrnstein & Murray, 1994) reignited this controversy by suggesting that African Americans were innately less intelligent than Caucasians while Caucasians were less intelligent than Asians. Research examining genetic influences on intelligence generally studies the heritability (i.e., the estimate of the genetic contribution to a given trait) of IQ using twin studies. Identical (monozygotic) and fraternal (dizygotic) twins reared together and reared apart present a unique research opportunity for examining the influence of both genetic and environmental contributions to a wide variety of traits. It has been estimated that the heritability of intelligence is between .40 and .80. Thus between 16 per cent and 64 per cent of the variance in intellectual ability is due to genetic influence. Research generally supports the notion of at least some significant genetic influence in intellectual ability. However, biological (e.g., prenatal care, genetics, nutrition), psychological (e.g., anxiety, motivation, self-esteem), and social (e.g., culture, socioeconomic status) influences all appear to be associated with intelligence or at least with IQ scores on standardised tests.

**(2) Is IQ Scores Stable Over Time?:** Measures of attention, memory, and other cognitive abilities assessed during the first year of life generally are moderately associated (i.e., r=.36) with intelligence fest scores assessed later in childhood. Often people assume that an IQ score obtained in childhood is stable over time. Thus, many people erroneously believe that someone who obtained an IQ of 120 in the first grade will also have an IQ of 120 in adulthood. Intelligence tests, however, provide an index of current functioning, and scores may change significantly over time. Many factors influence the stability of IQ scores. First, scores obtained when a child is very young (e.g., age 3) are likely to be less stable than scores obtained when a child is older (e.g., age 16). This is partly because early childhood tests focus on perceptual and motor skills, whereas tests for older children and adults focus more on verbal skills. Second, the longer the time between testing administrations, the more unstable the IQ score will appear. Thus, the difference between scores obtained at ages 3 and 30 is likely to be greater than the difference between scores obtained at ages 16 and 19. Furthermore, environmental factors such as stress, nutrition, educational opportunities, exposure to toxins such as lead, and illness, among other influences, all play a role in the determination of IQ scores.

**(3) Are IQ Scores Biased?:** Many people are concerned about potential bias in intelligence testing. For example, many feel that IQ testing may be biased in that children from high socioeconomic level homes tend to perform better on standardised tests than those from lower socioeconomic-level homes. Furthermore, some argue that currently, available intelligence tests may not be appropriate for use with individuals from many ethnic minority groups. California passed legislation that prohibited intelligence testing from being used for school placement of African-American children (Larry P vs Wilson Riles). The ruling suggested that intelligence testing was biased against African Americans and that they were disproportionately represented in educable mental retardation (EMR) classrooms. Bias is determined by examining the test's validity across different groups. A test is biased if the validity of the test varies from group to group. Research suggests that most standardised IQ tests such as the Wechsler and Stanford-Binet scales are not biased. However, tests can be misused by both unqualified and well-meaning people.

**(4) Should the Terms Intelligence Quotient or IQ Continue to be Used?:** Several misconceptions and myths about IQ exist. These include the notion that the IQ measures an innate or genetically-determined intelligence level, that IQ scores are fixed and never change, and that IQ scores generated from different tests mean the same thing. These concerns have led some experts to suggest that general IQ scores be eliminated in favour of standard scores that more accurately describe specific skills. Many recent tests of intellectual and cognitive ability have not used the terms intelligence quotient or IQ at all. These include the Woodcock-Johnson Psychoeducational Battery, the Kaufman Assessment Battery for Children, and the newest version of the Stanford-Binet. To be a top scorer–Read only GPH book.

**Q6. What do you mean by the abstract attitude?**

*Or*

**Define Abstract Attitude and its characteristics. Delineate the characteristics of test of Abstraction.** **[June-2021, Q.No.-7]**

**Ans.** An abstract attitude, as defined by Jung consists of "a view that is contrasted with concretism" which is thinking in a way that uses concrete, solid concepts related to direct observations or sensations instead of abstractions. This view equates having an "abstract" attitude about the world at large as being the opposite of a "concrete" point of view.

Abstract attitude can also refer to a concept introduced by psychiatrist Kurt Goldstein that describes the ability to use concepts to categorise things according to their specific attributes- thinking in a symbolic manner rather than in a concrete manner. The ability to do this can be impaired in individuals with brain damage or diseases.

**Characteristics of Abstract Attitude**

- To detach our ego from the outer world or inner experiences.
- To assume a mental set.
- To account for acts to oneself; to verbalise the account.
- To shift reflectively from one aspect of the situation to another.
- To hold in mind simultaneously various aspects.
- To grasp the essence of a given whole; to break up a given whole into parts, to isolate and synthesise them.
- To abstract common properties reflectively; to form hierarchic concepts.
- To plan ideationally; to assume an attitude towards the "merely possible" and to think or perform symbolically.

Based on these points, tests of abstraction can be said to have the following task characteristics.

**Characteristics of Tests of Abstraction**

- Learning to identify a relevant attribute or multiple attributes to solve a problem or make an accurate generalisation.
- Learning a rule or set of rules that solve a problem.
- Concept formation or spontaneous generation of hypotheses that relate disparate material.

- Inductive reasoning through the spontaneous formation of hypotheses that rule out alternative possibilities for a solution, and that finally lead to a correct solution.
- Having an "attitude towards the possible" or forming and manipulating a mental representation of an object that is not physically present.
- Spontaneous generation of plans that lead to the ultimate solution to a problem.
- The ability to shift, or change hypotheses or plans when the current one or the proponent response is not productive.

The large variety of cognitive and neuropsychological tests available makes it possible to identify procedures that provide assessments of all of these tasks. With respect to neuropsychology, patients with various forms of brain damage or disease lose all or some of these characteristics, as do some patients with psychiatric disorders, notably schizophrenia. Tests of abstract reasoning require to a greater or lesser degree the ability to maintain a mental set, to shift reflectively, to hold in mind simultaneously various aspects of a task (now known as dual processing), to abstract common properties, and to grasp essentials. Most scholars in the field would agree that these tests may be treated quantitatively, and would not agree with the relatively extreme view taken by Goldstein and Scheerer regarding numerical scoring. However, contemporary neuropsychology does not eschew the use of qualitative observation, and efforts are being made to make such observations objective, reliable, and perhaps quantifiable.

The distinction within abstract reasoning between those tasks in which the test taker has to generate concepts and those in which an established concept has to be identified through experiencing a series of positive and negative instances needs to be emphasised. Whereas self-initiated concept formation, attribute identification, and rule learning may all require the abstract attitude, they nevertheless appear to be separable cognitive abilities that may have different clinical and adaptive implications. Absence of the abstract attitude, and consequent concreteness, may prevent the solution of even the simplest conceptual tasks, but the capability of abstract reasoning can exist at numerous levels. Ability to identify relevant and irrelevant perceptual attributes and the ability to learn rules does not guarantee an intact ability to generate conceptual strategies in "open field" novel problem-solving situations.

The importance of flexibility is also important, because the attainment of a perfectly correct concept may not be adaptive when environmental circumstances necessitate a change. The Wisconsin Card Sorting Test stresses this latter consideration. The symptom of fixed preservative rigidity is perhaps the endpoint of this failure to reconceptualise under changing circumstances.

**Q7. What is measurement of conceptual thinking?**

**Ans.** The ADEPT-15 Conceptual scale measures how comfortable an individual is with long-term, big-picture, abstract thinking. At the low-scoring end of the dimension, the scale highlights the behaviours and the preferred approach which tend to be more pragmatic, concrete and of near-term concerns.

The purpose of these tests are, therefore, to help the psychologist observe the subject's thought processes and to discover the extent to which maladjustment or mental illness has impaired his conscious thinking, as revealed in efforts to solve problems requiring the formation of concepts.

In particular, these tests are intended to evaluate the subject's ability to deal with objects and situations on the abstract or conceptual level, as compared with the concrete. Ability to form concepts implies conscious reasoning at the abstract level; that is, transcending the immediate specific sensory situation, abstracting the common property from particular instances, analysing and synthesising, shifting from one aspect to another, keeping in mind several aspects simultaneously, planning ideationally, and self-criticism. An individual's behaviour at the concrete level, on the other hand, lacks these characteristics. The individual is then unreflective; he responds to the immediately given object or situation as something unique; he does not perceive an object or situation as one instance of a general class or category.

**Q8. Discuss the overview of tests.**

***Or***

**Describe Halstead Category Test and the Hanfmann Kasanin concept formation test.**

***Or***

**Give an overview of tests of abstract reasoning. [Dec-2020, Q.No.-3]**

**Ans.** Within neuropsychological assessment, there are specialised tests of abstract reasoning as well as tests generally classed as assessing other abilities that can be interpreted from the standpoint of abstract and concrete behaviour through qualitative observation. Although abstract reasoning may be involved in all these procedures, the specialised tests provide a direct assessment of the individual's ability to learn or form an abstract concept. Some of these procedures are paper and pencil tests that use language directly as the test medium.

**(1) Analogies and Proverb Tests:** The most commonly used tests of this type are analogies and proverbs tests. The Raven Progressive Matrices Test (1982) contains analogy items that use pictorial material, but factor analytic studies have shown that the test has a strong verbal component, apparently because many of the pictures of objects are nameable (Lezak, 1995). Proverbs tests, such as the one developed by Gorham (1956), test the ability to form verbal abstractions in either a free-response or multiple-choice form. Some items from the Comprehension subtest of the various Wechsler intelligence scales are proverbs that require a free verbal response. Interpretation of a proverb, such as "One swallow doesn't make a summer" requires the forming of an abstract generalisation from a metaphor.

**(2) Performance Tests (Sorting tests):** The tests used most commonly in the neuropsychological assessment are performance tests, which should not be characterised as nonverbal tests for various reasons, but which use nonverbal media, such as coloured blocks, or geometric forms. The major reason for not characterising these tests as nonverbal is that although the media used are generally not linguistic symbols, the test solution process may place heavy reliance on language. We will refer to them as performance tests, for want of a better term.

The most commonly used of these performance tests are sorting tasks. Many years ago Egon Weigl (1927) invented the prototype of these tasks that are still referred to as Weigl type sorting tests. The first tests developed were of the free sorting type in which a variety of objects are placed on a table, and the subject is asked to group the objects through such instructions as "Sort those figures which you think belong together," or "Put those together which you think can be grouped." After the first sorting, the subject is asked to put the objects together in another way.

The sorting tests first made generally available in a published form were those described in a monograph on abstract and concrete behaviour written by Kurt Goldstein and Martin Scheerer (1941). This monograph contains what is essentially a test manual for a series of procedures now known as The Goldstein Scheerer tests. In the Goldstein-Scheerer series, there is one relatively simple sorting task: The Weigl-Goldstein-Scheerer Colour Form Sorting Test, and two more complex tasks: the Gelb-Goldstein Colour Sorting Test and the Gelb, Goldstein, Weigl and Scheerer Object Sorting Test. The test method, however, is the same in all cases, the materials are set out, the subject is asked to sort them and then to report them. These tests assess the general capacities to form an abstraction or concept as the basis for the initial sorting and also evaluate cognitive flexibility, or the capacity to shift concepts.

**(3) Colour Sorting Tests:** The administration of the Colour Sorting Test is somewhat different from the other sorting tests. The test material consists of many skeins of wool (Holmgren Wools) that vary in hue and brightness. The subject is asked to select a skein of her or his preference, and to pick out the other skeins that can be grouped with it (e.g., different shades of green). When this procedure is completed, the examiner picks out a skein of a different hue and asks the subject to pick out the other skeins that go with it. This procedure is followed by triple matching. Three skeins at a time are placed before the subject varying in hue and brightness. The left and centre skeins have the same hue but different brightness, and the right skein has the same brightness as the centre skein but differs in hue. The examiner points to the left and right skein and asks about where the centre one belongs. The shift relates to whether the subject can sort according to hue and brightness. Shifting from hue to brightness is difficult for some normal people, and prompting about the idea of brightness is permissible, the point being whether the subject accepts the shift and the idea of common brightness. These free categorisation tests provide abundant opportunity for qualitative assessment and variations of the procedure to elicit various features of concreteness. However, they differ from the concept identification procedures to be described later in this unit in the sense that they are true measures of concept formation. "That is, the subject is provided with an array of diverse material out of which the abstraction has to be formed. The concept has to be self-initiated, and the subject makes up the rule that provides the basis for grouping. The rule may be simple (e.g., colour or shape) or quite complex as in the brightness or hue concept involved in the Colour Sorting Test. Nevertheless, the subject is required to initiate his or her categorisation or fail to do so.

**(4) Halstead Category Test:** The Goldstein-Scheerer tests are no longer commonly used, but their theoretical descendants are in common use. The most widely used ones are the Halstead Category Test (Halstead, 1947) and the Wisconsin Card Sorting Test (Grant& Berg, 1948; Heaton et al., 1993). Halstead (1947) was aware of Kurt Goldstein's theory of the abstract attitude, and it is historically important to note that the Wisconsin Card Sorting Test was first described as "a Weigl-type card-sorting problem." In these tests that followed the Weigl type sorting tests and the Goldstein Scheerer tests, there was an important change. The concepts in these tests are not formed by the subject but are inherent in the test materials themselves. The subject's task had changed from forming concepts to identifying concepts formed by the test maker.

Investigators in this area have therefore made a distinction between concept formation, which can be assessed with free sorting tests, and concept identification, which is what is involved in the Category and Card Sorting procedures.

In a series of experimental studies by Bourne and collaborators, the process of concept identification was intensively studied, mainly in normal individuals, to provide a detailed understanding of its relevant parameters, such as complexity and the role of informative feedback (Bourne, 1966). In a sense, the difference between a concept formation and a concept identification procedure is analogous to the difference between a projective and an objective test. In the former, the subject can exercise free self-expression; whereas the latter requires adherence to a particular structure. Perrine (1993) has made an important distinction in concept identification tests between attribute identification and rule learning. The Wisconsin Card Sorting Test stresses attribute identification. The correct answer is the stimulus attribute of form, colour, or number. In the case of the Category Test, the correct principle is a rule, regardless of the attributes of the stimuli. For example, the correct answer is the odd object in an array. Interestingly, Perrine reported only 30 per cent shared variance between the two procedures.

Brief descriptions of these two tests are as follows:

(i) **The Halstead Category Test** is administered through the use of an apparatus that displays the test stimuli and provides information to the subject regarding whether a response is correct. The subject looks at a screen below which are four numbered keys. The instructions are to look at the patterns on the screen and press the key that represents the right answer. If the correct key is pressed, the subject hears a pleasant chime. If the answer is incorrect, a rasping buzzer follows the response. The subject is told that he or she will be guessing at first, but when the concept or principle that unites the stimuli is learned, he or she will always get the chime. The test consists of seven subtests. The first of them is a familiarisation trial, and the second is a simple counting task. The remaining subtests require identification or learning of a concept, such as an oddity or spatial location. The most commonly used score for this test is total errors, but error scores can be obtained for each subtest and are sometimes useful clinically. For example, some of the concepts are spatial and some are numerical, each of which may have different implications for brain function.

**(ii) The Wisconsin card sort test (WCST**) was developed to examine concept formation and the ability of participants to overcome the tendency to perseverate. The Wisconsin Card Sorting Test in its original version consists of a deck of cards with coloured geometric forms printed on them. The cards vary about forms, colours, and several forms. Four of the cards are laid out as models, and the subject is given the deck. The general instruction is to place each card below the correct model card. After each placement, the examiner tells the subject whether the correct response was made. The task is to learn to sort the cards by form, colour, or number based on the pattern of right and wrong answers. When ten consecutive correct responses are made, the examiner, unbeknown to the subject, changes the concept. For example, if the colour was the correct response, the correct concept may be changed to form. The test continues until the subject correctly solves the six categories tested, or the supply of 128 cards is exhausted. Numerous scores are derived from this test, the most commonly used ones being the number of the six categories achieved, total errors, and preservative errors measuring persistence in sorting by a particular attribute after the relevant concept has been changed.

**(5) The Haufmann Kasanin Concept Formation Test (1937):** This is also known as the Vygotsky Test, and a recent modification called the Modified Vygotsky Concept Formation Test (MVCFT, Wang, 1983) represent tasks of that type. The Haufman Kasanin is a challenging procedure in which the subject is asked to perform several sorts, much like the Colour Form Sorting Test. However, there is a correct answer that the subject must learn through making sorts and obtaining information from the examiner concerning the correctness of the solution. The task is challenging because the concept is not a directly perceivable attribute, but is a second-order principle that has to be derived from the characteristics of multiple attributes. The MVCFT modifies the original procedure. It consists of 22 different blocks varying in colour, size, shape, and height. In the first part (convergent thinking), the examiner selects a target block and asks the participant to identify all other blocks that would belong with it, telling participants whether each response is right or wrong.

Participants are given correcting cues following each incorrect attempt. The procedure is repeated for four sets of blocks. A successful solution requires simultaneous consideration of the width and height of the blocks. Thus, the participant must combine abstract principles to determine the rule. When each complete set has been identified, the participant is then asked to state the sorting rule and then move on to the next set. Scores are based on the number of errors. After completion of this procedure, the examiner asks the participant to reclassify the blocks according to as many rules or ways as s/he can think of, one at a time (divergent thinking). After each classification, the examiner randomly mixes the blocks and asks for a new way of grouping. When the participant exhausts his/her means of classification, points are awarded for a total number of logical principles. This test contains concept formation and concept identification elements.

**(6) The Twenty Questions Task (Minshew, Siegel, Goldstein and Weldy, 1994):** This also has a correct answer, but the subject has to self-initiate sorting strategies to arrive at that answer. The procedure is much like the Twenty Questions parlour game in which a target object must be named based on questions that can be answered only yes or no.

The strategy for narrowing the possibilities and arriving at the right answer has to be formed by the player.

Another way of studying abstraction is through the examination of generalisation. When the same response is made to a continuum of stimuli, the phenomenon is referred to as stimulus generalisation. At a conceptual level, stimulus generalisation allows for classification, such that all objects with the same invariant characteristics may be classed into specific categories. Thus, a table is still a table regardless of wide variations in size, colour, shape, and other characteristics. When tasks are of a conceptual nature, stimulus generalisation is referred to as equivalence range (Gardner & Schoen, 1962).

Equivalence range problems assess an individual's tolerance for variability in stimulus characteristics within some category. In the case of the Colour Sorting Test, for example, the equivalence range is the amount of variation in brightness accepted to categorise a skein as being of a common hue. Generalisation procedures have been used mainly in research investigations.

In a study by Olson, Goldstein, Neuringer, and Shelly (1969), the task involved presenting geometric figures, half of which were permutations of a circle and the other half of which were permutations of a diamond. The permutations reduced the figures in width in the direction of a common shape. Subjects were shown the figures one at a time and asked to indicate whether it was a circle, a diamond, or neither. The measure of equivalence range was correctly classified figures. A modified version of the Colour Sorting Test was also administered. The literature suggested that brain-damaged individuals have narrow equivalence ranges, and that was what was found for both the colour sorting and visual forms tasks. Thus, it would appear that abstraction of common properties by brain-damaged individuals has a narrow focus, probably limited to specific, concrete, stimulus properties.

Another aspect of abstract reasoning relates to what K. Goldstein and Scheerer (1941) referred to as an "attitude towards the possible." It consists of the ability to form a central representation of an object that is not perceptually present. They used the Block Design Test (Kohs Blocks) for evaluating this aspect of abstract and concrete behaviour because it is necessary to form a changing representation of the individual blocks in space to match the model. As the model presented in their version of the test becomes more like the desired product with the blocks, by making it larger or drawing in lines between the blocks, the task becomes more concrete and simpler for patients.

Another form of abstract reasoning is challenged when a problem must be solved through logical inference. Situations requiring such processes generally require forming a plan or developing a strategy that ultimately leads to a solution. When lost in a forest, what is the best way of finding the way out? When shopping, what is the best way of completing errands in minimal time?

In trying to solve a problem, what inductive methods are best for solving the fewest steps? Psychological testing models for these abilities include searching strategy tests, the recently developed multiple errands tests (McCue et al., 1995), and game procedures in which a correct identification must be made with the fewest possible number of steps. The twenty questions game task, in which the test taker must identify an object contained in a large array of objects by asking as few questions as possible would be an example of a strategy task. (Minshew et al., 1994). The Tower of Hanoi or London problem is another strategy formation task. It is a puzzle in which rings are placed on pegs and the participant has to move the rings, one at a time, from one peg to another and put them in the same arrangement using the fewest possible moves (Shallice, 1982). The number of moves and time to solution is typically used as scores.

The Multiple Errands Test and the Modified Six Elements Test from the Behavioural Assessment of the Dysexecutive Syndrome tests (Wilson, Alderman, Burgess, Emslie, & Evans, 1996) are examples of such procedures. In both of them, the participant is assigned practical tasks and is scored for efficiency and success with which these tasks are performed. To be a top scorer–Read only GPH book.

**Q9. Discuss about cross cultural considerations and accommodations for persons with disabilities.**

**Ans.** Tests of cognitive functions do not rely heavily on language or knowledge of some specific environment or culture so they are called culturally fair. The stimuli used, usually geometric forms, do not include artifacts associated with some particular culture. Instructions written in English would have to be interpreted for patients who do not speak English. The major socio-cultural limitation would therefore relate mainly to general considerations concerning the meaning and acceptability of testing in different cultures.

These tests were designed for individuals with reasonably intact vision, hearing, and motor abilities. Typically, ad hoc accommodations are made for various disabilities where possible. There are two major issues about accommodation: testing of patients with severe sensory or motor handicaps of the upper extremities and of patients who are not ambulatory. In general, the former matter is dealt with on an *Adhoc* basis. There are no formal versions of the Category Test or the Wisconsin Card Sorting Test for the blind or the deaf.

However, the Wisconsin Card Sorting Test can be administered at the bedside, and this can be accomplished for the Category Test as well if one wishes to use the booklet version of this test, or a version that can be administered with a laptop computer. In the case of individuals who are severely visually impaired, the traditional methodology has been to substitute auditory modality tests. In the case of abstract reasoning, proverbs or analogies tests may be used. Using tests based on tactile perception is another useful strategy. The Halstead Tactual Performance Test may be administered to an individual who is blind and provides a good assessment of problem-solving ability. For patients with profound hearing loss, spoken instructions may be presented visually or any technology that provides sufficient amplification may be used.

**Q10. What do you mean by memory? Explain.**

*Or*

**Define memory. Elucidate the assessment of different memory systems. [June-2019, Q.No.-8]**

*Or*

**Write a short note on Explicit and Implicit Memory. [Dec-2019, Q.No.-12]**

*Or*

**Define Memory. Differentiate between explicit and implicit memory. [June-2021, Q.No.-8]**

**Ans.** Memory refers to the processes that are used to acquire, store, retain, and later retrieve information. There are three major processes involved in memory: encoding, storage, and retrieval. Human memory involves the ability to both preserve and recover information we have learned or experienced.

Neurocognitive research has indicated that it is more appropriate to consider the human memory as a collection of multiple but closely interacting systems than as a single and indivisible complex entity (e.g. Tulving, 1985a; Squire, 1992; Schacter & Tulving, 1994a). Different memory systems differ from one another in terms of the nature of representations they handle, the rules of their operations, and their neural substrates (e.g., Tulving, 1984; Weiskrantz, 1990; Tulving & Schacter, 1992; Schacter & Tulving, 1994b; Willingham, 1997).

Various classificatory schemes of human memory have been proposed so far. Undoubtedly, the two most influential and extended classifications are those postulated by Squire (1992) and Schacter and Tulving (1994a). Squire distinguishes two long-term memory systems: declarative and non-declarative (or procedural) memory; whereas Schacter and Tulving identify five major systems: procedural memory, perceptual representation system, semantic memory, short-term working memory and episodic memory. Related distinctions include explicit versus implicit memory, direct versus indirect memory, and memory with awareness versus memory without awareness. However, these latter dichotomies may not be memory systems, but rather forms of expression of memory. According to the Schacter and Tulving classification, retrieval operations in the procedural, perceptual representation and semantic systems are implicit, whereas in the working memory and episodic memory they are explicit. On the other hand, Squire considers declarative memory as an explicit system, whereas non-declarative memory is viewed as a heterogeneous collection of implicit abilities.

**Explicit and Implicit Memory:** Compelling evidence for the existence of multiple memory systems is provided by experimental findings of numerous convergent dissociations (functional, developmental, pharmacological, neuropsychological, neuroanatomical) between tasks of explicit and implicit memory (Schacter, 1987; Ruiz-Vargas, 1993; Nyberg & Tulving, 1996; Schacter, Wagner & Buckner, 2000).

- **Explicit Memory:** This is revealed by the intentional or conscious recollection of specific previous information, as expressed on traditional tests of free recall, cued recall and recognition. Although the relationships between cued recall, free recall, and recognition are highly complex, these three memory tests share an essential property: Success in them is predicated upon the subject's knowledge of events that occurred when s/he was personally present in a particular spatiotemporal context. Because the task instructions make explicit reference to an episode in the subject's personal history, such tasks have been referred to as autobiographical, direct, episodic, explicit or intentional memory tests.

- **Implicit Memory:** This is revealed by facilitation or change of performance on tests that do not require intentional or conscious recollection, such as perceptual identification, word stem completion, lexical decision, identification of fragmented pictures, mirror drawing, and so on. These tasks, classified as implicit, indirect, or incidental tests of memory, involve no reference to an event in the subject's personal history but are none the less influenced by such events. For example, prior experience with a particular word might later improve a subject's ability to identify that item under conditions of perceptual difficulty, restore deleted letters to complete that item, or make a decision concerning that item's lexical status. In general, such tasks require the subject to demonstrate conceptual, factual, lexical, perceptual, or procedural knowledge, or to make some form of affective or cognitive judgement. The measures of interest reflect a change in performance (e.g. change in accuracy and/or speed) as a function of some form of prior experience (e.g. experience with the task, with the test stimuli, or with related stimuli). When the prior experience occurs within the experimental context, it is possible to compare such measures of behavioural change with traditional measures of memory for the events causing that change.

Consider these two experimental situations:

- A list of 20 familiar words is presented to subjects who are instructed to pay attention to each word because, after the presentation, they will be asked to reproduce as many of the presented words as possible.

- A list of 20 familiar words is also presented to subjects who are instructed to perform an orienting task (e.g. pleasantness ratings).
- After this study phase, the subjects will be asked to say the first word that comes to mind in response to a series of three-letter word stems.

Some word stems can be completed with presented words, and some cannot. The first experimental situation reflects one of how psychologists have traditionally measured human memory: by assessing deliberate or explicit memory of subjects for items studied in a specific learning episode with a recall test. In the second situation, it is often observed that subjects show an enhanced tendency to complete word stems corresponding to studied words in comparison to 'new' word stems. This phenomenon is known as repetition priming or perceptual priming. Priming does not involve intentional or explicit recollection of the study episode, and thus it is assumed to reflect implicit memory for previously acquired information.

The distinction between explicit and implicit memory has had a profound impact on contemporary research and theorising of human memory. The finding that some products of memory are expressed with conscious awareness of the previous experience, and other ones without conscious awareness of the source of the information, has constituted a revolution in the way that we measure and interpret the influence of past events on current experience and behaviour' (Richardson-Klavehn & Bjork, 1988:475–476). Therefore, both experimenters and clinicians should take into account this distinction whenever they assess human memory.

**Memory Assessment:** The German philosopher Hermann Ebbinghaus (1850-1909) was the first to demonstrate that memory can be measured. His main contribution was methodological. Among his most important contributions were the study/test paradigm for the study of memory, the basic foundation of any memory experiment and test, and the savings method, currently considered as an implicit memory test, which was a couple of inventions of very large influence. Since then, memory assessment has undergone an extraordinary quantitative and qualitative advance.

Both the evolution and the accumulation of new memory tasks have defined the progress throughout the last century. The Ebbinghausian measure of serial recall led to new forms of testing recall (free recall, cued recall), and these measures fuelled new theoretical developments in the 1980s. Today, two major classes of memory measures are distinguished: tests of explicit memory and tests of implicit memory.

**Tests of Explicit Memory:** Tests are those in which the instructions in the test phase make explicit reference to an episode or experience in the subject's personal history. Thus, they require intentional or conscious recollection of previous information. Traditionally, these tests have been considered as the only memory tests. The table below provides a relatively extensive list of tests of explicit memory currently in use.

The RBMT is one of the few memory tests to have an aversion for children. However, recently some memory tests for use with children have been presented (e.g. The Children's test of Non-word Repetition (CNRep) constructed by Gathercole, Baddeley, Willis and Emslie; The Story Recall Test developed by Beardsworth and Bishop].

The tests of explicit memory include free recall, cued recall and recognition memory tasks. Prototypically, in tasks of free recall, subjects are shown a list of items (words, pictures, sentences) and are later asked to recall the items in any order that they choose. In cued recall, subjects are given explicit retrieval cues. The retrieval cues are prompts, reminders or any additional information that guides the search processes in memory (e.g. FRUITS for the to be recalled words 'apple', 'plum', 'grape', "kiwi'). In free and cued recall, memory performance is assessed simply by counting the number of to be remembered items recalled.

An exception to the prototypical tasks outlined above is serial recall, in which the subject is asked to recall the items in the order of presentation, and performance is assessed by the number of items recalled in the correct sequential order. This procedure allows the assessment of memory for order or temporal memory, one kind of memory especially relevant, for instance, in language perception and comprehension. A serial recall is also used in the well-known short-term memory task called digit span that has been traditionally included in tests of general intelligence such as Wechsler-batteries,

Atypical recognition task involves presenting a list containing the to-be-remembered or old items (e.g. words) just as in the presentation phase of recall tasks. However, in the subsequent test phase, subjects are shown a series of words, that is, old items mixed with new items or distracters and they are required to decide which the old ones are.

In the last few years, much research has also been devoted to the study of the subjective states of awareness associated with recognition memory. Tulving (1985b) introduced a new methodology to distinguish remember' (R) and know' (K) responses in recognition memory tests. An R response represents recognition with the conscious recollection of the item's prior occurrence; a K response represents recognition associated with feelings of familiarity in the absence of conscious recollection. Tulving proposed that these two states of awareness reflect two kinds of consciousness, autonoetic and noetic, which are respectively properties of episodic and semantic memory. The remember/know paradigm merits its consideration because several studies have demonstrated that the recollective experience of remembering is affected in different ways by many independent variables. For our purposes, its results are especially relevant to focus on different subject variables. There is now considerable evidence that age, Alzheimer's disease, amnesia, epilepsy, schizophrenia and autistic disorders have dissociative effects on Rand K responding. The general finding has been that, in the conditions mentioned, remember responses are selectively impaired and 'know responses are relatively spared (Gardiner & Richardson-Klavehn, 2000).

Finally, it cannot be ignored that an unlimited number of memory judgement tasks are also explicit memory tasks. For example, judgements of presentation frequency, judgements of temporal order or regency, judgements of input modality, judgements of source/reality monitoring, feeling-of-knowing judgements, and so on.

**Tests of Implicit Memory:** Implicit memory tests are those in which subjects are asked to respond to test stimuli (e.g. generate a word, classify an object, perform a motor task) without referring to prior events. The impressive experimental evidence available about dissociations between implicit and explicit memory tasks warrants the assumption that there are fundamental differences between mnemonic information assessed by implicit and explicit memory tests.

For example, numerous studies have documented across diverse tasks that amnesic patients (and other special populations) exhibit preserved mnemonic functioning when they are assessed with tests of implicit memory, and a memory severely impaired when tests of explicit memory are given. Studies with normal subjects have also shown that under some conditions (e.g. effects of alcohol, psychoactive drugs, general anaesthesia or certain experimental manipulations) normal's exhibit implicit memory for information that they cannot explicitly remember. The most important and theoretically relevant conclusion from these findings is that implicit memories are explicitly inaccessible and vice versa, because (i) different aspects of events are encoded by distinct but interacting neurocognitive systems, and (ii) diverse tasks tap different memory systems. Therefore, an adequate memory assessment requires of experimenters and clinicians to make use of explicit memory tests as well as implicit memory tests.

There are many implicit memory tests currently in use, and new tests are created every year. A general classification scheme that includes most of them has been recently proposed by Toth (2000). Implicit memory tests could be roughly organised in two major categories: verbal and non-verbal tests, and each one of them in its turn into three subclasses:

- **Perceptual tests** (e.g. perceptual identification, word stem completion, degraded word naming, object/non-object decision),
- **Conceptual tests** (e.g. word association, category instance generation, object categorisation, person/trait attributions), and
- **Procedural tests** (e.g. reading mirror-inverted text, probability judgements, mirror drawing, motor tracking), Generally speaking, the perceptual tests challenge the perceptual representation system, the conceptual tests involve the semantic memory system, and the procedural tests tap the procedural memory system.

**Assessment of Different Memory Systems:** From the multiple memory systems view, memory assessment must evolve to assess every single memory system. According to the five-fold classification system proposed by Schacter and Tulving, such systems are defined and could be assessed as follows:

- **The Procedural Memory System**: This is a behavioural action system concerned with the acquisition, retention and retrieval of the motor, perceptual and cognitive skills, simple conditioning, and non-associative forms of learning. These kinds of memory are measured by tests of implicit memory, such as the pursuit rotor task, maze learning, mirror reading, artificial grammar learning, tower of Hanoi, and so on.

- **The Perceptual Representation System (PRS)**: This encompasses various domain-specific subsystems that process and represent information about the form and structure of words and objects. The PRS is assessed with implicit memory tests, such as perceptual identification, word stem completion, homophone spelling, picture fragment completion, object/non-object decision, possible/impossible object decision, and many others.
- **The Semantic Memory System:** This is the system involved in the acquisition, retention and retrieval of general knowledge of the world. Therefore, the task of assessing the status of this complex and multi-faceted system seems an impressive one. This challenge could be overcome by using a multiplicity of types of tests, such as word fluency, vocabulary, word association, naming tasks (animals, objects, etc.), recognition of famous faces, category instance generation, fact generation, category verification, semantic anomaly detection, responses in recognition tests, and so on.
- **The Working Memory System (WM)**: This is a short-term system that makes possible the temporary maintenance and processing of information, and to manipulate that information. The WM is measured by explicit memory tests such as the Brown-Peterson task, various memory span tests (e.g. forward and backward digit span, word span, alpha span), the size of the recency effect, the release from proactive inhibition task, the Dobbs and Rule task, mental arithmetic, and others.

  As Craik et al. (1995) emphasise, because WM tests do not all measure the same component processes it is advisable to assess WM by using several tests rather than one global test.
- **The Episodic Memory System**: This is the system for personally experienced episodes. Episodic memories are assessed with tests of explicit memory for verbal and non-verbal materials, such as free recall (immediate and delayed), cued recall, recognition, R responses in recognition tests, generation task, and others. Different tasks may be used to

assess autobiographical memory, considered as a subtype of episodic memory, such as recall and recognition of famous events, the Crovitz-Schiffman technique or the cueing method, etc. In clinical contexts, the Autobiographical Memory Interview (AMI) provides relevant information about the deterioration of this kind of memory in patients.

At this point, it should be noted that remembering and the different memory systems summarised above all refer to the past. However, as everybody knows, people are also capable of remembering what they must do in the future. The former is called retrospective memory, and the latter, prospective memory.

Prospective memory is defined as the timely remembering of a planned action; everyday tasks such as remembering to phone one's sister at eleven o'clock, remembering to take medication after lunching, or remembering to reply to an email this evening are all significant memory acts common to everyday living. Because both observations in the real world, as well as laboratory studies, show that prospective memory declines with age, brain damages and progressive brain diseases, prospective memory tasks should be given whenever memory is assessed.

**Q11. What do you mean by the term creativity?**

*Or*

**Define creativity. Explain Torrance test of creative thinking.**

**[Dec-2019, Q.No.-8]**

*Or*

**Define creativity. Discuss the measures of creativity.**

**[Dec-2020, Q.No.-7]**

*Or*

**Explain Torrance Test of Creative Thinking. [June-2021, Q.No.-9]**

**Ans.** Creativity is a phenomenon whereby something somehow new and somehow valuable is formed. The created item may be intangible (such as an idea, a scientific theory, a musical composition, or a joke) or a physical object (such as an invention, a printed literary work, or a painting).

Scholarly interest in creativity is found in a number of disciplines, primarily psychology, business studies, and cognitive science, but also education, the humanities, technology, engineering, philosophy (particularly philosophy of science), theology, sociology, linguistics, the arts, economics, and mathematics, covering the relations between creativity and general intelligence, personality type, mental and neural processes, mental health, or artificial intelligence; the potential for fostering creativity through education and training; the fostering of creativity for national economic benefit, and the application of creative resources to improve the effectiveness of teaching and learning.

**Assessment of Creativity:** Psychologists wishing to assess individual differences in creativity have a tremendous range of instruments to choose from.

Therefore, before investigators can settle on any single test or battery of tests, it is first necessary that they address four major questions:

- What is the age of the target population? Some measures are specifically designed for school-age populations, whether children or adolescents, whereas other measures are targeted at adult populations.
- Which domain of creativity is to be assessed? Not only may creativity in the arts differ substantially from creativity in the sciences, but also there may appear significant contrasts within specific arts (e.g, music vs. literature) or sciences (e.g. mathematics vs. invention).
- What is the magnitude of creativity to be evaluated? At one extreme is the everyday problem-solving ability ('little c' creativity) were at the other extreme is eminent creativity that earns awards and honours appropriate to the domain ("Big C Creativity, or genius).
- Which manifestation of creativity is to be targeted? That is, the investigator must decide whether creativity manifests itself primarily as a product, a process, or a person. Some instruments postulate that creativity takes the form of a concrete product; others assume that creativity involves a particular type of cognitive process, while still others posit that creativity entails a personal disposition of some kind.

Of these four questions, it is the last that is perhaps the most crucial. Assessment strategies differ dramatically depending on whether creativity is best manifested as a product, process, or person. As a consequence, the description of creativity measures that follow will be divided into three subsections.

**Product Measures:** Ultimately, a creative idea should take some concrete form, such as a poem, story, painting, or design. Hence, one obvious approach to creativity assessment is to measure the quantity or quality of productive output. A case in point is the Consensual Assessment Technique devised by Amabile (1982). Here a research participant is asked to make some product, such as a collage or a poem, which is then assessed by an independent set of experts. This technique has proven especially useful in laboratory experiments on the social circumstances that are most likely to favour creative behaviour.

However, this approach has at least two disadvantages.

- First, the creativity of an individual is decided according to performance on a single task.
- Second, the assessment is based on a task that may not be representative of the domain in which the individual is most creative. For instance, a creative writer will not necessarily do well on a task in the visual arts, such as making collages.
- An alternative is to assess individual differences in creativity according to products that the person has spontaneously generated. For example, Lifetime Creativity Scales assess creative behaviour by asking participants to self-identify examples of their creative achievements (Richards et al., 1988).

According to this approach, creativity assessment is based on multiple products in the domain that the individual finds most germane to personal creative expression. Although this instrument has proven validity and utility, it can be objected that a product's creativity requires an external assessment, such as that provided in the Consensual Assessment Technique. Furthermore, this instrument is aimed at everyday creativity rather than creative output that is highly valued professionally or socially.

One way to assess such Big-C Creativity is to use some variety of productivity measure. Thus, the creativity of scientists may be gauged by journal articles and that of inventors by patents. Often such measures of the pure quantity of output are supplemented by evaluations of quality. For example, the quality of a scientist's productivity may be assessed by the number of citations to his or her work. Another approach is to assess creative impact in terms of awards and honours received or the evaluations of experts in the field, which tactic dates back to Francis Galton (1869). One especially innovative strategy is Ludwig's (1992) Creative Achievement Scale, which provides an objective approach to evaluating a creator's life work. This scale has proven useful in addressing the classic question of whether exceptional creativity is associated with some degree of psychopathology (the 'mad-genius' debate).

**Process Measures:** One major drawback of all product measures of creativity is that they appear barren of truly psychological content. These measures stress outward behaviour and its impact rather than internal mental states. Yet presumably there exist some special thought processes that underly these creative products. Accordingly, psychologists can instead devise instruments that tap into these crucial processes. For example, Mednick (1962) theorised that creativity requires the capacity to generate remote associations that can connect hitherto disparate ideas. He implemented this theory by devising the Remote Association Test, or RAT, that has seen considerable use in subsequent research. A person taking the RAT must identify a word that has an associative linkage with three separate stimulus words (e.g. associating the word 'chair' with the given words 'wheel, electric, high').

An even more popular set of measures was devised by Guilford (1967) in the context of his multidimensional theory of intelligence. These measures assess various kinds of divergent thinking, which is supposed to provide the basis for creativity. Divergent thinking is the capacity to generate a great variety of responses to a given set of stimuli. Unlike convergent thinking, which aims at the single most correct response, ideational productivity is emphasised. A specific instance is the Unusual Uses test, which asks research participants to come up with as many uses as possible for ordinary objects, such as a toothpick or paperclip. The participants' responses can then be scored for fluency (number of responses), flexibility (number of distinct categories to which the responses belong), and originality (how rare the response is relative to others taking the test).

Guilford's development of Divergent Thinking (DT) tests in the 1950s and 1960s are usually considered to be the launching point for serious development efforts and large-scale application. Among the first measures of divergent thinking were Guilford's (1967) Structure of the Intellect (SOI) divergent production tests, Wallach and Kogan's (1965) and Getzels and Jackson's (1962) divergent thinking tests, and Torrance's (1962, 1974) Tests of Creative Thinking (TTCT).

**The SOI Assessments (Structure of Intellect Assessments):** Guilford's (1967) Structure of the Intellect Model proposed 24 distinct types of divergent thinking: One type for each combination of four types of content (Figural, Symbolic, Semantic, Behavioural) and six types of product (Units, Classes, Relations, Systems, Transformations, Implications).

For example, the SOI DT battery (Structure of Intellect and Divergent Thinking) consists of several tests on which subjects are asked to exhibit evidence of divergent, production in several areas, including divergent production of semantic units (e.g., listing consequences of people no longer needing to sleep), of figural classes (finding as many classifications of sets of figures as is possible), and of figural units (taking a simple shape such as a circle and elaborating upon it as often as possible).

Another example is the Match Problem, which represented the divergent production of figural transformations. The Match Problem has several variations, but they tend to be variations on the basic theme of Match Problem I. In this test, 17 matches are placed to create a grid of two rows and three columns (i.e., six squares). Participants are asked to remove three matches so that the remaining matches form four complete squares.

Guilford noted that such tasks are characterised by the need for trial and error strategies and flexible thinking. Several other tests were also used to study figural transformations, all with the same basic requirements to come up with multiple ways to transform visual-spatial objects and relationships. Guilford believed that this particular group of tests assesses flexibility. Guilford's entire SOI divergent production battery consists of several dozen such tests corresponding to the various divergent thinking components.

**Torrance Tests of Creative Thinking (TTCT):** The Torrance Tests of Creative Thinking which are also based upon many aspects of the SOI battery are by far the most commonly used tests of divergent thinking and continue to enjoy widespread international use.

Over several decades, Torrance refined the administration and scoring of the TTCT, which may account for its enduring popularity. The battery includes Verbal (Thinking Creatively with Words) and Figure tests (Thinking Creatively with Pictures) that each includes a Form A and Form B that can be used alternately,

The Figural forms have three subtests:

- **Picture Construction**, in which a participant uses a basic shape and expands on it to create a picture;
- **Picture Completion,** in which a participant is asked to finish and title incomplete drawings; and
- **Lines/Circles,** in which a participant is asked to modify many different series of lines (Form A) or circles (Form B).

The Verbal form has seven subtests. For the first three tasks, the examiner is asked to refer to a picture at the beginning of the test booklet. For example, in Form A, the picture is of an elf staring at its reflection in a pool of water. These first three tasks are considered part of the Ask and Guess section:

- Asking, in which a participant asks as many questions as possible about the picture;
- Guessing Causes, in which a participant lists possible causes for the pictured action;
- Guessing Consequences, in which a participant lists possible consequences for the pictured action.

The final four verbal subtests are self-contained:

- Product Improvement, in which a participant is asked to make changes to improve a toy (e.g., a stuffed animal)
- Unusual Uses, in which a participant is asked to think of many different possible uses for an ordinary item (e.g., a cardboard box)
- Unusual Questions, in which a participant asks as many questions as possible about an ordinary item (this item does not appear in later editions); and
- Just suppose, in which a participant is asked to "just suppose" that an improbable situation has happened then list possible ramifications.

Administration, scoring, and score reporting of the various tests and forms are standardised, and detailed norms were created and revised accordingly. The original test produced scores in the traditional four DT areas, but the streamlined scoring system introduced in the 1984 revision made significant changes to the available scores. Under the streamlined system, the Figural tests can be scored for resistance to premature closure and abstractness of titles in addition to the familiar scores of fluency, elaboration, and originality. Flexibility was removed because those scores tended to be largely undifferentiated from fluency scores. Resistance to premature closure is determined by an examinee's tendency to not immediately close the incomplete figures on the Figural Picture Completion test. Torrance believed this tendency reflected the examinee's ability to keep open and delay closure long enough to make the mental leap that makes possible original ideas. Less creative persons tend to leap to conclusions prematurely without considering the available information" (Torrance & Ball, 1984).

**Person Measures:** Process measures of creativity operate under the assumption that creativity requires the capacity to engage in somewhat distinctive cognitive processes. Not all psychologists agree with this position. In the first place, often performance on process instruments can be enhanced by relatively straightforward training procedures, and sometimes performance enhancements can occur by changing the instructional set when administering the test (i.e. the command to be creative!). Also, creative individuals appear to have distinctive non-cognitive characteristics that set them apart from persons who fail to display creativity. This has led some psychologists to propose that creativity be assessed by person based measures.

The most frequently used instruments assess creativity via the personality characteristics that are strongly correlated with creative behaviour. These personality assessments are of three kinds. First, the assessment may simply depend on already established scales of standard tests, such as the Minnesota Multiphasic Personality Inventory or Eysenck's Personality Questionnaire. These measures will tend to yield the lowest validity coefficients.

Second, the assessment may be based on the construction of a specialised subscale of an already established personality test. For instance, Gough (1979) devised a Creative Personality Scale from his more general Adjective Check List. Third, the assessment may rely on a measure that is specially constructed to gauge individual differences in creative personality. An example is the How Do You Think questionnaire that gauges whether a person has the interests, values, energy, self-confidence, humour, flexibility, playfulness, unconventionality, and openness associated with creativity (Davis, 1975).

An alternative person-based approach is predicated on the assumption that creative potential emerges using a particular set of developmental experiences. These experiences may reflect either genetic predilections (nature)or acquired inclinations (nurture). For example, Schaefer and Anastasi (1968) designed a biographical inventory that identifies creativity in adolescent boys (see also Schaefer, 1970). The items tap such factors as family background, school activities, and extracurricular interests. Moreover, inventory discriminates not only creative from non-creative adolescents but also between scientific and artistic creativity. Similar biographical inventories have been devised for both children and adults. The box below presents a summary of representative creativity measures.

**Q12. What is cognitive testing? Discuss the utility of data from tests of cognitive functions.**

**Ans.** Cognitive tests are assessments of the cognitive capabilities of humans and other animals. Tests administered to humans include various forms of IQ tests; those administered to animals include the mirror test (a test of visual self-awareness) and the T maze test (which tests learning ability). Such study is important to research concerning the philosophy of mind and psychology, as well as determination of human and animal intelligence.

Modern cognitive tests originated through the work of James McKeen Cattell who coined the term "mental tests". They followed Francis Galton's development of physical and physiological tests. For example, Galton measured strength of grip and height and weight. He established an "Anthropometric Laboratory" in the 1880s where patrons paid to have physical and physiological attributes measured. Galton's measurements had an enormous influence on psychology. Cattell continued the measurement approach with simple measurements of perception. Cattell's tests were eventually abandoned in favour of the battery test approach developed by Alfred Binet.

**Utility of Data from Tests of Cognitive Functions**

**(1) Clinical Use of Intelligence Tests:** The intelligence test is a special measure that primarily helps to assess a wide spectrum of cognitive features. The manner in which such cognitive features operate for the patient needs to be delineated. One of the main assets of intelligence tests is their accuracy in predicting future behaviour. Initially, Binet was able to achieve a certain degree of predictive success with his scales, and, since that time, test procedures have become progressively more refined and accurate. More recent studies provide ample support that intelligence tests can predict an extremely wide number of variables. In particular, IQ tests are excellent predictors of academic achievement, occupational performance and are sensitive to the presence of neuropsychological deficit.

**(2) The Estimation of General Intellectual Level:** The most obvious use of an intelligence test is as a means for arriving at an estimate of the patient's general intellectual level. Frequently, the goal is the determination of how much general intelligence (g) a given person possesses. Often, the question is stated a bit differently-for example, what is the patient's intellectual potential? Posing the question in this way suggests that perhaps the person is not functioning as well as his or her potential would indicate. The potential can form a baseline against which to measure current achievements, thus providing information about the patient's current level of functioning. Many pitfalls and fallacies are associated with the pursuit of these goals.

**(3) The Case of Harold:** Harold was being routinely evaluated before transfer to a special class for advanced junior high school students. Rather surprisingly, his Full-Scale WISC-IV IQ turned out to be 107. This score was in the average range but below the cut-off point for admission to the class. It was also considerably below what his teachers had estimated based on his classroom performance. A closer look at his subtest scores revealed that his performances on Block Design and Coding were significantly below those on the other subtests. A follow-up interview with Harold was quite revealing. Since early childhood, he had suffered from muscular weakness in both arms and hands. This weakness prevented him from making fine, quick motor responses. However, he had developed several clever compensations to prevent others from guessing his limitation. For example, what had appeared to be slow, deliberate, even confused responses on Block Design were not that at all. He was feigning confusion to mask his difficulty with fine motor functions. Then, Harold's IQ score had been unduly affected by a motor weakness that had nothing to do with his ability to perform intellectually.

This example is but the tip of the iceberg. It does suggest, however, that obtaining an IQ is not the end of a clinician's task, but it is only the beginning. The IQ score must be interpreted. Only through knowledge of the patient's learning history and by observations made during the testing situation can that score be placed in an appropriate interpretive context and adequately evaluated.

**(4) Prediction of Academic Success:** As mentioned previously, some data demonstrate a relationship between intelligence test scores and school success (Neisser et al., 1996). To the extent that intelligence should logically reflect the capacity to do well in school, we are justified in expecting intelligence tests to predict school success. Not everyone would equate intelligence with scholastic aptitude, but the fact remains that a major function of intelligence tests is to predict school performance. One must remember, however, that intelligence and academic success are not conceptually identical.

**(5) Occupational Performance:** In addition to predicting academic achievement, IQ scores have also been correlated with the occupation, ranging from highly trained professionals with mean IQs of 125 to unskilled workers with mean IQs of 87 (Reynolds, Chastain, Kaufman, & McLean, 1987). Correlations between job proficiency and general intelligence have been highest in predicting relatively more complex jobs rather than less demanding occupations. J. Hunter (1986) reported moderately high correlations between general intelligence and success for managers (.53), salespersons (.61), and clerks (.54). For intellectually demanding tasks, nearly half the variance related to performance criteria can be accounted for by general intelligence (F. Schmidt, Ones, & Hunter, 1992). The use of intelligence tests for personnel selection has demonstrated financial efficacy for organisations (F. Schmidt & Hunter, 1998). Also, the accuracy of using IQ tests can be incrementally increased by combining the results with integrity tests, work samples, and structured interviews (F. Schmidt & Hunter, 1998).

**(6) The Appraisal of Style:** As we have noted, what is important is not only whether the client succeeds or fails on particular test items but also how that success or failure occurs. One of the major values of individual intelligence tests is that they permit us to observe the client or patient at work. Such observations can help us greatly in interpreting IQ. For example, did this child do as well as possible? Was there failure avoidance? Did the child struggle with most items, or was there easy success? Was the child unmotivated, and could this have detracted from the child's performance? Such questions and the ensuing interpretations breathe life into an otherwise inert IQ score.

The following simulated questions from the WAIS-II and a hypothetical patient's responses to them are examples of the data that can be obtained beyond the sheer correctness or incorrectness of a response:

- **Query**: Who wrote Paradise Lost? (Information subtest)
- **Answer:** Probably a Catholic. But since the Pope began changing things around, they retiled it.
- **Query**: What is the advantage of keeping money in a bank? (Comprehension subtest)
- **Answer**: There isn't. There are so damn many crooks. But they'll get theirs someday.
- **Query:** In what ways are a lion and a tiger alike? (Similarities subtest)
- **Answer:** Well, now, that's a long story. Do they look alike? They really can't breed together, you know.

(These simulated items were provided courtesy of The Psychological Corporation. The answers are based on responses to actual items.)

Some clinicians have ventured considerably beyond making a few limited personality inferences that would inject some added meaning into IQs and have based mental disorder diagnoses on the Stanford Binet and Wechsler scales. They believed that by examining patterns of scores (known as inter-test scatter); they could apply diagnostic labels to patients (e.g., schizophrenia or depression). Over the years, however, studies purporting to show the validity of these interpretations of intertest scatter could rarely be replicated. Thus, diagnoses cannot be reliably inferred from patterns of test performance. Another important asset of intelligence tests, particularly the WAIS-III and WISCIII, is that they provide valuable information about a person's cognitive strengths and weaknesses. They are standardised procedures whereby a person's performance in various areas can be compared with that of age-related peers. Also, useful comparisons can be made regarding a person's pattern of strengths and weaknesses. The WAIS-II, WISC-II, and other individually administered tests provide the examiner with a structured interview in which a variety of tasks can be used to observe the unique and personal ways the examinee approaches cognitive tasks. Through a client's interactions with both the examiner and the test materials, an initial impression can be made of the individual's self-esteem, behavioural idiosyncrasies, anxiety, social skills, and motivation, while also obtaining a specific picture of intellectual functioning.

Intelligence tests often provide clinicians, educators, and researchers with baseline measures for use in determining either the degree of change that has occurred in an individual over time or how an individual compares with other persons in a particular area or ability. This may have important implications for evaluating the effectiveness of an educational programme or for assessing the changing abilities of a specific student. In cases involving recovery from a head injury or readjustment following neurosurgery, it may be extremely helpful for clinicians to measure and follow the cognitive changes that occur in a patient. Furthermore, IQ assessments may be important in researching and understanding more adequately the effect on cognitive functioning of environmental variables, such as educational programs, family background, and nutrition. Thus, these assessments can provide useful information about cultural, biological, maturational, or treatment-related differences among individuals.

**Q13. What are the uses of neuropsychological assessment?**

**Ans.** Neuropsychological assessment is a performance-based method to assess cognitive functioning. This method is used to examine the cognitive consequences of brain damage, brain disease, and severe mental illness. There are several specific uses of neuropsychological assessment, including collection of diagnostic information, differential diagnostic information, assessment of treatment response, and prediction of functional potential and functional recovery. We anticipate that clinical neuropsychological assessment will continue to be used, even in the face of advances in imaging technology, because it is already well known that the presence of significant brain changes can be associated with nearly normal cognitive functioning, while individuals with no lesions detectable on imaging can have substantial cognitive and functional limitations.

**(1) Determining the Biological (I.E., Neuroanatomical, Physiological) Correlates of Test Results: Detection, Gradation and Localisation of Brain Damage:** After they have described the patient's behaviour, neuropsychologists typically try to determine whether the pattern of test results, Clinical behaviour, and particular historical context of the observations can be attributed to abnormal brain function. Such abnormalities may be the presence of a structural brain lesion, a developmental disorder, or in some cases, neurochemical lesion. Part of this determination is trying to ascertain what region of the brain is involved.

**(2) Determining Whether Changes are Associated with Neurological Disease, Psychiatric Conditions Developmental Disorders, or Non-Neurological Conditions:** The next kind of inference that clinical neuropsychologists often try to make or are asked to make concerns the likely a etiology or etiologies that produced the changes described. In the case of neurological disorder and known history, this can sometimes be done accurately. This is particularly true in cases in which the behavioural changes involve unusual and dramatic phenomena that have historically been related to the presence of lesions in specific parts of the brain and are usually caused by a highly limited set of etiologies. For example, non-fluent aphasia symptoms (e.g., hesitant, a grammatic speech) are most likely related to a limited **set** of diseases that, if present by history, can be considered causative of the observed changes in language.

Many changes in neuropsychological functions, however, may be caused by psychiatric, motivational, developmental, or cultural factors and may not be attributable to a specific neurological a etiology even when present by history. Often, neuropsychological test findings are nonspecific to a etiology and may be related to a host of factors, such as depression, anxiety, sleep deprivation, or even chronic pain. In these instances, the neuropsychologist must work as an investigator to review the test findings thoroughly in the context of the patient's history.

**(3) Assessing Changes over Time and Developing a Prognosis:** One of the most useful applications of neuropsychological assessment is to track improvements and decrements in performance over time. This helps in determining the etiology and progression of a disease, developing social or financial plans for a patient, and tracking whether treatment or efforts towards rehabilitation are effective.

**(4) Offering Guidelines for Rehabilitation, Vocational/Educational Planning, 'or A Combination of These':** 'The ability to provide inferences regarding a etiology and descriptive power has made neuropsychological assessment a popular tool in rehabilitation and educational planning. Therapists and teachers can often use a patient's profile of strengths and weaknesses to develop and optimise rehabilitation and educational programs. Knowledge of which problems or weaknesses are attributable to brain damage and which are likely the result of non-neurological sources can help a therapist allocate time and resources towards the treatment priorities that are most likely to be effective.

**(5) Providing Guidelines and Education for Family and Caregivers:** In a similar vein, neuropsychological data can help families and caregivers to understand the strengths and weaknesses of their loved ones and to cope with patients who may suffer from challenging limitations on independent functioning. Beleaguered family members are less likely to be angry with a patient when they understand that symptoms that appear to be related to motivation or personality are causally related to a disease state. An understanding of the prognosis of the illness can also be invaluable to families who must plan their use of finances and future care.

**(6) Planning for Discharge and Treatment Implementation:** Neuropsychological deficits can sometimes be insidious and difficult to describe, even for sophisticated clinicians. An understanding of a patient's capabilities can help the clinician assess the degree to which a patient is going to comply with treatment recommendations and medication use, as well as the extent to which the patient or the patient's family may need continued supervision after discharge.

**Q14. Write short notes on the followings:**

**(i) Behaviour Rating Inventory of Executive Function (BRIEF)**

**Ans.** The Behaviour Rating Inventory of Executive Function (BRIEF; Gioia, Isquith, Guy & Ken-worthy, 2000) is an individualised, norm-referenced measure of executive function behaviours designed for school-aged students from 5 to 18 years of age. The BRIEF is a questionnaire that is completed by parents or teachers (two different forms), who rate behaviours related to executive functions in eight scales (Inhibit, Shift, Emotional Control, Initiate, Working Memory, Plan/Organise, Organisation of Materials, and Monitor).

Results of the scales are combined to generate two index scores, Behavioural. Regulation/BRI (based on three scales) and Metacognition/MI (based on five scales), and an overall composite score, the Global Executive Composite/GEC. Standardisation of the BRIEF included individuals with a variety of developmental or neurological conditions, allowing for use of the inventory with a broad range of students. A Self-Report Form is also available for use with students 13 through 18 years of age, the Behaviour Rating Inventory of Executive Function-Self-Report Version (BRIEF-SR; Guy, Isquith, & Gioia, 2005).

**(ii) Behaviour Rating Inventory of Executive Function-Preschool Version (BRIEF-P)**

**Ans.** The Behaviour Rating Inventory of Executive Function-Preschool Version (BRIEF P; Gioia, Espy, & Isquith, 2003) is an individualised, norm-referenced measure of executive function behaviours for preschool-aged children from 2 years to 5 years-11 months of age. The BRIEFP, a questionnaire designed to be completed by parents or teachers (single form), rates behaviours related to various executive functions observed in the home and the preschool setting in five scales (Inhibit, Shift, Emotional Control, Working Memory, and Plan/Organise). Items are rated on a Likert scale (never, sometimes, often) comparing the significance of the child's behaviours to those of other children of the same age over a specified period.

Results of the scales are combined to generate three index scores, Inhibitory Self Control, Flexibility, and Emergent Meta cognition (each based on two scales), and an overall composite score, the Global Executive Composite/GEC. Standardisation of the BRIEF-P included individuals with a variety of developmental or neurological conditions and children considered at risk, allowing for use of the inventory with a broad range of students. Use of the BRIEF-P may facilitate early identification of children with potential problems in areas of self-regulation.

**(iii) Comprehensive Test of Nonverbal Intelligence (CTONI)**

**Ans.** The Comprehensive Test of Nonverbal Intelligence (CTONI; Hammill, Pearson, & Wiederholt, 1997) measures the nonverbal reasoning abilities of individuals aged 6-0 to 18-11. No oral responses, reading, writing, or manipulation of objects are required. The CTONI is useful for testing individuals with difficulties in language or fine-motor skills, including those who are bilingual, non-English-speaking, or have a motor or neurological disabilities. The test can be administered orally or through pantomime. The six subtests of the CTONI require subjects to view a group of pictures or designs and to solve problems involving analogies, categorisations, and sequences. The viewer simply indicates an answer by pointing to the answer. A computer-administered version of the test is available, the CTONI-CA. This is an interactive multimedia test that can be taken entirely on a computer. The programme gives all the instructions using a human voice; the examinee points the mouse and clicks on the answer. The book you can believe most–GPH book.

**(iv) Comprehensive Test of Phonological Processes (CTOPP)**

**Ans.** The Comprehensive Test of Phonological Processes (CTOPP, Wagner, Torgesen, & Rashotte, 1999) is an individually administered, norm-referenced measure of phonological awareness, phonological memory, and rapid naming, all foundational skill areas that are critical in learning to read. One form of the CTOPP is administered to children aged 5 and 6 years, focussing on the skills generally needed in kindergarten and first grade. It consists of seven core subtests and one supplemental subtest. A second form for individuals ranging from ages 7 through 24 years consists of six core subtests and eight supplemental subtests. The purposes of the CTOPP include identifying students who are behind in developing phonological skills and determining which skills have not been acquired or adequately developed. The supplemental tests allow for assessing specific strengths and weaknesses related to phonological processes. Subtests include subtests to measure rapid naming, blending and segmenting words and non-words, sound matching, and memory for digits. All subtests and composites (Phonological Awareness, Phonological Memory, and Rapid Naming) are reported in scaled scores, standard scores, and percentiles.

**(v) Das Naglieri Cognitive Assessment System (CAS)**

**Ans.** The Das Naglieri Cognitive Assessment System (CAS; Naglieri & Das, 1997) is an individually administered measure of cognitive ability designed to assess Planning, Attention, and Simultaneous and Successive (PASS) processes in individuals 5 years to 24 years-11 months old.

Planning tasks require the test taker to develop an approach to solving a task in an efficient and effective manner. Attention tasks require the individual to selectively attend to one and ignore the other aspect of a two-dimensional stimulus. Simultaneous tasks require the individual to interrelate the component parts of a particular item to arrive at the correct answer. Finally, successive tasks require the individual to either reproduce a particular sequence of events or answer questions that require correct interpretation of the linearity of events.

There are 8 subtests in the Basic Battery and 12 subtests in the Standard Battery. The CAS may be used for diagnosis, eligibility, determination of discrepancies, reevaluation, and instructional planning.

**(vi) Detroit Tests of Learning Aptitude-Fourth Edition (DTLA-4)**

**Ans.** The Detroit Tests of Learning Aptitude-Fourth Edition (DTLA-4; Hammill, 1998) is an individually administered measure of mental ability for individuals 6 to 17 years of age. It includes 10 subtests that may be combined to form 16 composites measuring both general intelligence and discrete ability areas. This test not only measures basic abilities but also shows the effects of language, attention, and motor abilities on test performance.

The DTLA-4 yields an Overall Composite comprised of standard scores of all 10 subtests in the battery. This composite is probably the best estimate of intelligence. The Optimal Level Composite includes the four highest standard scores on the subtests and is the best estimate of a person's overall "potential." The Domain Composites are contrasting composites provided for three domains: language, attention, and manual dexterity. DTLA 4 includes the following: Verbal Composite, Nonverbal Composite, Attention-Enhanced Composite, Attention Reduced Composite, Motor-Enhanced Composite, and Motor-Reduced Composite.

**(vii) Differential Ability Scales-Second Edition (DAS-II)**

**Ans.** The Differential Ability Scales-Second Edition (DAS-II; Elliott, 2007) is an individually administered norm-referenced battery of cognitive subtests for children and adolescents ages 2-6 through 17-11. Although most cognitive measures are truly language-free, the DAS-II controls for language loading by providing a special Nonverbal Index, and can be used easily with very young children and English Language Learners. It consists of two overlapping batteries, the Early Years Battery and the School-Age Battery. Several subtests within each battery can be used out of level for individuals working above or below typical levels by

The DAS-II yields (i) a composite score focussed on reasoning and conceptual abilities, the General Conceptual Ability (GCA) score; (ii) lower-level composite scores called cluster scores; and (iii) diverse, specific-ability measures, including the core subtests, which comprise the GCA and diagnostic subtests. Verbal Ability measures the child's acquired verbal concepts and knowledge. Nonverbal Ability represents complex, nonverbal, inductive reasoning requiring mental processing, Spatial Ability measures complex visual processing. Diagnostic Clusters include Working Memory, Processing Speed, and School Readiness. The DAS-II yields t-scores for sub-tests and standard scores and percentiles for cluster and index scores and the GCA.

**(viii) Kaufman Assessment Battery for Children-Second Edition (KABC-II)**

**Ans.** The Kaufman Assessment Battery for Children-Second Edition (KABC-II; Kaufman & Kaufman, 2004) is an individually administered measure of the cognitive processing abilities of children and adolescents aged three through 18. The KABC-II is a theory-based clinical instrument that contributes to culturally fair assessment. The KABC-II offers two global summaries: the Fluid Crystallised Index (FCI), which includes all five scales, and the Mental Processing Index (MPI), which includes the first four scales but not the Knowledge/Crystallised Ability Scale. The test manual states: "Measures of Gc (general cognition) should be excluded from any score that purports to measure a person's intelligence or overall cognitive ability whenever the measure of Gc is not likely to reflect that person's level of ability."

The KABC-II offers a Nonverbal Scale (NVI), which yields a nonverbal index to assess the processing and cognitive abilities of children with whom a nonverbal measure of cognitive ability is appropriate. The Sequential Processing/Short-Term Memory Scale is designed to measure the ability to solve problems by remembering and using an ordered series of images or ideas. The Simultaneous/Visual Processing Scale measures the ability to solve spatial, analogical, or organisational problems that require the processing of many stimuli at one time. The Learning Ability/Long-Term Storage and Retrieval Scale measures the ability to successfully complete different types of learning tasks. Immediate recall and delayed recall tasks are included in this scale.

The Planning Fluid Reasoning Scale measures the ability to solve nonverbal problems that are different from the kinds taught in school. Verbally mediated reasoning must be used to solve the problems. The Knowledge/Crystallised Ability Scale measures knowledge of words and facts using both verbal and pictorial stimuli and requiring either a verbal or pointing response.

**(ix) Leiter International Performance Scale-Revised (Leiter-R)**

**Ans.** The Leiter International Performance Scale-Revised (Leiter-R; Roid & Miller, 1998) is a standardised, individually administered, nonverbal test designed to assess cognitive functions in children and adolescents ages 2-0 to 20-11 years. The Leiter-R includes two groupings of subtests: the Visualisation and Reasoning Battery with 10 subtests of nonverbal intellectual ability related to visualisation, reasoning, and spatial ability; and the Attention and Memory Battery with 10 subtests of nonverbal attention and memory function.

The Fluid Reasoning composite is comprised of subtests that show evidence of providing a unique fluid measure of seriation, reasoning, and pattern generation. The Full IQ score represents a measure of general nonverbal intelligence. The IQ is the sum of the subtests that compose the IQ estimate, and the subtests represented vary depending on the age of the student. The IQ score includes diverse aspects of cognition and is comprised of highly correlated subtests to obtain a single measure of intellectual ability.

**(x) NEPSY, Second Edition (NEPSY-II)**

**Ans.** The NEPSY-II (Korkman, Kirk, & Kemp, 2007) is a comprehensive instrument designed to assess neuropsychological development in preschool and school-age children from 3 years to 16 years, 11 months. It has a strong theoretical foundation that emphasises the interrelatedness of brain operations. The full assessment evaluates six domains, including Executive Function and Attention, Language, Memory and Learning, Sensorimotor, Visuospatial Processing, and Social Perception. The Social Perception domain has been added to the original NEPSY. It includes Affect Recognition and Theory of Mind, which would be beneficial particularly for children with possible autism. Performance is reported in standard (scaled) scores, process scores, and percentiles. Behavioural observations are presented as cumulative percentages or base rates.

**(xi) Stanford-Binet Intelligence Scales-Fifth Edition (SB5)**

**Ans.** The Stanford-Binet-Fifth Edition (SB5; Roid, 2003) provides comprehensive coverage of five factors of cognitive ability: Fluid Reasoning, Quantitative Reasoning, Visual-Spatial Reasoning, Working Memory, and Knowledge. The SB5 scoring provides a Full-Scale IQ score, a Nonverbal IQ score, and a Verbal IQ score, which are reported in standard scores and percentiles and can be used to assess individuals from 2 years of age through 85 years. The SB5 Nonverbal IQ (NVIQ) is based on the nonverbal subtests of the five-factor index scales. It measures skills in solving abstract, picture-oriented problems; recalling facts and figures; solving quantitative problems shown in picture form; assembling designs; and recalling tapping sequences. The NVIQ measures the general ability to reason, solve problems, visualise, and recall information presented in pictorial, figural, and symbolic form, as opposed to information presented in the form of words and sentences.

The SB5 Verbal IQ (VIQ) provides a composite of all the cognitive skills required to solve the items in the five verbal subtests. The VIQ measures general ability to reason, solve problems, visualise, and recall important information presented in words and sentences (printed and spoken). Also, it reflects the examinee's ability to explain verbal response clearly, the present rationale for response choices, create stories, and explain spatial directions. General verbal ability, measured by VIQ, is one of the most powerful predictors of academic success in classrooms, because of the heavy reliance on language, reading, and writing.

Fluid Reasoning is the ability to solve verbal and nonverbal problems using inductive or deductive reasoning. Quantitative Reasoning is an individual's facility with numbers and numerical problem solving, whether word problems or picture relationships. Activities in the SB5 emphasise applied problem solving more than specific mathematical knowledge acquired through school learning. Visual-Spatial Processing measures an individual's ability to see patterns and relationships. Working Memory is a class of memory processes in which diverse information stored in short-term memory is inspected, sorted, or transformed. Knowledge is a person's accumulated fund of general information acquired at home, school, or work. Also called crystallised ability, it involves learned material such as vocabulary that has been acquired and stored in long-term memory. Verbal knowledge subtests fall under the narrow abilities of Lexical Knowledge and General Knowledge.

**(xii) Universal Nonverbal Intelligence Test (UNIT)**

**Ans.** The Universal Nonverbal Intelligence Test (UNIT; Bracken & McCallum, 1998) is a set of individually administered tasks that measure the general intelligence and cognitive abilities of children and adolescents from ages 5 through 17 years who may be disadvantaged by traditional verbal and language-loaded measures. As such, the UNIT provides a comprehensive assessment of general intelligence.

The UNIT offers three administration options: abbreviated battery (2 subtests), standard battery (4 subtests), and extended battery (6 subtests). The Nonverbal Intelligence Quotient (NIC) is, in most instances, the best index for measuring the ability to solve problems, or to reason, not requiring words. The Nonverbal Quotient (NIO) measures three cognitive abilities (analogical reasoning, categorical classifying, and sequential reasoning), all assessed in two contexts (pictorial objects and geometric designs). The Memory Quotient is an index of attending, organising, encoding, storing, and recalling information and experiences. The Reasoning Quotient provides a measurement of thinking skills, including the ability to use the information to solve problems. The Symbolic Quotient measures symbolic processing or mediation. Symbolic mediation represents the verbal component of a nonverbal task. The Nonsymbolic Quotient measures abilities of perception, recognition, sequencing, organisation, and integration. These skills encompass all aspects of cognition including reasoning and memory. Subtest scores are reported in standard scores and percentiles.

**(xiii) Wechsler Abbreviated Scale of Intelligence (WASI)**

**Ans.** The Wechsler Abbreviated Scale of Intelligence (WASI; Wechsler, 1999) is an individually administered, brief intelligence scale consisting of either two or four subtests designed to be used with individuals age 6 to 89. Subtests (from the WISC-IV and WAIS-III) are Vocabulary, Block Design, Similarities, and Matrix Reasoning. Subtest raw scores are converted to t-scores (mean of 50 and a standard deviation of 10). If two subtests are given, a Full-Scale IQ (reported as a standard score) can be derived. If four subtests are given, a Verbal IQ, Performance IQ, and Full-Scale IQ can be derived. The manual states that, "The WASI is appropriate for screening, estimating IQ when a full evaluation is not possible, revaluations when time is limited, research estimates of IQ, and other situations when a more comprehensive evaluation is not needed or not possible."

**(xiv) Wechsler Adult Intelligence Scale-Third Edition (WAIS-III)**

**Ans.** The Wechsler Adult Intelligence Scale-Third Revision (WAIS-III; Wechsler, 1997) is an individually administered, standardised test designed to measure general intelligence, or the overall ability of the individual "to act purposefully, to think rationally and to deal effectively with his environment" (Wechsler, 1999, p. 3). The WAIS-III covers an age range from 16 to 89 years. It contains 14 subtests, each yielding scaled scores with a mean of 10 and a standard deviation of 3. From these subtest scores, the WAIS-III provides three separate intelligence quotients (IQs): a Verbal Scale IQ, a Performance Scale IQ, and a Full-Scale IQ. Alternately, it may be scored using the Full-Scale IQ and the four Index Scores model used with the WISC-IV (Verbal Comprehension Index, Perceptual Organisation Index, Working Memory Index, and Processing Speed Index).

**(xv) Wechsler Intelligence Scale for Children-Fourth Edition (WISC-IV)**

**Ans.** The Wechsler Intelligence Scale for Children-Fourth Edition (WISC-IV; Wechsler, 2003) provides a measure of general intellectual functioning (Full Scale Intelligence Quotient (FSIQ]) and four index scores. It can be used to assess individuals between the ages of 6 and 16 years, 11 months. Its framework is based on theory and supported by clinical research and factor-analytic results. The four index scores are the Verbal Comprehension Index (VCI), the Perceptual Reasoning Index (PRI), the Working Memory Index (WMI), and the Processing Speed Index (PSI). The WISC-IV consists of 10 core subtests and five supplemental subtests. The VCI is composed of subtests measuring verbal abilities utilising reasoning, comprehension, and conceptualisation. The PRI is composed of subtests measuring perceptual reasoning and organisation. The WMI is composed of subtests measuring attention, concentration, and working memory. The PSI is composed of subtests measuring the speed of mental and graphomotor processing.

**(xvi) Wechsler Intelligence Scale for Children-Fourth Edition Integrated (WISC-IV Integrated)**

**Ans.** The Wechsler Intelligence Scale for Children-Fourth Edition (WISC-IV Integrated; Kaplan, Fein, Kramer, Delis, & Morris, 2004) enhances the WISC-IV by adding 16 process sub-tests, as well as qualitative and quantitative observations and error scores. The addition of more measures of cognitive processes allows for a broader definition of intelligence for individuals aged 6 years through 16-11. All or selected process subtests may be used when a low scaled score is obtained on a corresponding subtest or when a child displays inconsistent or atypical performance. Results may be used to investigate low scores and identify strengths and weaknesses in the corresponding areas.

To supplement the Verbal domain (VCI on WISC-IV), subtests include (i) Similarities Multiple Choice, (ii) Vocabulary Multiple Choice, (iii) Picture Vocabulary Multiple Choice, (iv) Comprehension Multiple Choice, and (v) Information Multiple Choice. To supplement the Performance domain (PRI on WISC IV), subtests include (i) Block Design Multiple Choice, (ii) Block Design Process Approach, and (iii) Elithorn Mazes. The six process subtests that enhance the Working Memory domain (WMI on WISC IV) include (i) Visual Digit Span, (ii) Spatial Span, (iii) Letter Span, (iv) Letter-Number Sequencing Process Approach, and (v) Elithorn Mazes. Finally, process subtests used to enhance the Processing Speed (PSI on WISC-IV) include Coding Recall and Coding Copy.

**(xvii) Wechsler Nonverbal Scale of Ability (WNV):** The Wechsler Nonverbal Scale of Ability (WNV; Wechsler & Naglieri, 2006) is an individually administered test of nonverbal intelligence for individuals from ages four through 21 years. When language poses a barrier to typical administration, or if traditional intellectual assessment results are questionable due to language-related difficulties, the WNV is appropriate.

The WNV uses subtests to determine a full-scale measure of cognitive ability. The subtests yield a raw score that is converted to a t-score, allowing a student's performance to be compared to that of his peers. T-scores have a mean of 50 and a standard deviation of 10. The t-scores of the subtests are totaled and converted to a full-scale score that is a standard score, with a mean of 100 and a standard deviation of 15. The subtests consist of (i) Matrices, (ii) Coding, (iii) Spatial Span (a visual memory measure corresponding to the auditory task in Digit Span), (iv) Spatial Span Forward, (v) Spatial Span Backwards, (vi) Picture Arrangement, (vii) Object Assembly, and (viii) Recognition.

**(xviii) Wechsler Preschool and Primary Scale of Intelligence-Third Edition (WPPSI-III)**

**Ans.** The Wechsler Preschool and Primary Scale of Intelligence-Third Edition (WWPSI III; Wechsler, 2002) is an individually administered, standardised instrument for assessing the intelligence of children aged 2-6 through 7-3. It includes short, game-like tasks that engage young children. The WPPSI-III provides a Full-Scale IQ (FSIQ), Verbal IQ (VIQ), and Performance IQ (PIQ) for ages 2-6 through 3-11 using four subtests. For ages 4-0 through 7-3, seven subtests are used to yield an FSIQ, VIQ, and PIQ. Optional subtests may be given to obtaining a General Language Composite for younger children or a Processing Speed Quotient for older children.

**(xix) Wide Range Assessment of Memory and Learning-Second Edition (WRAML-2)**

**ans.** The Wide Range Assessment of Memory and Learning-Second Edition (WRAML 2; Sheslow & Adams, 2004) is an individually administered measure of memory functions that may have a significant impact on learning and school-related problems. The WRAML-2 may be used with individuals from age 5 through 90. It provides a General Memory Index, three additional index scores (Verbal Memory, Visual Memory, and Attention and Concentration), and three supplemental index scores (Working Memory, Delayed Memory, and Recognition). Each index score is derived from performance on from two to four subtests, and all are reported in standard scores and percentile ranks. Standard scores have a mean of 100 and a standard deviation of 15.

**(xx) Woodcock-Johnson Tests of Cognitive Abilities-Third Edition Normative Update (WJ-III COG/NU)**

**Ans.** The Woodcock-Johnson III Tests of Cognitive Abilities (WJ-III COG/NU; Woodcock, McGrew, & Mather, 2005) is a comprehensive set of individually administered co-normed tests for measuring cognitive ability. The tests may be used from ages 2 through adult. The battery assesses general intellectual ability as well as specific cognitive abilities. Twenty individual tests and 20 Cluster scores provide broad estimates of cognitive abilities.

The Verbal Ability Cluster Score is a measure of language development that includes the comprehension of individual words and the comprehension of relationships among words. The Thinking Ability

Cluster Score represents a sampling of the thinking processes that may be invoked when information in short-term memory cannot be processed automatically. The scale includes samples of long-term retrieval, visual-spatial thinking, auditory processing, and fluid reasoning.

❑❑❑

# 4 PROJECTIVE TECHNIQUES IN PSYCHODIAGNOSTICS

## INTRODUCTION

In this chapter, we will first consider what projective testing is. Then we will discuss the categories and assumptions of projective tests. The main projective tests used to assess personality are described. We will briefly review the major testing approaches used in contemporary neuropsychology practice. After that, it deals with principles of measurement and projective techniques, current status with special reference to the Rorschach Test. When we read a story, we not only learn about the fictitious characters but also about the author. It will provide a comprehensive discussion of TAT in terms of its description, administration, scoring and psychometric properties. At last, it considers some of the most widely used objective measures of personality such as MMPI, MCMI, 16 PF, EPPS, CPI and NEO-PI-R.

**Q1. What do you mean by projective techniques?**

*Or*

**Discuss the various categories and basics assumptions of projective techniques.** **[June-2020, Q.No.-8]**

**Ans.** Projective techniques are indirect methods used in qualitative research. These techniques allow researchers to tap into consumers' deep motivations, beliefs, attitudes and values. This is important because psychology has told us for a long time that much of what drives behaviour can be emotional and irrational in nature. To some extent, these emotional drivers of behaviour lie below conscious awareness.

The projective technique is any personality test designed to yield information about someone's personality based on their unrestricted response to ambiguous objects or situations. Projective techniques are a set of instruments whose main objective is to describe and characterise personality. The adjective projective is a derivative of 'projection', a concept introduced by Freud in the vocabulary of psychology to describe the design of a defence mechanism leading the subject to transfer to another person, or thing, his urges, feelings, etc., that he cannot accept as belonging to him. However, this concept is not commonly used in the field of projective techniques. Rather, another concept with a less restrictive and specific meaning is used. This means that, in responding to the stimulus situation, the subject reveals or externalises aspects of his own life, such as motives, interests, feelings, emotions, conflicts and the like.

To a large extent, the characteristics of the stimuli of the projections are responsible for this externalisation and have an important effect on the nature and content of the subject's responses. Two such characteristics are the structure and ambiguity of stimuli. The structure refers to the degree of organisation of the stimulus: incompleteness, nearly an organised whole or fully divided, close to or far from being a real representation, etc. The ambiguity concerns the number and variability of responses each stimulus elicits.

**Important Projective Techniques:** The following are some of the major projective techniques:

- **Word Association Test**: An individual is given a clue or hint and asked to respond to the first thing that comes to mind. The association can take the shape of a picture or a word. There can be many interpretations of the same thing. A list of words is given and you don't know in which word they are most interested. The interviewer records the responses which reveal the inner feeling of the respondents. The frequency with which any word is given a response and the amount of time that elapses before the response is given is important for the researcher. For example: Out of 50 respondents 20 people associate the word "Fair" with "Complexion".

- **Completion Test:** In this, the respondents are asked to complete an incomplete sentence or story. The completion will reflect their attitude and state of mind.
- **Construction Test**: This is more or less like the completion test. They can give you a picture and you are asked to write a story about it. The initial structure is limited and not detailed like the completion test. For example, two cartoons are given and dialogue is to write.
- **Expression Techniques**: In this, people are asked to express the feeling or attitude of other people.

**Disadvantages of Projective Techniques**

- Highly trained interviewers and skilled interpreters are needed.
- Interpreters bias can be there.
- It is a costly method.
- The respondent selected may not be representative of the entire population.

**Categories of Projective Techniques:** For many years, the primary testing tools of clinical psychologists were projective techniques such as the Rorschach Inkblot Technique. These techniques have in common the presentation of ambiguous and malleable stimuli to which a large number of different responses can be made. Presumably, the specific responses given by a client reflect something about that individual's psychodynamic functioning. Projective techniques no longer occupy the dominant position they did years ago but continue to be used in clinical practice and research. Most projective techniques fall into one of five categories, viz.,

- **Associative Techniques:** The subject responds to a particular stimulus, such as an inkblot or a word, by indicating what the stimulus suggests. The Rorschach Inkblot Technique is a prime example

- **Construction Techniques:** The subject constructs a response, usually in the form of a story, to a stimulus, usually a picture. The prime example here is the Thematic Apperception Test (TAT).
- **Ordering Techniques:** This involves placing a set of stimuli in a particular order. Typically the stimuli are a set of pictures, very much like the panels of a newspaper comic strip but the panels are presented in random order, and they need to be placed to make a coherent sequence. The Picture Arrangement subtest of the WAIS is sometimes used as an ordering technique.
- **Completion Techniques:** Here the subject responds to a "partial" stimulus. For example, the subject may be given the beginning of a story to complete or a set of sentence stems (e.g., I am always...) to complete. Sentence completion tests are a prime example here.
- **Expressive Techniques:** The subject engages in some "creative" activity, such as drawing, finger painting, acting out certain feelings or situations (as in psychodrama). The Draw-A-Person test is a good example.

**Basic Assumptions:** In general, psychologists believe that behaviour is determined or can be explained by specific principles. If we observe a person verbally or physically attacking others, we label the behaviours as aggressive and we seek explanations for the behaviour, perhaps postulating "frustration" or looking for childhood developmental explanations or antecedent conditions. With projective tests, the assumption is that specific responses reflect the person's personality and/or psychodynamic functioning. This is based, however, on the questionable assumption that the test protocol presents a sufficiently extensive sampling of the client.

Second, we know that specific behaviours can be strongly influenced by transitory aspects. A person can do well academically in all courses except one, with performance in that course influenced by a dislike for the instructor or some other "chance" factor. Projective tests, however, assume that every response is indeed basic and reflective of some major personal themes.

The projective viewpoint further assumes that perception is an active and selective process, and thus what is perceived is influenced not only by the person's current needs and motivation but by that person's unique history and the person's habitual ways of dealing with the world. The more ambiguous a situation the more the responses will reflect individual differences in attempting to structure and respond to that situation. Thus, projective tests are seen as ideal miniature situations, where presentation can be controlled and resulting responses carefully observed.

**Q2. Write a note on projective testing.**

***Or***

**Discuss the application of Thematic Apperception Test.**

**[June-2019, Q.No.-6]**

***Or***

**Discuss any two projective tests. [Dec-2019, Q.No.-5]**

***Or***

**Write a short note on Projective Drawings. [Dec-2019, Q.No.-10]**

**Ans.** In psychology, a projective test is a personality test designed to let a person respond to ambiguous stimuli, presumably revealing hidden emotions and internal conflicts projected by the person into the test. This is sometimes contrasted with a so-called "objective test"/"self-report test", which adopt a "structured" approach as responses are analysed according to a presumed universal standard (for example, a multiple choice exam), and are limited to the content of the test. The responses to projective tests are content analysed for meaning rather than being based on presuppositions about meaning, as is the case with objective tests. Projective tests have their origins in psychoanalysis, which argues that humans have conscious and unconscious attitudes and motivations that are beyond or hidden from conscious awareness.

**(1) The Rorschach Test:** The Rorschach Test is the famous inkblot test (Rorschach, 1921/1942, 1951). Many people are fascinated by the idea of using inkblots to investigate personality and psychological functioning. Of course, many people (including psychologists) are skeptical of projective techniques such as the Rorschach, questioning its validity as a measure of psychological functioning.

The Rorschach consists of 10 symmetrical inkblots; that is, the left side of each card is essentially a mirror image of the right side. The same 10 inkblots have been used in the same order of presentation) since they were first developed by Herman Rorschach in 1921 (Rorschach, 1921/1942). Half of the cards are black, white, and grey, and half use colour. While there are several different ways to administer the Rorschach and score, the vast majority of psychologists today use the method developed by John Exner (Exner, 1974, 1976, 1986, 1993, 2003; Exner & Weiner, 1995). Each card is handed to the patient with the question, "What might this be?" The psychologist writes down everything the patient says verbatim. During this free association portion of the test, the psychologist does not question the patient. After all, 10 cards are administered; the psychologist shows the patient each card a second time and asks questions that will help in scoring the test. For example, the psychologist might say, "Now I'd like to show you the cards once again and ask you several questions about each card so that I can be sure that I see it as you do."

With each card, he or she asks a non-leading question such as, "What about the card made it look like a - to you?" The psychologist looks for answers that will help him or her score the test in several categories such as location (i.e., the area of the blot being used), content (i.e., the nature of the object being described, such as a person, animal, or element of nature), determinants (i.e., the parts of the blot that the patient used in the response, such as form, colour, shading, and movement), and popular (i.e., the responses are typically seen by others). This portion of the test is referred to as the inquiry. Once the test is completed, scoring involves a highly complex system and analysis. Each response is carefully scored based on the content, location, determinants, and quality of the response.

Various aspects of the Rorschach responses are associated with psychological functioning. For example, the frequent use of shading is generally considered to be reflective of anxiety and depression. The use of human movement and an adequate number of popular responses are usually associated with adaptive and well-integrated psychological functioning. Numerous responses that attend to minor details of the blots often reflect obsessive-compulsive traits. Frequent use of the whitespace around the blot is generally associated with oppositionality and/or avoidance.

**(2) The Thematic Apperception Test (TAT):** The TAT (Murray & Bellack, 1942; Tomkins, 1947) was developed during the late 1930s by Henry Murray and Christiana Morgan at Harvard University. The TAT was originally designed to measure personality factors in research settings. Specifically, it was used to investigate goals, central conflicts, needs, press (i.e., factors that facilitate or impede progress towards reaching goals) and achievement strivings associated with Henry Murray's theory of *personology* (Murray, 1938). The TAT consists of 31 pictures (one of which is blank), almost all of which depict people rather than objects. Some of the pictures are designed to be administered to males, some to females, and others to both genders. Generally, only a selected number of cards (e.g., 10) are administered to any one patient.

The psychologist introduces the test by telling the patient that he or she will be given a series of pictures and requested to tell a story about each. The patient is instructed to make up a story that reflects what the people in the picture are thinking, feeling, and doing and also to speculate on what led up to the events depicted in the picture and what will happen in the future. After each card is presented to the patient, the psychologist writes down everything that is said verbatim.

Although a variety of complex scoring approaches have been developed.... (Murray, 1943; Shneidman, 1951), most clinicians use their clinical experience and judgement to analyse the themes that emerge from the patient's stories. Since clinicians generally do not officially score the TAT, conducting reliability and validity research is challenging.

Other tests similar to the TAT have been developed for special populations, such as Robert's Apperception Test for Children (RATC; McArthur & Roberts, 1982) for use with elementary school children. The 27 pictures depict children interacting with parents, teachers, and peers. The Children's Apperception Test (CAT, Bellak, 1986) was developed for very young children and depicts animals interacting in various ways.

**(3) Projective Drawings:** Many clinician's ask both children and adults to draw pictures to assess their psychological functioning. Typically, people are asked to draw a house, a tree, a person, and their family doing something together. For the Draw a Person test (Machover, 1949), the House Tree Person Technique (Buck, 1948), and the Kinetic Family Drawing Technique, the patient is instructed to draw each picture in pencil on a separate blank piece of paper and to avoid the use of stick figures.

On the assumption that a drawing tells us something about its creator, clinicians often ask clients to draw human figures and talk about them. Evaluations of these drawings are based on the details and shape of the drawing, solidity of the pencil line, location of the drawing on the paper, size of the figures, features of the figures, use of background, and comments made by the respondent during the drawing task. In the *Draw a Person (DAP) Test,* the most popular of the drawing tests, subjects are first told to draw "a person," and they are instructed to draw another person of the opposite sex.

**(4) Sentence Completion Techniques:** Another projective technique involves the use of sentence completion. There are many different versions of this technique (e.g., Forer, 1957; P. A. Goldberg, 1965;

Lanyon & Lanyon, 1980; Rotter, 1954; Rotter & Rafferty, 1950). The patient is presented (either orally by the examiner or in writing through a questionnaire) a series of sentence fragments. These might include items such as, "When he answered the phone he.." or "Most mothers are The patient is asked to give the first response that he or she thinks of and complete the sentence. Again, like projective drawings and the TAT, several scoring systems have been developed to assist in interpretation. "

However, these scoring approaches are generally used only in research settings. Most clinicians prefer to use their own experience and clinical judgement to interpret the themes that emerge from the completed sentences.

**Merits of Projective Tests:** Until the 1950s, projective tests were the most common technique for assessing personality. In recent years, however, clinicians and researchers have relied on them largely to gain "supplementary" insights. One reason for this shift is that practitioners who follow the newer models have less use for the tests than psychodynamic clinicians do. Even more important, the tests have rarely demonstrated much reliability or validity:

In reliability studies, different clinicians have tended to score the same person's projective test quite differently. Standardised procedures for administering and scoring the tests have been developed to improve scoring consistency, but research suggests that the reliability of projective tests remains weak even when such procedures are used (Wood et al., 2000; Lilienfeld et al., 2000).

Research has also challenged the validity of projective tests. When clinician's try to describe a client's personality and feelings based on responses to projective tests, their conclusions often fail to match the self-report of the client, the view of the psychotherapist, or the picture gathered from the extensive case history. Another validity problem is that projective tests are sometimes biased against minority ethnic groups.

**Q3. Discuss the concept of Neuropsychological assessment and Neuropsychological testing.**

***Or***

**Discuss Neuropsychological testing. [June-2019, Q.No.-5]**

**Ans.** Neuropsychological assessment is a performance-based method to assess cognitive functioning. This method is used to examine the cognitive consequences of brain damage, brain disease, and severe mental illness. There are several specific uses of neuropsychological assessment, including collection of diagnostic information, differential diagnostic information, assessment of treatment response, and prediction of functional potential and functional recovery. We anticipate that clinical neuropsychological assessment will continue to be used, even in the face of advances in imaging technology, because it is already well known that the presence of significant brain changes can be associated with nearly normal cognitive functioning, while individuals with no lesions detectable on imaging can have substantial cognitive and functional limitations.

To illustrate this, consider the case of a young man who has sustained a head injury in an assault. A year after the incident he has made a good physical recovery, but is very aggressive and has lost his job as a sales manager because of hostility towards colleagues and a general lack of organisation in his work. These problems might, on the one hand, arise from organic damage to regions of the brain involved in the genesis or inhibition of aggression, or, on the other, be a psychological reaction to some more subtle cognitive deficit such as a generalised reduction in the efficiency with which information is processed or mild but specific impairment of memory. In the former case, a pharmacological treatment to control the emotional reactions might be most appropriate, whilst in the latter, it would be more relevant to address the underlying cognitive deficit directly and or help the patient adjust his lifestyle and outlook to his new limitations.

***Purposes of Neuropsychological Assessment*:** The form taken by any neuropsychological assessment wills depends critically on the question which is to be answered. The frequent purpose of assessment includes the following:

- Description and measurement of organically based cognitive deficits.
- Differential diagnosis (e.g. to ascertain whether memory problems arise from organic injury or mood disturbances).
- Prediction of the consequences of neurosurgical excision of brain tissue (e.g. the cost-benefits likely to accrue from a temporal lobotomy).
- Monitoring improvement or deterioration associated with recovery from, or exacerbation of, a neurological condition.
- Evaluation of the neuropsychological effects, positive or adverse, of pharmacological and non-pharmacological treatments (e.g. to determine whether a psychological intervention has improved attention, or whether an anticonvulsant might impair learning).
- Guiding rehabilitation strategies.
- Predicting or explaining deficits in social, educational, or occupational functioning. Medico-legal evaluations (e.g. contributing to the determination of compensation awards, ascertaining fitness to plead.

***Dimensions and Level of Assessment*:** The extensiveness of, and methods employed within, any individual assessment will be largely determined by the specific referral question, though a wide range of other factors will also be influential. These will include characteristics of the patient which affect his or her ability or willingness to carry out certain tests, as well as resource-based considerations, such as the location in which the assessment is to take place, or the amount of time which is available.

A major element of many neuropsychological assessments is evaluation of the patient's intellectual functioning, usually tested via formal pen and paper or computerised test procedures. However, this is neither the only form of assessment used nor necessarily the most important. If the presenting problem is one of behavioural or emotional disturbance, the assessment may concentrate on the systematic collection of information either from the patient or from others concerning factors which may influence its occurrence. Thus, although neuropsychological assessment is often perceived as a special form of cognitive assessment, it is very often much broader than this. In practice, a referral to a neuropsychologist will often result in a multidimensional assessment in which the presenting problem is analysed from several perspectives rather than just one. Sometimes there may be no formal testing if the pertinent information can be gleaned from systematic behavioural observations and interviews.

At a general level, the purpose of neuropsychological assessment may be categorised into those which are primarily descriptive and those which are explanatory. The former represents an attempt to identify the type and severity of any problems, while the latter entails more theoretically driven procedures designed to illuminate the causes or consequences of an observed deficit. These two aspects will be differentially important depending on the nature of the initial question. So, if the purpose of the assessment is to quantify the extent of any memory deficits (e.g. for monitoring change over time, or for medico-legal purposes), then a standardised measurement of different aspects of the patient's memory relative to their general intellectual level may suffice. By contrast, if the purpose of the assessment is to determine why the patient has difficulty in remembering information in daily life and to make therapeutic recommendations, then more detailed probing of potential causes for the memory problem become relevant. For instance, it may be that the memory deficit is secondary to poor concentration or impaired perception, or that it is related to the form in which the information is presented (e.g. verbally vs. visually). If the assessment clarifies the mechanisms underlying the patient's problems, then treatment can focus specifically on these.

Descriptive assessments will also vary in terms of their breadth, and this again is likely to reflect the referral question. In one case the requirement may be to determine whether a brain injury has resulted in any impairment, whilst in another, the emphasis may be particularly on a certain aspect of the patient's functioning. The basis for focussing on one aspect more than on others may consist in observations which have already been made (e.g. that the patient appears forgetful) or based on what is known about the a etiology or location of the brain injury (e.g. that there is a focal lesion to a part of the brain which is implicated in memory functions). The prediction of neuropsychological sequelae which are likely to arise from damage to specified areas of the brain has become an increasingly sophisticated exercise over the last decade with the emergence of complex information processing models of cognitive function.

**Neuropsychological Testing:** Brain impairment due to head injury, substance abuse, stroke, or other illnesses and injuries often impact the cognitive ability to use language, think and make appropriate judgements, adequately perceive and respond to stimuli, and remember old or new information. Neuropsychological testing assesses brain behaviour skills such as intellectual, abstract reasoning, memory, visual-perceptual, attention, concentration, gross and fine motor, and language functioning.

Neuropsychological tests include test batteries as well as individual tests. The Halstead Reitan Battery (Boll, 1981; Halstead, 1947, Reitan& Davison, 1974) and the Luria Nebraska Battery (Golden, Hammeke, & Purisch, 1980) are the most commonly used test batteries with adults. The Halstead Reitan Battery can be administered to persons aged 15 through adulthood and consists of 12 separate tests along with the administration of the MMPI-2 and the WAIS-HI. The battery takes approximately 6 to 8 hours to administer and provides an overall impairment index as well as separate scores on each subtest assessing skill such as memory, sensory-perceptual skills, and the ability to solve new learning problems. Other versions of the test are available for children between ages 5and 14.

The Luria Nebraska Battery consists of 11 subtests for a total of 269 separate testing tasks. The subtests assess reading, writing, receptive and expressive speech, memory, arithmetic, and other skills. The Luria Nebraska battery takes about 2.5 hours to administer.

Another neuropsychological testing approach is represented by the Boston Process Approach (Delis, Kaplan, & Kramer, 2001; Goodglass, 1986; E. Kaplan et al., 1991; Milberg, Hebben, & Kaplan, 1986). The Boston process approach uses a variety of different tests depending upon the nature of the referral question. Rather than using a standard test battery, the Boston Process Approach uses a subset of a wide variety of tests to answer specific neuropsychological questions. Performance on one test determines which tests or subtests if any, will be used next. The testing process could be short or long involving few or many tests and subtests depending upon what is needed to adequately evaluate strengths and weaknesses in functioning. For example, if a neuropsychological evaluation of a head-injured patient was to focus on memory skills following a car accident, several tests would be considered for use. These might include the Benton Visual Retention Test, the Wechsler Memory Scale-III, and the Wisconsin Card Sorting Test. Each of these tests measures a different facet of memory functioning. Results provide a clearer picture of short and long-term memory as well as visual, auditory, and sensory memory. If during testing, language problems were detected, the receptive and expressive language sections of the Luria Nebraska might be added to the battery to assess language skills. The language assessment might help to better understand the relationship between memory and language skills in this patient.

Some of the commonly used individual neuropsychological tests include the Wechsler Memory Scale-III (Wechsler, 1997), the Benton Visual Retention Test (Benton, 1991), the WAIS-R as a Neuro psychological Instrument (E. Kaplan et al., 1991), the WISC-III as a Process Instrument (E. Kaplan et al., 1999), the Kaufman Short Neuropsychological Assessment Procedure (K-SNAP; Kaufman & Kaufman, 1994), the California Verbal Learning Test (Delis, Kramer, Kaplan, & Ober, 1987, 2000) and the California Verbal Learning Test Children's Version (Delis, Kramer, Kaplan, & Ober, 1994), and the Wisconsin Card Sorting Test (Grant & Berg, 1993).

The Delis Kaplan Executive Function System (D-KEFS; Delis, Kaplan, & Kramer, 2001) provides a comprehensive evaluation of executive functioning or high-level thinking and processing as well as cognitive flexibility. It can be administered to both children and adults from ages 8 through 89. It assesses the integrity of the frontal lobe area of the brain and examines potential deficits in abstract and creative thinking. The D-KEFS consists of 9 subtests including the Sorting, Trail Making, Verbal Fluency, Design Fluency, Colour-Word Interference, Tower, 20 Questions, Word Context, and the Proverb tests. These tests measure various aspects of cognitive functioning that reflect the strengths and weaknesses associated with brain-behaviour relationships. Results from these tests are compared with norms to develop a clearer understanding of the interaction between brain functioning and behaviour, emotions, and thoughts as well as to help locate the site of brain impairment.

Some authors have suggested that physiological tests such as evoked potentials, electroencephalography (EEG), and reaction time measures may be useful in the assessment of intelligence and cognitive abilities (Matarazzo,1992; Reed & Jensen, 1991). Evoked potentials assess the brain's ability to process the perception of a stimulus, and EEG measures the electrical activity of the brain. Although psychologists are currently not licenced to administer or interpret neuroimaging techniques such as computerised axial tomography (CAT), magnetic resonance imaging (MRI), and positron emission tomography (PET), these techniques allow examination of brain structure and function, which is useful in assessing brain behaviour relationships such as cognitive abilities. For example, cortical atrophy, shrinkage, or actual loss of brain tissue has been associated with schizophrenia, Alzheimer's disease, anorexia nervosa, alcoholism, and mood disorders.

Contemporary neuropsychological testing integrates specialised tests along with additional sources of information. The tests are often used in conjunction with data obtained from clinical interviews, behavioural observations, and other cognitive, personality, and physiological assessment tools. Thus, neuropsychological testing is not isolated from other evaluation techniques used by contemporary clinical psychologists. While the neuropsychological assessment is a subspecialty of clinical psychology, it overlaps with many of the skills and techniques of general clinical psychologists. In addition to specialised testing, neuropsychologists must have a high level of understanding of brain structure and functioning.

***Limitations:*** Neuropsychological tests in general have several limitations. Prigatano and Redner (1993) identify four major ones:

- Not all changes associated with brain injury are reflected in changed test performance;
- Test findings do not automatically indicate the reason for the specific performance;
- Neuropsychological test batteries are long to administer and therefore expensive, and

- A patient's performance is influenced not just by brain dysfunction but also by a variety of other variables such as age and education.

**Q4. Describe the nature and clinical usefulness of projective tests.**

**Ans.** A major distinguishing feature of projective techniques is to be found in their assignment of a relatively unstructured task, i.e., a task that permits an almost unlimited variety of possible responses. In order to allow free play to the individual fantasy, only brief, general instructions are provided. For the same reason, the test stimuli are usually vague or ambiguous. The underlying hypothesis is that the way in which the individual perceives and interprets the test material, or structures the situation, will reflect fundamental aspects of her or his psychological functioning. In other words, it is expected that the test materials will serve as a sort of screen on which respondents project their characteristic thought processes, needs, anxieties, and conflicts.

Typically, projective instruments also represent disguised testing procedures, insofar as test takers are rarely aware of the type of psychological interpretation that will be made of their responses. Projective techniques are likewise characterised by a global approach to the appraisal of personality. Attention is focussed on a composite of the whole personality, rather than on the measurement of separate traits. Finally, projective techniques are usually regarded by their exponents as especially effective in revealing covert, latent, or unconscious aspects of personality. Moreover, the more unstructured the test, it is argued, the more sensitive it is to such covert material. This follows from the assumption that the more unstructured or ambiguous the stimuli, the less likely they are to evoke defensive reactions on the part of the respondent.

For some, the definition of a projective test resides in Freudian notions regarding the nature of ego defences and unconscious processes. However, these do not seem to be essential characteristics.

Over the years, many definitions have been offered. Perhaps the easiest solution is a pragmatic one that comes from consulting the English and English (1958) psychological dictionary, which defines a projective technique as "a procedure for discovering a person's characteristic modes of behaviour by observing his behaviour in response to a situation that does not elicit or compel a particular response." Projective techniques, taken as a whole, tend to have the following distinguishing characteristics (Rotter, 1954):

- In response to an unstructured or ambiguous stimulus, examinees are *forced to impose their structure* and, in so doing, reveal something of themselves (such as needs, wishes, or conflicts).
- The stimulus material is *unstructured.* This is a very tenuous criterion, even though it is widely assumed to reflect the essence of projective techniques.

  For example, if 70 per cent of all examinees perceive Card V on the Rorschach as a bat, then we can hardly say that the stimulus is unstructured. Thus, whether a test is projective or not depends on the kinds of responses that the individual is encouraged to give and on how those responses are used. The instructions are an important element. If a patient is asked to classify the people in a set of TAT cards as men or women, then there is a great deal of structure, that is the test is far from ambiguous. However, if the patient is asked what the people on the card are saying, the task has suddenly become quite ambiguous indeed.
- The method is *indirect.* To some degree or other, examinees are not aware of the purposes of the test; at least, the purposes are disguised. Although patients may know that the test has something to do with adjustment maladjustment, they are not usually aware in detail of the significance of their responses. There is no attempt to ask patients directly about their needs or troubles; the route is indirect, and the hope is that this very indirectness will make it more difficult for patients to censor the data they provide.
- There is *freedom of response.* Whereas questionnaire methods may allow only for a "yes" or a "no", response, projections permit a nearly infinite range of responses.
- Response interpretation deals with *more variables.* Since the range of possible responses is so broad, the clinician can make interpretations along multiple dimensions (needs, adjustment, diagnostic category, ego defences, and so on). Many objective tests, in contrast, provide but a single score (such as degree of

psychological distress), or scores on a fixed number of dimensions or scales.

**Clinical Usefulness:** There is little doubt that in the hands of a skilled and sensitive clinician, projective techniques can yield useful information and individual practitioners can utilise these measures to elicit superb psychodynamic portraits of a patient, and to make accurate predictions about future behaviour. Given this, why is there a need for scientific validation? MacFarlane and Tuddenham (1951) provided five basic answers to this question;

- **A Social Responsibility:** Projective tests are misused, and we need to know which types of statements can be supported by the scientific literature and which cannot.
- **A Professional Responsibility:** Errors of interpretation can be reduced and interpretive skills sharpened by having objective validity data.
- **A Teaching Responsibility:** If we cannot communicate the basis for making specific inferences, such as "this type of response to card 6 on the Rorschach typically means that...," then we cannot train future clinicians in these techniques,
- **Advancement of Knowledge:** Validity data can advance our understanding of personality functioning, psychopathology, etc.
- **A Challenge to Research Skills:** As scientists, we ought to be able to make explicit what clinicians use intuitively and implicitly.

**Q5. Briefly discuss standardisation, reliability and validity of projective techniques.**

**Ans.** There is a striking contrast between objective tests and projective tests. The former, by their very nature, lend themselves to an actuarial interpretive approach. Norms, reliability, and even validity seem easier to manage. The projective tests, by their very nature, seem to resist psychometric evaluation. Indeed, some clinicians reject even the suggestion that a test such as the Rorschach should be subjected to the indignities of psychometrics; they would see this as an assault upon their intuitive art. In this section, we offer several general observations about the difficulties involved in evaluating the psychometric properties of projective tests.

**Standardisation:** There are surely many reasons for standardisation of projective techniques. Such standardisation would facilitate communication and would also serve as a check against the biases and the interpretive zeal of some clinicians. Furthermore, the enthusiastic proponents of projective tests usually act as if they have norms (implicit though these may be) so that there seems to be no good reason not to attempt the standardisation of those norms. Of course, research of problems with projective tests can be formidable.

The dissenters argue that interpretations from projective tests cannot be sized. Every person is unique, and any normative descriptions will inevitably be misleading. There are so many interacting variables that standardised interpretive approaches would surely destroy the holistic nature of projective tests. After all, they say, interpretation is an art.

**Reliability:** Even the determination of reliability turns out not to be simple. For example, it is surely too much to expect an individual to produce, word for word, the same TAT story on two different occasions. Yet how many differences between the two stories are permissible? Of course, one can bypass test responses altogether and deal only with the reliability of the personality interpretations made by clinicians. However, this may confound the reliability of the test with the reliability of the judge. Also, test-retest reliability may be affected by psychological changes in the individual, particularly when dealing with patient populations. Clinicians can indeed opt for establishing reliability through the use of alternate forms. However, how do they decide that alternate forms for TAT cards or inkblots are equivalent? Even split-half reliability is difficult to ascertain because of the difficulty of demonstrating the equivalence of the two halves of each test.

**Validity:** Because projective tests have been used for such a multiplicity of purposes, there is little point in asking general questions: Is the TAT valid? Is the Rorschach a good personality test? The book you can believe most–GPH book.

**Q6. Explain Rorschach test and Rorschach Inkblot method.**

*Or*

**Discuss the reliability and validity of Rorschach scores.**

*Or*

**Give a description of administration and scoring of Rorschach test.**
**[Dec-2020, Q.No.-8]**

**Ans.** The Rorschach test is a psychological test in which subjects' perceptions of inkblots are recorded and then analysed using psychological interpretation, complex algorithms, or both. Some psychologists use this test to examine a person's personality characteristics and emotional functioning. It has been employed to detect underlying thought disorder, especially in cases where patients are reluctant to describe their thinking processes openly. The test is named after its creator, Swiss psychologist Hermann Rorschach. The Rorschach can be thought of as a psychometric examination of pareidolia, the active pattern of perceiving objects, shapes, or scenery as meaningful things to the observer's experience, the most common being faces or other pattern of forms that are not present at the time of the observation. In the 1960s, the Rorschach was the most widely used projective test.[

Although the Exner Scoring System (developed since the 1960s) claims to have addressed and often refuted many criticisms of the original testing system with an extensive body of research, some researchers continue to raise questions. The areas of dispute include the objectivity of testers, inter-rater reliability, the verifiability and general validity of the test, bias of the test's pathology scales towards greater numbers of responses, the limited number of psychological conditions which it accurately diagnoses, the inability to replicate the test's norms, its use in court-ordered evaluations, and the proliferation of the ten inkblot images, potentially invalidating the test for those who have been exposed to them.

**Administration:** There are various techniques for administering the Rorschach Test. However, for many clinicians, the process goes something like this. The clinician hands the patient the first card and says, "Tell me what you see. What it might be for you. There are no right or wrong answers. Just tell me what it looks like to you."

All of the subsequent cards are administered in order. The clinician takes down verbatim everything the patient says. Some clinicians also record the length of time it takes the patient to make the first response to each card as well as the total time spent on each card. Some patients produce many responses per card, and others produce very few. The clinician also notes the position of the card as each response is given (right side up, upside down, or sideways). All spontaneous remarks or exclamations are also recorded.

Following this phase, the clinician moves to what is called the Inquiry. Here, the patient is reminded of all previous responses, one by one, and asked what it was that prompted each response. The patient is also asked to indicate for each card the exact location of the various responses. This is also a time when the patient may elaborate or clarify responses.

**Scoring:** Although Rorschach scoring techniques varies, most employ three major criteria.

- Location refers to the area of the card, to which the patient responded. The whole blot, a large detail, a small detail, white space, and so on.
- Content refers to the nature of the object seen (an animal, a person, a rock, fog, clothing, etc.)
- Determinants refer to those aspects of the card that prompted the patient's response (the form of the blot, its colour, texture, apparent movement, shading, etc.).

Some systems also score popular responses and original responses (often based on the relative frequency of certain responses in the general population). Currently, Exner's Comprehensive System of scoring is the most frequently used (Exner, 1974, 1993). Although the specifics of this scoring system are beyond the scope of this unit (a total of 54 indices are calculated in Exner's Structural Summary), several resources are available that provide details on the Comprehensive System (including Exner, 1991, 1993). The actual scoring of the Rorschach Test involves such things as compiling the number of determinants, computing their percentages based on the total number of responses, and computing the ratio of one set of responses to another set (e.g., computing the total number of movement responses divided by the number of colour responses). Indeed, the layperson is often surprised to learn that orthodox scoring of the Rorschach Test is much more concerned with the formal determinants than with the actual content of the responses. However, many contemporary clinicians do not bother with formal scoring at all, preferring to rely on the informal notation of determinants. Furthermore, these clinicians tend to make heavy use of content in their interpretations. As mentioned earlier, the Rorschach Test interpretation can be a complex process. For example, a patient's overuse of form may suggest conformity. Poor form, coupled with unusual responses, may hint at psychosis. Colour is said to relate to emotionality, and if it is not accompanied by a good form, it may often indicate impulsivity. Extensive use of white spaces has been interpreted as indicative of oppositional or even psychopathic qualities. Use of the whole blot points to a tendency to be concerned with integration and to be well organised. Extensive use of details is thought to be correlated with compulsivity or obsessional tendencies. But content is also important. Seeing small animals might mean passivity. Responses of blood, claws, teeth, or similar images could suggest hostility and aggression. Even turning a card over and examining the back might lead to an interpretation of suspiciousness. However, the student must treat these as examples of potential interpretations or hypotheses and not as successfully validated facts!

We conclude our discussion of the Rorschach test with some general evaluative comments. As previously mentioned, the most comprehensive approach to scoring has been developed by Exner (1974, 1993). His system incorporates elements from the scoring systems of other clinicians. Exner and his associates have offered a substantial amount of psychometric data, evidence of stable test-retest reliability, and construct validity studies. It is a promising, research-based approach that warrants careful attention from clinicians who choose to use the Rorschach Test.

**Reliability and Validity of Rorschach Scores:** Research-oriented clinical psychologists have questioned the reliability of the Rorschach Test scores for years (Wood et al., 2003). As we mentioned previously, at the most basic level, one should be confident that the Rorschach Test responses can be scored reliably across raters. If the same Rorschach Test responses cannot be scored similarly by different raters using the same scoring system, then it is hard to imagine that the instrument would have much utility in clinical prediction situations. Unfortunately, the extent which the Rorschach Test scoring systems meet acceptable standards for this most basic and straightforward form of reliability remains contentious. For example, in a recent rather heated exchange, Meyer (1997a, 1997b) reported that evidence indicates "excellent inter-rater reliability for Exner's scoring system, but Wood, Nezworski, and Stejskal (1997) remained unconvinced by his new reliability analyses and results.

Although inter scorer reliability is important to address, we must also evaluate the consistency of an individual's scores across time or test conditions as well as the reliability of score interpretations. Weiner (1995) argues that frequent retests (even daily) are possible because the basic structure and thematic focus of their Rorschach data tend to remain the same". However, we are not aware of a large body of empirical studies that support the stability of Rorschach summary scores. The limited available evidence does tend to support the stability over time of summary scores believed to reflect trait-like dispositions (Meyer, 1997a; Weiner, Spielberger, & Abeles, 2002), but more evidence is needed to address this question but the relatively neglected type of reliability is crucial for measures like the Rorschach.. It is quite probable that two clinicians trained together over several years can achieve reliability in their interpretations. However, what about two clinicians with no common training? The proliferation of formal scoring systems, coupled with the tendency of so many clinicians to use freewheeling interpretive approaches, makes the calculation of this type of reliability difficult.

As for the validity of the Rorschach Test scores and interpretations, there have been many testimonials over the years. When skilled, experienced clinicians speak highly of an instrument, those in the field listen. But at some point, these testimonials must give way to hard evidence. From the vast Rorschach literature, it is apparent that the test is not equally valid for all purposes. The problem is not one of determining whether the Rorschach is valid but of differentiating the conditions under which it is useful from those under which it is not. For many years, a procedure involving the interpretation of the Rorschach Test responses with almost no other information about the patient was used to assess Rorschach Test validity. Even when Rorschach response protocols are submitted for analysis in this manner, however, identifying cues are often present. For example, the Rorschach protocols of 10-year olds may be combined in one study with those of 60-year-olds. Sometimes the protocols are sent to former teachers or friends so that there may be a higher than usual level of agreement. Just knowing that the protocols came from Hospital X may provide important clues about the nature of the patients.

Other studies have used a matching technique, that is specifically, the matching of the Rorschach Test protocols with case histories, to assess the validity of the Rorschach test results interpretations. However, there are also problems with these studies. Correct matching may be a function of one or two strikingly deviant variables. Consequently, what has been validated? There have even been instances in which the person who had administered the Rorschach Test was subsequently asked to match it with the correct case history. Thus, a correct match may have been determined by the recall of patient characteristics observed during the testing,

Despite the questions raised about the validity of the Rorschach Test, several surveys have placed the Rorschach Test in a favourable light (e.g., Atkinson, 1986; Parker, 1983; Parker et al., 1988). For example, Parker et al. (1988), in a broad survey of Rorschach studies, found the average validity coefficient across a variety of Rorschach scales to be .41. Also, both inter judge reliability and test-retest reliability were in the mid-80s. Still, many remain critical of the quality of the individual studies that have been cited as supporting the validity of the Rorschach Test scores (e.g., Wood et al., 1996; Wood et al., 2003). Perhaps most important, a recent reanalysis of the studies included in Parker et al.'s (1988) meta-analysis arrived at a different conclusion. Garb et al. (1998), using data from the same studies reviewed by Parker et al., reported significantly lower validity estimates for the Rorschach Test scores (validity coefficient of.29 vs. the Previous estimate of .41). Further, the revised, corrected estimate of the Rorschach Test validity was significantly lower than that of the MMPI (-48). These findings, in addition to findings that fail to support the incremental validity of the Rorschach Test scores (Archer & Krishnamurthy, 1997; Garb, 1984, 1998), led the authors to "recommend that less emphasis be placed on training in the use of the Rorschach" (p. 404). It remains to be seen whether clinical psychology programs will heed this call.

The debate over the utility of the Rorschach Test in clinical assessment continues (Meyer, 1999, 2001; Wood et al. 2003). Advocates (Stricker & Gold, 1999; advocates (Stricker & Gold 1999. Viglione, 1999; Viglione & Hilsenroth, 2001; Weiner et al. 2002) argue that the Rorschach Test is useful when the focus is on the unconscious functioning and problem-solving styles of individuals. However, critics remain sceptical of the clinical utility of Rorschach scores (Hunsley & Bailey, 1999, 2001) or their incremental validity (Dawes, 1999; Garb, 2003).

**Rorschach Inkblot "Method":** Weiner (1991) has argued that the Rorschach Test is best conceptualised as a *method* of data collection, not a test.

The Rorschach is not a test because it does not test anything. A test is intended to measure whether something is present or not and in what quantity. But with the Rorschach Test, which has traditionally been classified as a test of personality, we do not measure whether people have a personality or how much personality they have (p. 499).

Several implications are as follow:

First, Weiner argues that data generated from the Rorschach Test method can be interpreted from a variety of theoretical positions. These data suggest how the respondent typically solves problems or makes decisions (cognitive structuring processes) as well as the meanings that are assigned to these perceptions (associational processes). Weiner calls this an "integrationist" view of the Rorschach Test because the method provides data relevant to both the structure and dynamics of personality. According to Weiner, a second, practical implication is that viewing the Rorschach as a method allows one to fully use all aspects of the data that are generated, resulting in a more thorough diagnostic evaluation.

The influence and utility of this reconceptualisation remain to be seen. In any case, empirical data supporting the utility and incremental validity of data generated by the Rorschach Test method" are still necessary before its routine use in clinical settings can be advocated.

**Q7. Discuss the concept of 'Thematic Apperception Test'.**

**Ans.** Thematic apperception test (TAT) is a projective psychological test developed during the 1930s by Henry A. Murray and Christiana D. Morgan at Harvard University. A thematic apperception test involves showing the subject several pictures (which are engaging but broad and open to interpretation) and having the subject tell a story for each picture. The subject is encouraged to use as much detail as possible. For example: What is happening in the picture? What events occurred before what is happening in the picture? What will happen afterward? Why are the characters acting and feeling the way they are?

It is difficult to generalise the results of a thematic apperception test. The results are often subjective and do not use any formal type of scoring system. However, a close analysis of the stories told by the subject normally gives the tester a decent idea of the traits mentioned above (personality, emotional control, and attitudes towards aspects of everyday life).

Companies sometimes use thematic apperception tests to screen potential employees. These tests can determine (to a certain extent) whether the potential employee is likely to succeed at a certain position. For example: Can they handle stressful situations? How will they react to emotional conflicts? Will they fit in well with the general atmosphere and attitude of the company?

The Thematic Apperception Test (TAT) is comparable to the Rorschach Test in many ways, including its importance and psychometric problems. As with the Rorschach Test, the use of the TAT grew rapidly after its introduction. Except for the Rorschach Test, the TAT is used more than any other projective test (Wood et al., 2003). Though its psychometric adequacy was (and still is) vigourously debated, unlike the Rorschach, the TAT has been relatively well-received by the scientific community.

Also, the TAT is based on Murray's (1938) theory of needs, whereas the Rorschach is theoretical. The TAT and the Rorschach differ in other respects as well. The TAT authors were conservative in their evaluation of the TAT and scientific in their outlook. The TAT was not oversold as was the Rorschach, and no extravagant claims were made. Unlike the Rorschach, the TAT was not billed as a diagnostic instrument, that is, a test of disordered emotional states. Instead, the TAT was presented as an instrument for evaluating human personality characteristics. This test also differs from the Rorschach Test because the TAT'S non-clinical uses are just as important as its clinical ones. Indeed, the TAT is one of the most important techniques used in personality research (Abrams, 1999; Bellak, 1999; Cramer & Blatt, 1990; McClelland, 1999).

As stated, the TAT is based on Murray's (1938) theory, which distinguishes 28 human needs, including the needs for sex, affiliation, and dominance. Many of these needs have been extensively researched through the use of the TAT (McClelland, 1999). The theoretical need for achievement that is the desire or tendency to do things as rapidly and/or as well as possible" (Murray, 1938, p. 164)-alone has generated a very large number of studies involving the TAT,

The TAT measure of the achievement need has been related to factors such as parental perceptions, parental expectations, and parental attitudes towards offspring. Need achievement is also related to the standards that you as a student set for yourself (for example, academic standards). The higher your need for achievement, the more likely you are to study and ultimately achieve a high economic and social position in society. Studies such as those on the achievement motive have provided construct related evidence for validity and have increased the scientific respectability of the TAT.

**Administration:** Although, theoretically the TAT could be used with children, it is typically used with adolescents and adults. The original manual (H. A. Murray, 1943) does have standardised instructions, but typically examiners use their versions. What is necessary is that the instructions include the points that:

- the client is to make up an imaginative or dramatic story;
- the story is to include what is happening, what led to what is happening, and what will happen,
- Finally, it should include what the story characters are feeling and thinking.

As part of the administration, the examiner unobtrusively records the response latency of each card, i.e., how long it takes the subject to begin a story. The examiner writes down the story as accurately as possible, noting any other responses (such as nervous laughter, facial expressions, etc.). Some examiners use a tape recorder, but such a device may significantly alter the test situation (R. M. Ryan, 1987). The examiner also records the *reaction time that* is the time interval between the initial presentation of a card and the subject's first response. By recording reaction time, the examiner can determine whether the subject has difficulty with a particular card. Because each card is designed to elicit its themes, needs, and conflicts, an abnormally long reaction time may indicate a specific problem. If, for example, the reaction time substantially increases for all cards involving heterosexual relationships, then the examiner may hypothesise that the subject is experiencing difficulty in this area.

Often, after all the stories have been elicited, there is an inquiry phase, where the examiner may attempt to obtain additional information about the stories the client has given. A variety of techniques are used by different examiners, including asking the client to identify the least preferred and most preferred cards.

**Pull of TAT Cards:** TAT cards elicit "typical" responses from many subjects, somewhat like the popular responses on the Rorschach Test. This is called the "pull" of the card, and some have argued that this pull is the most important determinant of a TAT response (Murstein, 1963). Many of the TAT cards are from woodcuts and other art media, with lots of shadings and dark, sometimes indistinguishable details. Because of this stimulus pull, many of the cards elicit stories that are gloomy or melancholic. There is some evidence to suggest that the actual TAT card may be more important than the respondent's "projections" in determining the actual emotional tone of the story (Eron, Terry, & Callahan, 1950).

**Scoring:** H. A. Murray (1938) developed the TAT in the context of a personality theory that saw behaviour as the result of psychobiological and environmental aspects. Thus not only are there *needs* that a person has (both biological needs, such as the need for food and psychological, such as the need to achieve or the need for control), but there are also forces in the environment, called *press*, that can affect the individual. Presumably, the stories given by the individual reflect the combination of such needs and presses, both in an objective sense and as perceived by the person.

There were several attempts to develop comprehensive scoring systems for the TAT. Several manuals are available that can be used (Henry, 1956; Stein, 1981), although none have become the standard way, and ultimately the scoring reflects the examiner's clinical skills and theoretical perspective.

Almost all methods of TAT interpretation take into account the *hero, needs, press, themes,* and *outcomes*. The *hero* is the character in each picture with whom the subject seems to identify. In most cases, the story revolves around one easily recognisable character. If more than one character seems to be important, then the character most like the storyteller is selected as the hero. Of particular importance are the motives and *needs* of the hero. Most systems, including Murray's original, consider the intensity, duration, and frequency of each need to indicate the importance and relevance of that need. In TAT interpretation, *the press* refers to the environmental forces that interfere with or facilitate satisfaction of the various needs. Again, factors such as frequency, intensity, and duration are used to judge the relative importance of these factors. The frequency of various *themes* (for example, depression) and *outcomes* (for example, failures) also indicates their importance.

Analysis of TAT protocols is often impressionistic that is a subjective, intuitive approach where the TAT protocol is perused for such things as repetitive themes, conflicts, slips of the tongue, degree of emotional control, the sequence of stories, etc. As with the Rorschach, the interpretation is not to be done blindly but in accord with other information derived from interviews with the client, other test results, etc.

The utility of the TAT is, in large part, a function of both the specific scoring procedure used and the talent and sensitivity of the individual clinician. Many specific scoring guidelines have also been developed that focus on the measurement of a specific dimension, such as gender identity (May 1966) or achievement motivation (McClelland, Atkinson, Clark, et al., 1953). A recent example is a scoring system designed to measure how people are likely to resolve personal problems; for each card, a total score, as well as four subscale scores, are obtained, and these are aggregated across cards (Ronan, Colavito, & Hammontree, 1993).

**What does the TAT Measure?:** First and foremost, TAT stories are samples of the subject's verbal behaviour. Thus, they can be used to assess the person's intellectual competence, verbal fluency, the capacity to think abstractly, and other cognitive aspects. Second, the TAT represents an ambiguous situation presented by an authority" figure, to which the subject must somehow respond. Thus, some insight can be gained about the person's coping resources, interpersonal skills, and so on. Finally, the TAT responses can be assumed to reflect the individual's psychological functioning, and the needs, conflicts, feelings, etc., expressed in the stories are presumed to reflect the client's perception of the world and inner psychodynamic functioning. TAT stories are said to yield information about the people:

- Thought organisation,
- Emotional responsiveness,
- Psychological needs,
- View of the world,
- Interpersonal relationships,
- Self-concept and

- Coping patterns.

Holt pointed out that the responses to the TAT not only are potentially reflective of a person's unconscious functioning, in a manner parallel to dreams, but there are several determinants" that impact upon the responses obtained. For example, the situational context is very important. Whether a subject is being evaluated as part of court-mandated proceedings or whether the person is an introductory psychology volunteer can make a substantial difference. The "directing set" is also important, i.e., the preconceptions that the person has of what the test, tester, and testing situations are like.

**Reliability:** The determination of the reliability and validity) of the TAT is a rather complex matter because we must ask which scoring system is being used, which variables are scored, and perhaps even what aspects of specific examinees and examiners are involved.

Eron (1955) pointed out that the TAT was a research tool, one of many techniques used to study the fantasy of normal individuals, but that it was quickly adopted for use in the clinic without any serious test of the reliability and validity of the many methods of analysis that were proposed. He pointed out that there are as many ways of analysing TAT stories as there are practitioners, and that few of these methods have been demonstrated to be reliable.

Some would argue that the concept of reliability is meaningless when applied to projective techniques. Even if we don't accept that argument, it is clear that the standard methods of determining reliability are not particularly applicable to the TAT. Each of the TAT cards is unique, so neither split-half nor parallel-form reliability is appropriate. Test-retest reliability is also limited because on the one hand, the test should be sensitive to changes over time, and on the other, the subject may focus on different aspects of the stimulus from one time to another.

The determination of reliability also assumes that extraneous sources of variation are held in check, i.e., the test is standardised. This is not the case with the TAT, where instructions, the sequence of cards, scoring procedure, etc., can vary.

**Validity:** Validity is also a very complex issue, with studies that support the validity of the TAT and studies that do not. Varble (1971) reviewed this issue and indicated that:

- the TAT is not well suited or useful for differential diagnosis;

- the TAT can be useful in the identification of personality variables, although there are studies that support this conclusion and studies that do not;
- different reviewers come to different conclusions ranging from the validity of the TAT is practically nil" to "there is impressive evidence for its validity."

Holt (1951) pointed out that the TAT is not a test in the same sense that an intelligence scale is, but that the TAT reflects a segment of human behaviour that can be analysed in many ways. One might as well ask what is the reliability and validity of everyday behaviour. It is interesting to note that Bellak's (1986) book on the TAT, which is quite comprehensive and often used as a training manual, does not list either reliability or validity in its index. To be a top scorer–Read only GPH book.

**Q8. State the applications and alternative apperception procedures of TAT.**

*Or*

**Write a short note on children's appreciation test.**

**[June-2021, Q.No.-12]**

**Ans.** TAT continues to be used as a tool for research into areas of psychology such as dreams, fantasies, mate selection and what motivates people to choose their occupation. Sometimes it is used in a psychiatric or psychological context to assess personality disorders, thought disorders, in forensic examinations to evaluate crime suspects, or to screen candidates for high-stress occupations. It is also commonly used in routine psychological evaluations, typically without a formal scoring system, as a way to explore emotional conflicts and object relations.

TAT is widely used in France and Argentina using a psychodynamic approach.

David McClelland and Ruth Jacobs conducted a 12-year longitudinal study of leadership using TAT and found no gender differences in motivational predictors of attained management level. The content analysis, however, "revealed 2 distinct styles of power-related themes that distinguished the successful men from the successful women. The successful male managers were more likely to use reactive power [that is, aggressive] themes while the successful female managers were more likely to use resourceful [that is, nurturing] power themes. Differences between the sexes in the power themes were less pronounced among the managers who had remained in lower levels of management."

The TAT is often used in individual assessments of candidates for employment in fields requiring a high degree of skill in dealing with other people and/or ability to cope with high levels of psychological stress, for example, law enforcement, military leadership positions, religious ministry, education, diplomatic service, etc.

Although the TAT should not be used in the differential diagnosis of mental disorders, it is often administered to individuals who have already received a diagnosis to match them with the type of psychological treatment that is best suited to their personalities.

Lastly, the TAT is sometimes used for forensic purposes in evaluating the motivations and general attitudes of persons accused of violent crimes. For example, the TAT was recently administered to a 24-year-old man in prison for a series of sexual murders. The results indicated that his attitudes towards other people are not only outside normal limits but are similar to those of other persons found guilty of the same type of crime.

The TAT can be given repeatedly to an individual as a way of measuring progress in psychotherapy or, in some cases, to help the therapist understand why the treatment seems to be stalled or blocked.

In addition to its application in individual assessments, the TAT is frequently used for research into specific aspects of human personality, most often needs for achievement, fears of failure, hostility and aggression, and interpersonal object relations. "Object relations" is a phrase used in psychiatry and psychology to refer to the ways people internalise their relationships with others and the emotional tone of their relationships.

Research into object relations using the TAT investigates a variety of different topics, including:

- the extent to which people are emotionally involved in relationships with others.
- in their ability to understand the complexities of human relationships.
- their ability to distinguish between their viewpoint on a situation and the perspectives of others involved.
- their ability to control aggressive impulses.

- Self-esteem issues; and issues of personal identity.

For example, one recent study compared responses to the TAT from a group of psychiatric inpatients diagnosed with dissociative disorders with responses from a group of non-dissociative inpatients, to investigate some of the controversies about dissociative identity disorder (formerly called multiple personality disorder).

The versatility and usefulness of the TAT approach are illustrated not only by attempts such as those of Ritzler et al. (1980) to update the test but also by the availability of special forms of the TAT for children and others for the elderly. The Children's Apperception Test (CAT) was created to meet the special needs of children ages three through 10 (Bellak, 1975). The CAT stimuli contain animal rather than human figures as in the TAT. A special children's apperception test has been developed specifically for Latino and Latina children (Malgady, Constantino, & Rogler, 1984).

***Tell Me a Story Test*:** This is a multicultural thematic apperception test designed to use with minority and non-minority children and adolescents with a set of stimulus cards and extensive normative data for each group. The stimulus cards are structured to elicit specific responses and are in colour to facilitate verbalisation and projection of emotional states. It differs from the TAT is the following aspects:

- It focuses on personality functions as manifested in internalised interpersonal relationships rather than on intrapsychic dynamics.
- It consists of 23 cards with chromatic pictures while the TAT has 19 achromatic pictures and one blank card.
- Tell me a story test attempts to elicit meaningful stories indicating conflict resolution of bipolar personality functions while the TAT uses ambiguous stimuli to elicit meaningful stories.
- The Tell me a story stimulus represents the polarities of negative and positive emotions cognitions and interpersonal functions, while the TAT is primarily weighted to represent negative emotions, depressive mood and hostility.
- The Tell Me a Story test stimulus cards are culturally relevant, gender-sensitive and have diminished ambiguity.

The Gerontological Apperception Test uses stimuli in which one or more elderly individuals are involved in a scene with a theme relevant to the concerns of the elderly, such as loneliness and family conflicts (Wolk & Wolk, 1971). The Senior Apperception Technique is an alternative to the Gerontological Apperception Test and is parallel in content (Bellak, 1975; Bellak & Bellak, 1973).

This test measures the experience es of older persons. The scoring criteria were developed to reflect the interpersonal, health-related and intrapsychic dimensions of the experience of later life. There are a total of 20 items. Stories based on the pictures were written down verbatim. The stories received a score of 0 for tolerance and 1 for lack of tolerance. The sample items for the elderly included the following:

- Tolerates loneliness/separateness
- Concern for affiliation with others
- Fear of losing one's place/status in the community
- Concern for heterosexuality-sexual
- Concern for heterosexuality-companionship/sociability

**The Children's Apperception Test (The CAT):** The Children's Apperception Test, often abbreviated as CAT, is an individually administered projective personality test appropriate for children aged three to 10 years.

The CAT is intended to measure the personality traits, attitudes, and psychodynamic processes evident in prepubertal children. By presenting a series of pictures and asking a child to describe the situations and makeup stories about the people or animals in the pictures, an examiner can elicit this information about the child.

The CAT was originally developed to assess psychosexual conflicts related to certain stages of a child's development. Examples of these conflicts include relationship issues, sibling rivalry, and aggression. Today, the CAT is more often used as an assessment technique in clinical evaluation. Clinical diagnoses can be based in part on the Children's Apperception Test and other projective techniques

**Description of CAT:** The Children's Apperception Test was developed by Leopold Bellak and Sonya Sorel Bellak. It was an offshoot of the Thematic Apperception Test(TAT), which was based on Henry Murray's need-based theory of personality. Bellak and Bellak developed the CAT because they saw a need for an apperception test specifically designed for children. The most recent revision of the CAT was published in 1996.

The original CAT featured ten pictures of animals in such human social contexts as playing games or sleeping in a bed. Today, this version is known as the CAT or the CAT-A (for the animal). Animals were chosen for the pictures because it was believed that young children relate better to animals than humans. Each picture is presented by a test administrator in the form of a card. The test is always administered to an individual child; it should never be given in group form. The test is not timed but normally takes 20-30 minutes. It should be given in a quiet room in which the administrator and the child will not be disturbed by other people or activities.

The second version of the CAT, the CAT-H includes ten pictures of human beings in the same situations as the animals in the original CAT. The CAT-H was designed for the same age group as the CAT-A but appeals especially to children aged seven to 10, who may prefer pictures of humans to pictures of animals.

The pictures on the CAT were chosen to draw out children's fantasies and encourage storytelling. Descriptions of the ten pictures are as follows: baby chicks seated around a table with an adult chicken appearing in the background; a large bear and a baby bear playing tug-of-war, a lion sitting on a throne being watched by a mouse through a peephole; a mother kangaroo with a joey (baby kangaroo) in her pouch and an older joey beside her; two baby bears sleeping on a small bed in front of a larger bed containing two bulges, a cave in which two large bears are lying down next to a baby bear; a ferocious tiger leaping towards a monkey who is trying to climb a tree; two adult monkeys sitting on a sofa while another adult monkey talks to a baby monkey; a rabbit sitting on a child's bed viewed through a doorway; and a puppy being spanked by an adult dog in front of a bathroom. The cards in the human version substitute human adults and children for the animals but the situations are the same. Gender identity, however, is more ambiguous in animal pictures than in the human ones. The ambiguity of gender can allow for children to relate to all the child animals in the pictures rather than just the human beings of their sex.

The pictures are meant to encourage the children to tell stories related to competition, illness, injuries, body image, family life, and school situations. The CAT test manual suggests that the administrator should consider the following variables when analysing a child's story about a particular card: the protagonist (the main character) of the story; the primary needs of the protagonist; and the relationship of the main character to his or her environment. The pictures also draw out a child's anxieties, fears, and psychological defences.

**Scoring of CAT:** Scoring of the Children's Apperception Test is not based on objective scales; it must be performed by a trained test administrator or scorer. The scorer's interpretation should take into account the following variables: the story's primary theme; the story's hero or heroine; the needs or drives of the hero or heroine; the environment in which the story takes place; the child's perception of the figures in the picture; the main conflicts in the story; the anxieties and defences expressed in the story; the function of the child's superego; and the integration of the child's ego.

Consider, for example, the card in which a ferocious tiger leaps towards a monkey who is trying to climb a tree. A child may talk about his or her fears of aggression or punishment. The monkey may be described as a hero escaping punishment from the evil tiger. This storyline may represent the child's perceived need to escape punishment from an angry parent or a bully. Conversely, a child may perceive the picture in a relatively harmless way, perhaps seeing the monkey and tiger playing an innocent game.

A projective test like the CAT allows for a wide variety of acceptable responses. There is no "incorrect" response to the pictures. The scorer is responsible for coherently interpreting the child's responses to make the test useful as a clinical assessment technique. It is recommended practice for the administrator to obtain the child's personal and medical history before giving the CAT, to provide a context for what might otherwise appear to be abnormal responses. For example, it would be normal under the circumstances for a child whose pet has just died to tell stories that include themes of grief or loss even though most children would not respond to the cards in that way.

A person scoring the CAT has considerable flexibility in interpretation. He or she can use the analysis of a child's responses to support a psychological diagnosis, provide a basis for a clinical evaluation, or gain insight into the child's internal psychological structure.

**Precautions:** A psychologist or other professional person who is administering the CAT must be trained in its usage and interpretation and should be familiar with the psychological theories underlying the pictures. Because of the subjective nature of interpreting and analysing CAT results, caution should be used in concluding the test results. Most clinical psychologists recommend using the CAT in conjunction with other psychological tests designed for children. The CAT is frequently criticised for its lack of objective scoring, its reliance on the scorer's scoring method and bias, and the lack of accepted evidence for its reliability (consistency of results) and validity (effectiveness in measuring what it was designed to measure). For example, no clear evidence exists that the test measure's needs, conflicts, or other processes related to human motivations validly and reliably.

**Q9. What is the meaning and procedure of personality testing?**

***Or***

**Write a short note on 'the sixteen personality factor (16PF).**

**[June-2019, Q.No.-10]**

***Or***

**Explain the concept of personality and psychological functioning in personality testing.** **[Dec-2020, Q.No.-9]**

**Ans.** A personality test is a method of assessing human personality constructs. Most personality assessment instruments (despite being loosely referred to as "personality tests") are in fact introspective (i.e., subjective) self-report questionnaire (Q-data, in terms of LOTS data) measures or reports from life records (L-data) such as rating scales. Attempts to construct actual performance tests of personality have been very limited even though Raymond Cattell with his colleague Frank Warburton compiled a list of over 2000 separate objective tests that could be used in constructing objective personality tests. One exception however, was the Objective-Analytic Test Battery, a performance test designed to quantitatively measure 10 factor-analytically discerned personality trait dimensions. A major problem with both L-data and Q-data methods is that because of item transparency, rating scales and self-report questionnaires are highly susceptible to motivational and response distortion ranging all the way from lack of adequate self-insight (or biased perceptions of others) to downright dissimulation (faking good/faking bad) depending on the reason/motivation for the assessment being undertaken.

**Personality and Psychological Functioning:** Each human being has a unique manner of interacting with the world. Some people tend to be shy and withdrawn, while others are generally outgoing and gregarious. Some tend to be anxious worriers, while others are generally calm and relaxed. Some are highly organised and pay attention to detail, while others are disorganised and impressionistic.

Personality refers to the enduring styles of thinking and behaving when interacting with the world (Hogan, Hogan, & Roberts, 1996; MacKinnon, 1944; McCrae & Costa, 2003). Thus, it includes characteristic patterns that make each person unique. These characteristics can be assessed and compared with those of others. Personality is influenced by biological, psychological, and social factors. For example, research has shown that between 20 per cent and 60 per cent of the variance in personality traits (e.g., extroversion, sociability) are influenced by genetic factors, with the remainder influenced by psychosocial factors (e.g., relationships that develop with parents, siblings, and friends, as well as life events. While the nature versus nurture debate rages on well beyond statistical models, personality development clearly reflects biological, psychological and social factors.

**Personality Inventories:** Personality theories provide a way to understand how people develop, change, and experience generally stable and enduring behaviour and thinking patterns. These theories also help us to understand the differences among people that make each person unique. Ultimately, personality theory is used to understand and predict behaviour. This understanding is then used to develop intervention strategies to help people change problematic patterns.

Psychological functioning is a more general term referring to the individual's cognitive personality, and emotional worlds. Thus, psychological functioning includes personality as well as other aspects of emotional, behavioural, cognitive, and interpersonal functioning.

Here psychological functioning refers to particularly non-cognitive areas of functioning such as mood and interpersonal relationships. For example, while anxiety, depression, and anger may all be enduring personality traits, they can also be temporary mood states. Someone facing stressful life events, such as the death of a loved one or criminal victimisation, may experience severe anxiety, depression, or anger. However, these mood states may not be associated with enduring personality characteristics. Thus, the individual may feel and behave in an anxious or depressed manner as a reaction to the stressful event(s) but does not tend to be anxious or depressed most of the time. Therefore, psychological functioning can be viewed as encompassing the gamut of component psychological processes as they impact one's ability to cope with life's pleasures and demands and uniquely combine to define personality

A review of the empirical literature on the dimensional models pertinent to individuals' mental representations of self and others and subsequent empirical analyses suggest that the following components are most central in comprising a personality functioning continuum:

(1) **Identity**: Experience of oneself as unique, with boundaries between self and others; a coherent sense of time and personal history; stability and accuracy of self-appraisal and self-esteem; capacity for a range of emotional experience and its regulation. *Self-direction:* Pursuit of coherent and meaningful short-term and life goals; utilisation of constructive and prosocial internal standards of behaviour, ability to self-reflect productively.

(2) **Interpersonal**

  (i) **Empathy:** Comprehension and appreciation of others' experiences and motivations; tolerance of differing perspectives; understanding of social causality.

  (ii) **Intimacy:** Depth and duration of connection with others; desire and capacity for closeness; mutuality of regard reflected in interpersonal behaviour.

In applying these dimensions, self and interpersonal difficulties should not be better understood as a norm within an individual's dominant culture.

**Self and Interpersonal Functioning Continuum:** Although the degree of disturbance of the self and interpersonal domains is continuously distributed, in practice it is useful to consider levels of impairment in functioning for efficient clinical characterisation and treatment planning and prognosis. Patients' conceptualisation of self and others affects the nature of interaction with mental health professionals and can have a significant impact on treatment efficacy and outcome. The following continuum uses each of the dimensions listed above to differentiate five levels of self-interpersonal functioning impairment: No impairment, Mild impairment, Moderate impairment

In addition to using interviews, observations, checklists, inventories, and even biological assessments (e.g., neuroimaging techniques such as PET scans), clinical psychologists generally use a range of tests to assess personality and psychological functioning. *M*ost of these tests can be classified as either objective or projective.

Objective testing presents very specific questions (e.g., Do you feel sad more days than not?) or statements (e.g., I feel rested) to which the person responds by using specific answers (e.g., yes/no, true/false, multiple-choice) or a rating scale (e.g., 1 = strongly disagree, 10 = strongly agree). Scores are tabulated and then compared with those of reference groups, using national norms. Thus, scores that reflect specific constructs (e.g., anxiety, depression, psychotic thinking, stress) may be compared to determine exactly how anxious, depressed, psychotic, or stressed someone might be relative to the norm.

Projective testing uses ambiguous or unstructured testing stimuli such as inkblots, incomplete sentences, or pictures of people engaged in various activities. Rather than answering specific questions using specific structured responses (e.g., yes/no, true/false, agree/disagree) subjects are asked to respond freely to the testing stimuli. For example, they are asked to tell stories about pictures or describe what they see in an inkblot, or say the first thing that comes to their mind when hearing a word or sentence fragment. The theory behind projective testing is that unconscious or conscious needs, interests, dynamics, and motivations are projected onto the ambiguous testing stimuli, thereby revealing the internal dynamics of personality. Projective responses are generally much more challenging to score and interpret than objective responses.

**Objective Testing:** There are hundreds of objective tests of personality and psychological functioning. Clinical psychologists usually employ a small set of objective tests to evaluate personality and psychological functioning. By far the most commonly used testis the Minnesota Multi Phasic Personality Inventory (MMPI), now in its second edition (MMPI-2). The MMPI also includes an adolescent version called the Minnesota Multiphasic Personality Inventory-Adolescents (MMPIA).

**The Minnesota Multiphasic Personality Inventory (MMPI, MMPI-2, MMPIA):** The original MMPI was developed during the late 1930s and published in 1943 by psychologist Starke Hathaway and psychiatrist J. C. McKinley. The MMPI was revised and became available as the MMPI-2 in 1989. The original MMPI consisted of 550 true/false items. The items were selected from a series of other personality tests and the developer's clinical experience to provide psychiatric diagnoses for mental patients. The original pool of about 1000 test items was considered and about 500 items were administered to psychiatric patients and visitors at the University of Minnesota hospitals. The MMPI was designed to be used with individuals ages 16 through adulthood. However, the test has been frequently used with adolescents younger than 16. The MMPI takes about one to one-and-a-half hours to complete.

Scoring the MMPI results in four validity measures and ten clinical measures. The validity measures include the? (Cannot Say), L(Lie), F (Validity), and K (Correction) scales. Admitting too many problems or "faking bad" is reflected in an inverted V configuration with low scores on the L and K scales and a high score on the F scale. Presenting oneself in a favourable light or "faking good" is reflected in a V configuration with high scores on the L and K scales and a low score on the F scale. The clinical scales include Hypochondriasis (Hs), Depression (D), Conversion Hysteria (Hy), Psychopathic deviate (Pd), Masculinity/femininity (Mf), Paranoia (Pa), Psychasthenia (Pt), Schizophrenia (Sc), Hypomania (Ma), and Social Introversion (Si). Scores are normed using standardised *T*-scores, meaning that each scale has a mean of 50 and a standard deviation of 10. Scores above 65 (representing one and one half standard deviations above the mean) are considered elevated and in the clinical range. While 65 is the cut-off score on the MMPI-2 and MMPI-A, *70* is used with the original MMPI. Since the MMPI was originally published, several additional subscales have been developed, including measures such as Repression, Anxiety, Ego Strength, Over controlled Hostility, and Dominance. It has been estimated that there are over 400 subtests of the MMPI (Dahlstrom, Welsh, & Dahlstrom, 1975). The MMPI has been used in well over 10,000 studies that examine a wide range of clinical issues and problems (Graham, 1990).

Although the original MMPI was the most widely used psychological test, a revision was needed. For example, the MMPI did not use a representative sample when it was constructed. The original sample included Caucasians living in the Minneapolis, Minnesota, area who were either patients or visitors at the University of Minnesota hospitals. Also, many of the more sophisticated methods of test construction and analysis used today were not available in the late 1930s when the test was developed. Therefore, during the late 1980s, the test was re standardised and many of the test items were rewritten. Furthermore, many new test items were added, and outdated items were eliminated. The resulting MMPI 2 consists of 567 items and can be used with individuals aged 18through adulthood. The MMPI-2 uses the same validity and clinical scale names as the MMPI. Importantly, many have noted that the names reflecting each of the MMPI (or MMPI-2) scales are misleading. For example, a high score on the Schizophrenia (Sc) scale does not necessarily mean that the person who completed the test is Projective Techniques in Psychodiagnostics schizophrenic. Therefore, many clinicians and researchers prefer to ignore the scale names and use numbers to reflect each scale instead. For example, the Schizophrenia (Sc) scale is referred to as Scale 8.

Like the original MMPI, the MMPI-2 has numerous subscales, including measures such as Type A behaviour, post-traumatic stress, obsessions, and fears.

**The Minnesota Multiphasic Personality Inventory Adolescent (MMPI-A) (Butcher et al., 1992):** This was developed for use with teens between the ages of 14 and 18. The MMPI-A has 478 true/false items and includes several validity measures in addition to those available in the MMPI and MMPI-2. The MMPI, MMPI 2, and MMPI-A can be scored by hand using templates for each scale or they can be computer scored. Most commercially available computer scoring programs offer in-depth interpretive reports that fully describe the testing results and offer suggestions for treatment or other interventions. Scores are typically interpreted by reviewing the entire resulting profile rather than individual scale scores. Profile analysis is highlighted by examining pairs of high scores combinations. For example, high scores on the first three scales of the MMPI are referred to as the neurotic triad reflecting anxiety, depression, and somatic complaints. Research indicates that the MMPI, MMPI-2, and MMPI-A have acceptable reliability, stability, and validity (Butcher et al., 1989; Butcher et al., 1992; Graham, 1990; Parker et al., 1988).

However, controversy exists concerning many aspects of the test. For example, the Mac Andrew Scale was designed as a supplementary scale to classify those people with alcohol-related problems. The validity of the scale has been criticised and some authors have suggested that the scale no longer be used to examine alcohol problems (Gottesman & Prescott, 1989).

**The Millon Clinical Multiaxial Inventories:** The Millon Clinical Multiaxial Inventories (MCMI) include several tests that assess personality functioning using the *DSM-IV* classification system and the Theodore Millon theory of personality (Millon, 1981). Unlike the MMPI-2, the Millon was specifically designed to assess personality disorders outlined in the DSM such as histrionic, borderline, paranoid, and obsessive-compulsive personalities. The first Millon test was published in 1982; additional tests and revisions quickly developed during the 1980sand 1990s. The current tests include the Milion Clinical Multiaxial Inventory-III (MCM HI; Millon, Millon, & Davis, 1994), the Millon Adolescent Clinical Inventory (MACI; Millon et al., 1994), the Millon Behavioural Health Inventory (MBHI; Millon, Green, & Meagher, 1982), the Millon Clinical Multiaxial Inventory-II (MCMI-II; Millon, 1987), and the Millon Adolescent Personality Inventory (MAPI; Millon, Millon, & Davis, 1982).

The MBHI, however, is a health behaviour inventory and not a measure of personality or psychological functioning per se. The *M*CMI-II will be highlighted here. The MCMI-III is a 175 true/false item questionnaire designed for persons aged 18 through adulthood and takes approximately 30 minutes to complete. It was designed to assess personality disorders and syndromes based on the *DSM IV* system of classification. The MCMI-III includes 24scales, including 14 personality pattern scales and 10 clinical syndrome scales. Furthermore, the MCMI-III also includes several validity measures.

**The Sixteen Personality Factors (16PF):** The 16PF was developed by Raymond Cattell and colleagues and is currently in its fifth edition (Cattell, Cattell, & Cattell, 1993). It is a 185 item multiple-choice questionnaire that takes approximately 45 minutes to complete. The 16 PF is administered to individuals aged 16 years through adulthood. Scoring the 16PF results in 16 primary personality traits (e.g., apprehension prone) and five global -factors that assess second-order personality characteristics (e.g., anxiety). Standardised scores from 1 to 10 or ten scores are used with means set at 5 and a standard deviation of 2. The 16 PF has been found to have acceptable stability, reliability, and validity (Anastasi & Urbina, 1996; Cattell et al., 1993).

**The Neo-Personality Inventory-Revised:** The NEO-PI-R (Costa & McCrae, 1985, 1989, 1992) is a 240 item questionnaire that uses a 5-point rating system. A brief 60-item version of the NEO-PI-R called the NEO-Five Factor Inventory (NEO-FF) is also available as well as an observer rating version (Form R). The NEO-PI-R measures the big five personality dimensions: neuroticism, extroversion, openness, agreeableness, and conscientiousness. The *big five* or the five-factor model is consistent personality dimensions from factor analytic research conducted for over 40 years and across many cultures (Digman, 1990; McCrae & Costa, 2003). To be a top scorer–Read only GPH book.

**Q10. Write short notes on the followings:**

**(i) The Edwards Personal Preference Schedule (EPPS)**

**Ans.** Two theoretical influences resulted in the creation of the EPPS. The first is the theory proposed by Henry Murray (1938) which, among other aspects, catalogued a set of needs as primary dimensions of behaviour, for example, need achievement, need affiliation, need heterosexuality. A second theoretical focus is the issue of *social desirability*. A. L. Edwards (1957) argued that a person's response to a typical personality inventory item may be more reflective of how desirable that response is than the actual behaviour of the person. Thus a true response to the item, "I am loyal to my friends" may be given not because the person is loyal, but because the person perceives that saying "true" is socially desirable.

A. L. Edwards developed a pool of items designed to assess 15 needs taken from Murray's system. Each of the items was rated by a group of judges as to how socially desirable endorsing the item would be. Edwards then placed together pairs of items that were judged to be equivalent in social desirability, and the task for the subject was to choose one item from each pair.

Each of the scales on the EPPS is then composed of 28 forced-choice items, where an item to measure need Achievement, for example, is paired off with items representative of each of the other 14 needs, and this done twice per comparison. Subjects choose from each pair the one statement that is more characteristic of them, and the chosen underlying need is given one point. The EPPS, like most other personality inventories, is commercially available, a group test, a self-report paper and pencil inventory, with no time limit, designed to assess what the subject typically does, rather than maximal performance.

The EPPS is designed primarily for research and counselling purposes, and the 15 needs (such as Achievement, Deference, Order, Exhibition, Autonomy, Affiliation, Interception) that are scaled are presumed to be relatively independent normal personality variables. The EPPS is easy to administer and is designed to be administered within the typical 50 minute class hour. There are two answer sheets available, one for hand scoring and one for machine scoring. The test manual gives both internal consistency (corrected split-half coefficients based on a sample of 1,509 subjects), and test-retest coefficients (1-week interval, $n = 89$); the ' corrected split-half coefficients range from +.60for the need Deference scale to +.87 for the need Heterosexuality scale. The test-retest coefficients range from +.74 for need Achievement and need Exhibition, to +.88 for need basement. The test manual presents little data on validity, and many subsequent studies that have used the EPPS have assumed that the scales were valid. The results do seem to support that assumption, although there is little direct evidence of the validity of the EPPS.

**(ii) The California Psychological Inventory (CPI)**

**Ans.** The California Psychological Inventory (CPI) is a self-report inventory created by Harrison G. Gough and currently published by Consulting Psychologists Press. The text containing the test was first published in 1956, and the most recent revision was published in 1996. It was created in a similar manner to the Minnesota Multiphasic Personality Inventory (MMPI)—with which it shares 194 items. But unlike the MMPI, which focuses on maladjustment or clinical diagnosis, the CPI was created to assess the everyday "folk-concepts" that ordinary people use to describe the behaviour of the people around them.

The CPI is usually presented as an example of a strictly empirical inventory, but that is not quite correct. First of all, of the 18 original scales, 5 were constructed rationally, and 4 of these 5 were constructed using the method of internal consistency analysis. Second, although 13 of the scales were constructed empirically, for many of them there was an explicit theoretical framework that guided the development; for example, the

Socialisation scale came out of a role theory framework. Finally, with the 1987 revision, there is now a very explicit theory of human functioning incorporated in the inventory. The 20 scales (for example Dominance, Capacity, Sociability, Responsibility, Socialisation, etc.) are arranged in four groups; these groupings are the result of logical analyses and are intended to aid in the interpretation of the profile, although the groupings are also supported by the results of factor analyses. Group I scales measure interpersonal style and orientation, and relate to such aspects as self-confidence, poise, and interpersonal skills. Group II scales relate to normative values and orientation, to such aspects as responsibility and rule respecting behaviour. Group III scales are related to cognitive intellectual functioning. Finally, Group IV scales measure personal style. The basic goal of the CPI is to assess those everyday variables that ordinary people use to understand and predict their behaviour and that of others. This is termed by Gough as folk concepts. These folk concepts are presumed to be universal, found in all cultures, and therefore relevant to both personal and interpersonal behaviour. The CPI then is a personality inventory designed to be taken by a "normal" adolescent or adult person, with no time limit, but usually taking 45 to 60 minutes. In addition to the 20 standard scales, there are currently some 13 "special purpose scales" such as, for example, a "work orientation" scale (Gough, 1985) and a "creative temperament" scale (Gough, 1992). The 1987 revision of the CPI also included three "vector" or structural scales, which taken together generate a theoretical model of personality.

The first vector scale called "v1" relates to introversion extraversion, while the second vector scale, "v2," relates to norm accepting vs. norm questioning behaviour. Classification of individuals according to these two vectors yields a four-fold typology. According to this typology, people can be broadly classified into one of four types: the alphas who are typically leaders and doers, who are action-oriented, and rule respecting; the betas who also rule respecting but are more reserved and benevolent; the gammas, who are the sceptics and innovators, and finally, the deltas who focus more on their private world and maybe visionary or maladapted.

Finally, a third vector scale, "v3," was developed with higher scores on this scale relating to a stronger sense of self-realisation and fulfilment. These three vector scales, which are relatively uncorrelated with each other, lead to what Gough (1987) calls the cuboid model. The raw scores on "v3" can be changed into one of seven different levels, from door to superior each level defined in terms of the degree of self-realisation and fulfilment achieved. Thus the actual behaviour of each of the four basic types is also a function of the level reached on "v3"; a delta at the lower levels may be quite maladapted and enmeshed in conflicts while a delta at the higher levels may be highly imaginative and creative.

As with other personality inventories described so far, the CPI requires little by way of administrative skills. It can be administered to one individual or hundreds of subjects at a sitting. The directions are clear and the inventory can be typically completed in 45 to 60 minutes. The CPI has been translated into several different languages, including Italian, French, German, Japanese, and Mandarin Chinese.

The CPI can be scored manually through the use of templates or by machine. Several computer services are available, including scoring of the standard scales, the vector scales, and several special-purpose scales, as well as detailed computer-generated reports, describing with almost uncanny accuracy what the client is like. The scores are plotted on a profile sheet so that raw scores are transformed into *T*-scores. The book you can believe most–GPH book.

# *QUESTION PAPERS*

# Psychodiagnostics: MPCE-12

## June, 2019

*Note: All sections are compulsory.*

### SECTION – A

**Answer any two from the following questions in about 450 words each:**

**Q1. Discuss the various stages in psychodiagnostic assessment.**

**Ans.** Psychological assessment is a process of testing that uses a combination of techniques to help arrive at some hypotheses about a person and their behaviour, personality and capabilities. The process involves various stages or steps as outlined below. A psychological assessment can be most useful when it addresses specific individual problems and provides guidelines for decision making regarding these problems. Therefore, throughout these phases, psychologist integrates data and serves as an expert on human behaviour rather than merely an interpreter of test scores.

These steps are looked at separately so that they are easy to understand. However, practically they often occur together and may interact with each other:

**(1) Prepare for the assessment:** The psychologist prepares to undertake the assessment. For this he understands the patient's problem, evaluates the referral question and plans rest of the assessment process.

***Understand the Problem:*** The clinician goes through the history of the patient, and uses other methods to develop a perspective on the problem. Clinician is aware of the advantages and limitations of psychological tests, and they are responsible for providing useful information, therefore, it is his duty to clarify the received requests. He may need to uncover hidden agendas, unspoken expectations, and complex interpersonal relationships, as well as explain the specific limitations of psychological tests.

***Evaluating the Referral Question:*** Many of the practical limitations of psychological evaluations result from an inadequate clarification of the problem. Clinicians rarely are asked to give a general or global assessment, but instead are asked to answer specific questions. To address these questions, it is sometimes helpful to contact the referral source at different stages in the assessment process. The information derived from such an observation might be relayed back to the referral source for further clarification or modification of the referral question.

***Plan the Assessment Process:*** *Based* on his learning from the previous steps the clinician plans the rest of the assessment process. He needs to take decisions regarding gathering data, and how to interpret it and finally how to use the output.

**(2) Gather Inputs:** Once he has sufficient understanding of the problem, the next step for the clinician is to gather inputs related to the problem. For this he conducts a Mental Status Examination and deploys measures to acquire knowledge related to the content of the problem. The data collected during the process contributes to the differential diagnosis for the patient.

***Mental Status Examination:*** MSE is a subjective method of collecting data about the patient. It starts with observing the patient the minute he enters the office and moves onto an interview. The clinician tries to gather data related to patient's thought process, patient history, social history, the patient's affect, his sensorium and cognition.

***Build Content Knowledge:*** It is essential that clinicians have in-depth knowledge about the variables they are measuring or their evaluations are likely to be extremely limited.

Clinicians may need to refer both the test manual and additional outside sources. Clinicians should be familiar with operational definitions for problems such as anxiety disorders, psychoses, personality disorders, or organic impairment so that they can be alert to their possible expression during the assessment procedure.

Examiner also needs to consider the problem in relation to the adequacy of the test and decide whether a specific test or tests can be appropriately used on an individual or group. This demands knowledge in such areas as the client's age, sex, ethnicity, race, educational background, motivation for testing, anticipated level of resistance, social environment, and interpersonal relationships. Finally, clinicians need to assess the effectiveness or utility of the test in aiding the treatment process.

***Data Collection:*** Next the clinicians proceed with the actual collection of information. This may come from a wide variety of sources, the most frequent of which are test scores, personal history, behavioural observations, and interview data. Clinicians may also find it useful to obtain school records, previous psychological observations, medical records, police reports, or discuss the client with parents or teachers.

The case history provides a context for understanding the client's current problems and, through this understanding, renders the test scores meaningful. For specific problem solving and decision making, clinicians must rely on multiple sources and, using these sources, assess the consistency of the observations they make.

**(3) Processing the data and interpreting it to get the output:** Once the data is collected. It is organised, analysed and then interpreted to get output. Once the output is ready it is to be communicated and decisions on further clinical actions are made.

The end product of assessment should be a description of the client's present level of functioning, considerations relating to etiology, prognosis, and treatment recommendations. Further elaborations may also attempt to assess the person from a systems perspective - patterns of interaction, mutual two-way influences, and the specifics of circular information feedback.

An additional crucial area is to use the data to develop an effective plan for intervention.

The description should rather provide a deeper and more accurate understanding of the person which allows the examiner to perceive new facets of the person in terms of both his or her internal experience and his or her relationships with others. To develop these descriptions, clinicians must make inferences from their test data.

The process of developing hypotheses, obtaining support for these hypotheses, and integrating the conclusions is dependent on the experience and training of the clinician. Maloney and Ward (1976) have conceptualised a seven-phase approach to evaluating data as explained below:

Phase 1: Collect data about the client

Phase 2: Develop inferences about the client

Phase 3: Accept, reject or modify the inferences

Phase 4: Develop and begin to elaborate on statements relating to the client.

Phase 5: Integration and correlation of the client's characteristics to develop a dynamic model of the person

Phase 6: place this comprehensive description of the person into a situational context

Phase 7: makes specific predictions regarding his or her behaviour.

**Q2. Elucidate the various types of interviews conducted by clinical psychologists.**

**Ans.** There are many different forms of interviews conducted by psychologists. Some interviews are conducted prior to admission to a clinic or hospital, some are conducted to determine if a patient is in danger of injuring themselves or someone else, some are conducted to determine a diagnosis. Whereas some Interviews are highly structured with specific questions asked for all patients, others are unstructured and spontaneous. In this section the common forms of clinical interviews will be briefly discussed. Some important forms of interview are:

- The intake/admission interview
- The case history interview
- Mental status examination interview
- The crisis interview
- Diagnostic interview
- Structured interview

**The Intake/Admission Interview**

According to Watson; "This type of interview is usually concerned with clarification of the patient's percentage complaints,the steps he has taken previously to resolve his difficulties and his expectances in regard to what may be done for him".

The purpose of the initial intake interview or admission interview is to develop a better understanding of the patient's symptoms or concerns in order to recommend the most appropriate treatment or intervention plan. Whether the interview is conducted for admission to a hospital, an outpatient clinic, a private practice, or some other setting the initial interview attempts to evaluate the patient's situation as efficiently as possible.

Ordinarily a psychiatric social worker conducts this interview; however, upon occasion, the psychologist, one of the physician, or a psychiatric nurse may serve as intake interviewer. The basic question to be dealt with is "Why is the patient here?, i.e., what doe she says is the matter with him? Important but secondary questions involve information about previous hospitalisation, the name of his doctors, what the patient expect from treatment, his availability for treatment, and the like.

**Case History Interview:** In many hospitals and clinics the intake or admission interview is followed immediately by the personal and social history interview. The same person usually a psychiatric social worker, commonly conduct both interviews, often in one sitting. Sources of information other then the patient himself are, of course, utilised when completing a personal and social history report. Frequently, the patient does not remember or cannot for other reasons communicate material which may have a bearing upon his problem. Thus, information from friends, relatives, hospital, military, and other records are also used for the history. But whatever the source of information, the purposes of the social and personal history report is to gather information which will be helpful in diagnosing and treating the patient's disorder.

Frequent job changes, for example, may be evidence of general instability. The adult schizophrenic who showed marked apathy and withdrawal symptoms as a preschool child is probably more severely afflicted than patients whom symptoms appeared more recently. Neurotic symptoms which appear after the divorce of parents may have different etiology than similar symptoms which appear after the head injury.

In most instances a standardised form or social history guide of some sort is used. There are advantages in using a standardised printed form, as Louttite has noted in that pertinent information will not be skipped; however as he also notes, a rigid dependency upon the form may ensue. Certain obvious information may not be recorded because the form does not call for it or details which are unimportant for a particular case may be set down in time wasting abundance. Obviously the common sense of the interviewer is the answer to such problems.

**Mental Status Examination Interview:** Often a mental status examination interview is conducted to screen the patient's level of psychological functioning and the presence or absence of abnormal mental phenomena such as delusions, delirium, or dementia. Mental status exams include a brief evaluation and observation of the patient's appearance and manner, speech characteristics, mood, thought processes, insight, judgement, attention, concentration, memory, and orientation.

Results from the mental status examination provide preliminary information about the likely psychiatric diagnosis experienced by the patient as well as offering some direction for further assessment and intervention (e.g. referred to a specialist, admission to psychiatric unit, and evaluation for medical problems that impact psychological functioning). For instance, mental status interviews typically include questions and tasks to determine orientation to time (e.g., "what day is it? What month is it?), place (e.g., Where are you now? Which hospital are you in?"), and person ("who am I who is the president of United States?"). Also, the mental status interview asses short-term memory (e.g. "I am going to name three objects I'd like you to try and remember: dog, pencil, and vase") and attention- concentration (e.g., "count down by 7s starting at 100. For example 100, 93, and so forth").

**The Crisis Interview:** A crisis interview occur when the patient is in the middle of a significant and often traumatic or life threatening crisis. The psychologists or the mental health professionals (e.g., a trained volunteer) might encounter such a situation while working at a suicide or poison control hotline, an emergency room, a community mental health clinic, a student health service on campus, or in many other settings. The nature of the emergency dictates a rapid, "get to the point" style of interview as well as quick decision making in the context of a calming style. For example, it may be critical to determine whether the person is at significant risk of hurting him-or herself or others. Or it may be important to determine whether the alcohol, drugs, or any other substances are used, so as to make sure that the clinician interviews the person in a calming and clear headed manner while asking critical questions in order to deal with the situation effectively.

The interviewer may need to be more directive (e.g., encouraging the person to phone the police, unload a gun, provide instructions to induce vomiting, or step away from a tall building or bridge); break confidentiality if the person (or someone else, such as a child) is in serious and immediate danger, or enlist the help of others (e.g., police department, ambulance).

**The Diagnostic Interview:** The purpose of the screening or diagnostic interview is to assist the clinician in his attempt to understand the patient.

If the level of diagnostic understanding required is merely a separation of the fit from the unfit, as in military neuro-psychiatric examinations, the interview task is one of screening. That is, after a brief interview the interviewee be adjusted fit for specific duties, such as a regular military assignment, or he may be referred for prolonged observation and extended psychological testing. Occasionally, limit or trial duty may be recommended as an alternative to regular duty of psychological observation. Upon other occasions the diagnostic task is highly specific, and a detailed level of understanding is required. This may involve a diagnostic label as categorised as "paranoid schizophrenia" and a description of personality dynamics. In the later case primary dependence is not placed upon the interview alone, for psychological tests play a most important role in such detailed diagnostic procedures.

In the diagnostic interview, while the examination progresses, the interviewer observes the interviewee's behaviour as well as noticing the content of his answers. Thus thighs pressed together, a mincing walk, and fluttery feminine gestures in a male should lead the interviewer to suspect and investigate the possibility of homosexuality. The bubbling, enthusiastic replies and exaggerated gestures in another interview should lead the interviewer to hypothesise tentatively a manic condition and seek further evidence. Similarly, as Wittson, et al. noted, the psychopath often gives evidence of his deviation by his utter impersonality or even belligerence towards the interviewer.

**Structured Interview:** In an effort to increase the reliability and validity of clinical interviews, a number of structured interviews have been developed. These interviews include very specific questions asked in a detailed flow chart format. The goal is to obtain necessary information, to make an appropriate diagnosis, to determine whether a patient is appropriate for a specific treatment or research program, and to secure critical data that are needed for patient care. The questions are generally organised and developed in a decision tree format. If a patient answers yes to particular questions (for example, about panic), the list of additional questions might be asked to obtain details and clarification.

**Q3. Discuss ethical issues in assessment.**

**Ans.** Refer to Chapter-1, Q.No.-14

**Q4. Trace the historical development of intelligence assessment. Elucidate Wechsler scales for adults.**

**Ans.** Refer to Chapter-3, Q.No.-1, 2

## SECTION – B

**Answer any four of the following questions in about 250 words each:**

**Q5. Discuss Neuropsychological testing.**

**Ans.** Refer to Chapter-4, Q.No.-3

**Q6. Discuss the application of Thematic Apperception Test.**

**Ans.** Refer to Chapter-4, Q.No.-2

**Q7. Discuss the various controversies with regard to IQ testing.**

**Ans.** Refer to Chapter-3, Q.No.-5

**Q8. Define memory. Elucidate the assessment of different memory systems.**

**Ans.** Refer to Chapter-3, Q.No.-10

**Q9. Discuss the format for writing psychological report.**

**Ans.** Refer to Chapter-2, Q.No.-13

## SECTION – C

**Write short notes on any two of the following in about 100 words each:**

**Q10. The Sixteen Personality Factor (16PF)**

**Ans.** Refer to Chapter-4, Q.No.-9

**Q11. Disguised field observations**

**Ans.** Refer to Chapter-1, Q.No.-7

**Q12. Invasion of privacy**

**Ans.** Refer to Chapter-1, Q.No.-14

# Psychodiagnostics: MPCE-012

## December, 2019

*Note: All sections are compulsory.*

### SECTION – A

**Answer any two from the following questions in about 450 words each:**

**Q1. What are the characteristics of tests of abstraction? Discuss the specialised tests of abstract reasoning and concrete behaviour.**

**Ans.** Refer to Chapter-3, Q.No.-6, 8

**Q2. Explain the measurement of personality and psychological functioning. Discuss any one objective measure of personality testing.**

**Ans.** Refer to Chapter-4, Q.No.-9

**Q3. Discuss the general guidelines for writing a psychological report.**

**Ans.** Refer to Chapter-2, Q.No.-13

**Q4. Discuss the mental status examination in psychodiagnostics. What are the specific areas to cover in mental status examination?**

**Ans.** Refer to Chapter-2, Q.No.-6

### SECTION – B

**Answer any four of the following questions in about 250 words each:**

**Q5. Discuss any two projective tests.**

**Ans.** Refer to Chapter-4, Q.No.-2

**Q6. What do you understand by psychological assessment in clinical context? Discuss the practical application of psychological assessment.**

**Ans.** Refer to Chapter-1, Q.No.-4

**Q7. Describe Wechsler's scales for children.**

**Ans.** Refer to Chapter-3, Q.No.-2

**Q8. Define creativity. Explain Torrance test of creative thinking.**

**Ans.** Refer to Chapter-3, Q.No.-11

**Q9. Discuss the areas to be covered in a diagnostic interview.**

**Ans.** Refer to Chapter-2, Q.No.-1 (vii)

## SECTION – C

**Write short notes on any two of the following in about 100 words each:**

**Q10. Projective Drawings**

**Ans.** Refer to Chapter-4, Q.No.-2

**Q11. Psychophysiological Assessment**

**Ans.** Refer to Chapter-1, Q.No.-8

**Q12. Explicit and Implicit Memory**

**Ans.** Refer to Chapter-3, Q.No.-10

❑❑❑

**Education's purpose is to replace an empty mind with an open one.**

# Psychodiagnostics: MPCE-012

## June, 2020

*Note: All sections are compulsory.*

### SECTION – A

**Answer any two from the following questions in about 450 words each:**

**Q1. Discuss the importance of interview in clinical assessments. Describe the skills and techniques required for effective interviewing.**

**Ans.** The clinical interview is the most widely used method of clinical assessment and is particularly advantageous in the early stages of assessment. The most salient of its advantages is flexibility. The typical interview begins with a broad-based inquiry regarding the client's functioning. As the interview progresses, it becomes more focussed on specific problems and potential controlling variables. Interviewing also provides an opportunity to directly observe the client's behaviour, and to begin developing a therapeutic relationship.

The clinical interview also has important disadvantages. Interviews elicit information from memory that can be subject to errors, omissions, or distortions. Additionally, the interview often relies heavily on the clinician to make subjective judgements in selecting those issues that warrant further assessment or inquiry. One could reasonably expect that different clinicians could emerge from a clinical interview with very different conceptualisations of the client. Structured and semi-structured interviews were developed to facilitate consistency across interviewers.

**Now,** Refer to Chapter-2, Q.No.-8

**Q2. Explain the role of psychological assessment in deciding, planning, conducting and evaluating therapy.**

**Ans.** Refer to Chapter-1, Q.No.-11

**Q3. Describe the characteristics of teats of abstraction. Give a description of any two tests and highlight the limitations and cross-cultural considerations.**

**Ans.** Refer to Chapter-3, Q.No.-6, 8, 9

**Q4. Describe self-report inventory highlighting its strengths and weaknesses. Discuss the various formats of self-report inventory.**

**Ans.** Refer to Chapter-1, Q.No.-6

## SECTION – B

**Answer any four of the following questions in about 250 words each:**

**Q5. Differentiate between psychodiagnostic assessment and psychiatric consultation. Describe the application of psychodiagnostic testing.**

**Ans.** Refer to Chapter-2, Q.No.-1 (i), (iv)

**Q6. What is a test battery? Discuss its uses.**

**Ans.** Refer to Chapter-2, Q.No.-7

**Q7. Discuss the questions and controversies connecting the IQ testing.**

**Ans.** Refer to Chapter-3, Q.No.-5

**Q8. Discuss the various categories and basic assumptions of projective techniques.**

**Ans.** Refer to Chapter-4, Q.No.-1

**Q9. Define personality testing. Discuss any two objective tests of gersonality.**

**Ans.** Refer to Chapter-4, Q.No.-9, 10

## SECTION – C

**Write short notes on any two of the following in about 100 words each:**

**Q10. Cognitive Assessment.**

**Ans.** Refer to Chapter-2, Q.No.-3

**Q11. Addiction Assessment.**

**Ans.** Refer to Chapter-1, Q.No.-10

**Q12. Perfect Conditions Fallacy.**

**Ans.** Refer to Chapter-1, Q.No.-12

# Psychodiagnostics: MPCE-012

## December, 2020

*Note: All sections are compulsory.*

### SECTION – A

**Answer any two from the following questions in about 450 words each:**

**Q1. Describe psychodiagnostic assessment. Discuss the specific types of assessment.**

**Ans.** Refer to Chapter-1, Q.No.-1 and Chapter-2, Q.No.-3

**Q2. Critically discuss the measurement of memory.**

**Ans.** There are many techniques for measuring memory. Some methods are highly specialised, either for the purpose of addressing a particular research question or for diagnosing a specific memory dysfunction, but most measurement procedures are variants of the basic techniques described in this entry.

**Measures of Recall**

- ***Immediate Serial Recall: Memory Span:*** In the most commonly used version of this task, a randomly ordered sequence of digits (e.g., 4-7-8-2-5-9) is read once to the participant, who is required to repeat them in the same order. The resulting measure is known as the digit span, defined as the number of digits that can be repeated in the correct order without error. An immediate difficulty is that an individual's performance may fluctuate slightly from one occasion to the next, six digits being correctly repeated on one occasion, for example, and seven on the next. The formal measurement of span is therefore usually taken as the number of digits that can be correctly recalled on 50 per cent of occasions.
- ***Free Recall:*** In free recall, a list of items is presented and the task is to recall them in any order. The measure of memory is the number (or proportion) of these items recalled. If people are allowed to begin recalling immediately after the presentation of

the last item, this simple measure is subject to a strong recency effect: The last few items in the list will be recalled very well (and usually recalled first). There is also a weaker primacy effect: The first few items in the list will be better recalled than those in the middle positions.

- ***Cued Recall:*** In cued recall, the task is to recall each item in response to a cue provided by the tester. This cue may have been presented along with the item at the time of study (an intra-list cue) or be an item not studied before (an extra-list cue). For example, a participant may study word pairs such as dog-tail and when tested be given the intralist cue dog and asked to recall the word with which it was paired. Alternatively, he or she may study a list of single words (including tail but not dog) and when tested be given the extra-list cue dog as a potential aid to recall.

**Measures of Recognition Memory**

- ***Forced-Choice Recognition:*** In this procedure memory is measured by presenting each of the previously studied items (the "old" items) with one or more new items or "lures" and instructing the participant to choose which of these items is old. The measure is then the number or proportion of items correctly identified as old. There are two difficulties with this measure. Guessing poses an obvious problem because in the case of a two-alternative forced choice, someone who remembered nothing at all could guess correctly half the time. Increasing the number of lures reduces the expected rate of correct guessing but does not eliminate the problem entirely. Researchers have proposed various methods of "correcting for guessing," but they are often not used, partly because the problem of guessing is not as serious as it may seem.
- ***Single-Item (Yes/No) Recognition Tests:*** In what may seem the simplest form of a recognition test, participants are shown each test item in turn and asked to respond "yes" if they have seen it before (an old item) and "no" if they have not (a new item). The test list contains a mixture of old and new items. A possible measure of memory would be the proportion of items correctly identified as old, a measure referred to as the hit rate. However,

this measure has a serious shortcoming: It will be influenced by the participant's criterion for saying "yes." Adopting a lax criterion (that is, saying "old" even if the item is only faintly familiar) can yield a high hit rate, usually at the expense of mistakenly saying "old" to a large number of new items. Such errors are termed false positives or false alarms.

**Q3. Give an overview of tests of abstract reasoning.**

**Ans.** Refer to Chapter-3, Q.No.-8

**Q4. Discuss the formats and types of Interview.**

**Ans.** Refer to Chapter-2, Q.No.-9

## SECTION – B

**Answer any four of the following questions in about 250 words each:**

**Q5. Describe the general guidelines for writing psychological report.**

**Ans.** Refer to Chapter-2, Q.No.-13

**Q6. Discuss the application of psychological assessment.**

**Ans.** Refer to Chapter-1, Q.No.-4

**Q7. Define creativity. Discuss the measures of creativity.**

**Ans.** Refer to Chapter-3, Q.No.-11

**Q8. Give a description of administration and scoring of Rorschach test.**

**Ans.** Refer to Chapter-4, Q.No.-6

**Q9. Explain the concept of personality and psychological functioning in personality testing.**

**Ans.** Refer to Chapter-4, Q.No.-9

## SECTION – C

**Write short notes on any two of the following in about 100 words each:**

**Q10. Use of personality assessment as treatment.**

**Ans.** Refer to Chapter-2, Q.No.-4 (iv)

**Q11. Analogue observation.**

**Ans.** Refer to Chapter-1, Q.No.-7

**Q12. Mental Status Examination.**

**Ans.** Refer to Chapter-2, Q.No.-6

# Psychodiagnostics: MPCE-012

## June, 2021

*Note: All sections are compulsory.*

## SECTION – A

**Answer any two from the following questions in about 450 words each:**

**Q1. Define Psychodiagnostics. Discuss the various date sources for psychological assessment.**

**Ans.** Refer to Chapter-1, Q.No.-1, 3

**Q2. Describe Wechsler scales for adults (WAIS III), its administration and scoring.**

**Ans.** Refer to Chapter-3, Q.No.-2

**Q3. Discuss the nature of projective tests and their measurement and standardisation.**

**Ans.** Refer to Chapter-4, Q.No.-4, 5

**Q4. Discuss ethical issues in assessment.**

**Ans.** Refer to Chapter-1, Q.No.-14

## SECTION – B

**Answer any four of the following questions in about 250 words each:**

**Q5. Discuss the phase of planning, conducting and evaluating therapy in Clinical Psychology.**

**Ans.** Refer to Chapter-1, Q.No.-11

**Q6. Elucidate the purpose and areas to be covered in diagnostic interview.**

**Ans.** Refer to Chapter-2, Q.No.-1 (vi), (vii)

**Q7. Define Abstract Attitude and its characteristics. Delineate the characteristics of test of Abstraction.**

**Ans.** Refer to Chapter-3, Q.No.-6

**Q8. Define Memory. Differentiate between explicit and implicit memory.**

**Ans.** Refer to Chapter-3, Q.No.-10

**Q9. Explain Torrance Test of Creative Thinking.**

**Ans.** Refer to Chapter-3, Q.No.-11

## SECTION – C

**Write short notes on any two of the following in about 100 words each:**

**Q10. Disguised Field Observations**

**Ans.** Refer to Chapter-1, Q.No.-7

**Q11. Computer Assisted Interviews**

**Ans.** Refer to Chapter-2, Q.No.-9

**Q12. Children's Apperception Test**

**Ans.** Refer to Chapter-4, Q.No.-8

❑❑❑

*The true purpose of education is to make minds, not careers*

# Psychodiagnostics: MPCE-012

## December, 2021

*Note: All sections are compulsory.*

### SECTION A

**Answer any two of the following questions in about 450 words each:**

**Q1. Discuss measurement of personality and psychological functioning. Describe MMPI and what it measures.**

**Ans.** Refer to Chapter-4, Q.No.-9

**Q2. Describe in detail the Rorschach Inkblot Test.**

**Ans.** Refer to Chapter-4, Q.No.-2 and Q.No.-6

**Q3. Describe the instruments of cognitive functioning.**

**Ans.** Refer to Chapter-3, Q.No.-14

**Q4. Describe the tests used in neuropsychological assessment.**

**Ans.** Refer to Chapter-3, Q.No.-13

### SECTION B

**Answer any four of the following questions in about 250 words each:**

**Q5. Elucidate the formats used in self-report inventories.**

**Ans.** Refer to Chapter-1, Q.No.-6

**Q6. Describe the skills and techniques required in interviewing.**

**Ans.** Refer to Chapter-2, Q.No.-8

**Q7. Explain the categories and basic assumptions of projective techniques.**

**Ans.** Refer to Chapter-4, Q.No.-1

**Q8. Describe Performance (Sorting) tests and Colour Sorting tests for assessment of conceptual thinking.**

**Ans.** Refer to Chapter-3, Q.No.-8

**Q9. Define implicit memory and discuss the tests for measuring the same.**

**Ans.** Refer to Chapter-3, Q.No.-10

### SECTION C

**Write short notes on any two of the following in about 100 words each:**

**Q10. Uncertain Gate-keeping**

**Ans.** Refer to Chapter-1, Q.No.-12

**Q11. Applications of Psychodiagnostic Testing**

**Ans.** Refer to Chapter-2, Q.No.-1(iv)

**Q12. Self and Interpersonal Functioning Continuum**

**Ans.** Refer to Chapter-4, Q.No.-9

# Psychodiagnostics: MPCE-012

## June, 2022

*Note: All sections are compulsory.*

### SECTION A

**Answer any two of the following questions in about 450 words each:**

**Q1. Describe the various formats of self-report inventories.**

**Ans.** Refer to Chapter-1, Q.No.-6

**Q2. Discuss the specific types of assessment.**

**Ans.** Refer to Chapter-2, Q.No.-3

**Q3. How is creativity assessed? Describe subsections of creativity measures.**

**Ans.** Refer to Chapter-3, Q.No.-11

**Q4. Explain the administration and scoring of Rorschach Test.**

**Ans.** Refer to Chapter-4, Q.No.-6

### SECTION B

**Answer any four of the following questions in about 250 words each:**

**Q5. Differentiate between Descriptive assessments and Prediction assessments.**

**Ans.** Refer to Chapter-2, Q.No.-2

**Q6. Elucidate the skills and techniques required in an interview.**

**Ans.** Refer to Chapter-2, Q.No.-8

**Q7. Define Abstract Attitude. Explain the characteristics of tests of abstraction.**

**Ans.** Refer to Chapter-3, Q.No.-6

**Q8. What does Thematic Apperception Test measure? Discuss its reliability and validity.**

**Ans.** Refer to Chapter-4, Q.No.-7

**Q9. Describe any two objective personality tests.**

**Ans.** Refer to Chapter-4, Q.No.-10

## SECTION C

**Write short notes on any two of the following in about 100 words each:**

**Q10. Confirmation Bias**

**Ans.** Refer to Chapter-1, Q.No.-12

**Q11. Adlerian Theory of Counselling**

**Ans.** Refer to Chapter-2, Q.No.-5

**Q12. Precautions in Children's Apperception Test**

**Ans.** Refer to Chapter-4, Q.No.-8

# Psychodiagnostics: MPCE-012

## December, 2022

*Note: All sections are compulsory.*

### SECTION A

**Note: Answer any two of the following questions in about 450 words each.**

**Q1. Discuss the common fallacies and pitfalls in psychological testing and assessment.**

**Ans.** Refer to Chapter-1, Q.No.-12 (Pg. No.-44)

**Q2. Describe mental status examination.**

**Ans.** Refer to Chapter-2, Q.No.-6 (Pg. No.-85)

**Q3. Discuss any two measures of intelligence.**

**Ans.** Refer to Chapter-3, Q.No.-2 (Pg. No.-123)

**Q4. Explain the administration and application of Thematic Apperception Test.**

**Ans.** Refer to Chapter-4, Q.No.-7 (Pg. No.-204)

### SECTION B

**Note: Answer any four of the following questions in about 250 words each.**

**Q5. Elucidate the phases in delivering psychological treatment.**

**Ans.** Refer to Chapter-1, Q.No.-11 (Pg. No.-39)

**Q6. Describe any two types of interviews conducted by a psychologist.**

**Ans.** Refer to June-2019, Q.No.-2 (Pg. No.-232)

**Q7. Explain the uses of neurological assessment.**

**Ans.** Refer to Chapter-3, Q.No.-13 (Pg. No.-166)

**Q8. Discuss the reliability and validity of Rorschach scores.**

**Ans.** Refer to Chapter-4, Q.No.-6 (Pg. No.-198)

**Q9. Describe California Psychological Inventory.**

**Ans.** Refer to Chapter-4, Q.No.-10(ii) (Pg. No.-224)

### SECTION C

**Note: Write short notes on any two from the following in about 100 words each.**

**Q10. Assessment in vocational guidance testing and job placement.**

**Ans.** Refer to Chapter-1, Q.No.-4 (Pg. No.-12)

**Q11. Use of test batteries**

**Ans.** Refer to Chapter-2, Q.No.-7 (Pg. No.-97)

**Q12. Structure of intellect assessments**

**Ans.** Refer to Chapter-3, Q.No.-11 (Pg. No.-155)

# Psychodiagnostics: MPCE-012

## June, 2023

*Note: All sections are compulsory.*

### SECTION A

**Note : Answer any two of the following questions in about 450 words each.**

**Q1. Discuss the various data sources for psychological assessment.**

**Q2. Define psychological assessment. Discuss the purpose of psychological assessment.**

**Q3. Describe the stages in psychodiagnostics.**

**Q4. Explain the skills and techniques for assessment interviews.**

### SECTION B

**Note : Answer any four of the following questions in about 250 words each.**

**Q5. Differentiate between descriptive assessment and predictive assessment.**

**Q6. Describe the various uses of neuropsychological assessment.**

**Q7. Describe projective techniques and discuss the categories of projective techniques.**

**Q8. Discuss the current status and future prospects of Rorschach Test.**

**Q9. Discuss the ethical issues in assessment.**

### SECTION C

**Note : Write short notes on any two of the following in about 100 words each.**

**Q10. Precaution in administering children's Apperception Test**

**Q11. Torrance Tests of Creative Thinking (TTCT)**

**Q12. Neo-Personality Inventory**

❑❑❑

www.ingramcontent.com/pod-product-compliance
Ingram Content Group UK Ltd.
Pitfield, Milton Keynes, MK11 3LW, UK
UKHW021705190726
13853UKWH00001B/429

9 789390 557349